Volume 6

MINNESOTA MONOGRAPHS IN THE HUMANITIES

Gerhard Weiss, founding editor

Leonard Unger, editor

ALDOUS
HUXLEY ✀ ✀

Satirist and Novelist

BY PETER FIRCHOW

UNIVERSITY OF MINNESOTA PRESS
Minneapolis

© Copyright 1972 by Peter Firchow. "Sitting Round the Cauldron,"
by Aldous Huxley, copyright © 1972 by Laura Archera Huxley.
All rights reserved.
Printed in the United States of America at
Jones Press, Minneapolis
Published in the United Kingdom and India by the Oxford
University Press, London and Delhi, and in
Canada by the Copp Clark Publishing Co. Limited, Toronto

Library of Congress Catalog Card Number: 74-187165
ISBN 0-8166-0635-8

For my parents
Paul and Marta Firchow

Acknowledgments

In writing and researching this book, I have incurred some obligations which I am pleased to discharge now. My thanks go to Miss Patricia Palmer and Mr. Brooke Whiting of the Stanford and UCLA libraries, and their staffs, for generous assistance in helping me find my way through their manuscript collections; to the Graduate School of the University of Minnesota for making it financially possible for me to travel to those collections; to the Department of English of the University of Minnesota for providing me with occasional help in typing; and to my wife for being my most generous critic.

Acknowledgment should also be made to the following for permission to use certain materials in the book:

To Mrs. Laura Archera Huxley, Chatto and Windus Ltd., and Harper and Row, Publishers, Inc., for permission to quote from the following works by Aldous Huxley: *Verses and a Comedy, Crome Yellow, Antic Hay, Those Barren Leaves, Point Counter Point, Music at Night, Brave New World, Eyeless in Gaza, Ends and Means, After Many a Summer, Time Must Have a Stop,* and *The Genius and the Goddess.*

To Mrs. Laura Archera Huxley, for permission to quote from the *Letters of Aldous Huxley,* ed. Grover Smith; from a manuscript notebook of Aldous Huxley's in the Stanford Uni-

versity Library; and from the fragmentary novel by Aldous Huxley contained in her *This Timeless Moment* (Farrar, Straus and
Giroux).

To the University Library of the University of California,
Los Angeles, for permission to quote from materials in its possession.

To the Aldous Huxley Collection of the Felton Collection
in the Manuscript Division of the Department of Special Collections of the Stanford University Libraries, for permission to quote
from manuscripts in their possession.

To Mr. Christopher Isherwood, for permission to quote
from a letter to me, dated February 28, 1971.

To *Modern Fiction Studies* and the copyright holder, the
Purdue Research Foundation, for permission to include in chap-
ter V parts of my article on *Brave New World*, published in
MFS, 12 (Winter 1966–67), 451–460.

Contents

ALDOUS HUXLEY, SATIRIST AND NOVELIST

Introduction

ALMOST by definition, the act of criticism is one of the smaller attempting to encompass the larger, of the smaller fish trying to swallow the larger one. When this actually happens, it is like a miracle, but like miracles, it rarely, if ever, does occur. This is no doubt why criticism so seldom seems a satisfactory enterprise, at least in the sense of appeasing one's hunger for a fullness of understanding. Criticism only infrequently ventures beyond the analytical hors d'oeuvres because the critic, perhaps by nature, is a half-hearted cannibal who finds only certain parts of the anatomy of his victim to his taste. He may give us an admirable dissertation on the heart, rump, solar plexus, even occasionally the brain, but almost never on all of them together, never on the totality of the original man. It was probably this realization, or something resembling it, that caused Friedrich Schlegel to suggest that the critic, like the cow, should have several stomachs; but the process of natural selection among critics has not yet reached this stage of development. Meanwhile, the temporary solution to this problem has been to allow each critic to present us with, as it were, *une tranche de son auteur*, cooked to his own order. We look in vain for the great postprandial summation which would evoke the spirit, if not the reality, of the whole.

Still, this approach, regrettable as it is in its assumption that a single perspective can offer a complete view, or a single dish take the place of an entire cuisine, is — for want of a better procedure — the one that has been adopted here. With the difference, however, that the slice of Huxley presented here is a cross section, a possibility in this instance because Huxley is primarily a satirist and because satire is an attitude and not a form, because satire is — to conclude the culinary metaphor — a flavor which tinges (bitterly, one might add) the entire corpus of Huxley's work. In other words, Huxley is a satirist even when he is a novelist, poet, essayist; and although satire is not his only perspective on life, it is certainly the only one that is continuous and fundamental in his work.

Except for Jerome Meckier's *Aldous Huxley, Satire and Structure* (London, 1969), no book-length study devoted primarily to Huxley the satirist has been published, and even Meckier casts a wider net than his title suggests. Rather than concentrating on the sources of Huxley's literary and intellectual inspiration, what I have attempted to do here is isolate and analyze the main techniques and victims of Huxley's satire, tracing their development from his first poems and short stories through all of his novels. I have hoped in this way to present a coherent view of Huxley's achievement as a satirist.

Some readers will undoubtedly feel that such a view cannot be arrived at without first considering where Huxley fits into the tradition of satire, English and Continental. If I have chosen to omit such a disquisition, it is not because I do not feel the force of such an objection, but because I realize that the task of putting Huxley in his proper historical place can only be dealt with adequately in a separate book. Confronted with the alternatives of history or analysis, I have preferred the latter. My excuse, if I must have one, is that Huxley — even the Huxley whittled down to satirist — is, after all, large enough to accommodate many volumes.

Among these future volumes, certainly one of the most interesting will be the study of Huxley's critical reputation. For as anyone who has bothered to lift the lid of this Pandora's box soon realizes, a great part of what was said about Huxley by his contemporaries, especially distinguished ones like Eliot, Gide, Maugham, and Virginia Woolf, has been more or less unfavorable. Nor, until relatively recently, have succeeding generations been particularly willing to revise their verdict. Eminent critics like David Daiches, Arnold Kettle, Cyril Connolly, and Sean O'Faolain have joined the chorus of voices which have found Huxley wanting.

To be sure, no serious author who has achieved popularity and prominence as quickly as did Huxley has ever escaped the pursuit of detractors. By his very magnitude, Huxley presented a tempting target to would-be giant killers. This, of course, holds true for some of his literary ill-wishers, like Gide and Eliot, as well. Not that Huxley apparently minded what was said about him, for he claimed never to have read his critics — an assertion which, though no doubt true on the surface, is belied on a deeper level by the preoccupations of some of his personae in novels like *Point Counter Point* and *Eyeless in Gaza.* There Philip Quarles and Anthony Beavis, both of whom are easily recognizable self-portraits, go to some lengths to justify the kind of fiction Huxley is writing. And Anthony Beavis, along with William Propter, Huxley's mouthpiece in *After Many a Summer,* goes even further than Quarles in denying the truth and usefulness of the conventional work of fiction.

What was it (or is it) in Huxley's writing that made him at once so popular, and so distasteful to so many serious critics? Frank Swinnerton's reply to this question was that Huxley had been dismissed in the best circles because he had dared to laugh at the first rate people who inhabited them, especially in Bloomsbury.[1] This notion may have been partly true of those "first rate" people whom Huxley actually put in and down in his novels but, generalized into a secret conspiracy to denigrate Huxley, it becomes nothing more than a rather absurd, if touching, gesture on the part of Huxley's old friend and former editor to account for what seemed to him otherwise inexplicable. Bloomsbury, after all, has come and gone — and so, for that matter, has Aldous Huxley — and yet the critical attack, although in much diminished form, goes on.

Though it has borne many different names and has come from a variety of directions, the basic objection to Huxley as a writer was always much the same: he was not a novelist. Broadly defined, what this meant was that Huxley was incapable of conceiving of and creating "real" human beings. His characters, so this line of criticism ran (and still runs), were either mere allegorical statements of moral or intellectual positions or else, what was even worse, mouthpieces for Huxley's own ideas, which could be and often were much more efficiently and appropriately presented in essay form. That there was a good deal of truth in this criticism, Huxley himself recognized. In an entry in his notebook in *Point Counter Point,* Philip Quarles admits to not being a "congenital novelist," and Huxley himself, when prodded on this point in an interview given four years before his death, confessed to being still of the same mind.

But what is a "congenital novelist"? In Huxley's own view, it is a writer who has no interests outside of fiction. For such a man, Huxley told his interviewers, writing novels is "an absorbing thing which fills up his mind and takes all his energy, whereas someone else with a different kind of mind has these other, extracurricular activities going on."[2] Extracurricular was surely a modest way of describing the multitude of activities and interests which absorbed Huxley's extraordinarily rich and supple mind. For him, though he was usually too self-effacing to say so outright, being a novelist was not enough. What he sought to be was at the same time a philosopher, a critic, a scientist, an economist, a moralist — and, yes, even a human being. Hence the odd and, in some respects, frustratingly encyclopedic nature of his fiction.

It was no doubt Huxley's misfortune — literarily speaking, at least — to have been born in an age which had little use for such a writer. The eighteenth century would have provided a much more congenial environment, as Huxley, with his liking for

Swift, Fielding, and Voltaire, seems to have intuited. These were "novelists," as he was later to observe in an essay called "Tragedy and the Whole Truth" (but which might just as easily have been entitled "Congenital Novelists and the Whole Truth"), who preferred to render the totality of human experience, from its grossest bodily functions to its noblest flights of fancy, rather than confine it within an arbitrarily constructed and allegedly "pure" bed of Procrustes. The first half of the twentieth century, which refused to consider Swift a novelist and placed Fielding and Voltaire beyond the pale of the "Great Tradition," filed Huxley away in the category of the misfits. From a Jamesian perspective that insisted on rigidly delimiting a fictional world through a filtering consciousness with which the reader was asked to identify but could never wholly rely on, Huxley the novelist was inevitably unsatisfactory.

And even on less theoretical grounds Huxley frequently proved disappointing. On the one hand, his novels usually presupposed a familiarity with Western (and later Eastern) literature, philosophy, and history which only a relatively few readers could have possessed. His audience, in this respect, seemed identical to the one tenth of one percent of humanity about which, in the guise of Philip Quarles, Huxley claimed to be writing, and which must have been roughly the equivalent of these readers of *The Waste Land* who could manage to get through the poem without explanatory notes. But on the other hand, Huxley's novels often lacked what Eliot's poems (to use the same point of reference) were so well supplied with, namely density and ambiguity.

Even better perhaps, a comparison with D. H. Lawrence might illustrate what I mean. For example, a novel like *The Rainbow,* though by no means lacking in intellectual pretensions, has an emotional impact which is never equaled by any of Huxley's novels (excepting possibly *Eyeless in Gaza).* The reason for this, I suppose, is that Lawrence the congenital novelist, while never striving for obscurity for its own sake, understands that an experience must be rendered symbolically as well as intellectually. Consequently, *The Rainbow* abounds with strange and powerful and difficult scenes which do not yield to immediate rational analysis: obscure pagan dances of fertility, deathly prostrations before the moon, or, most striking, a haunting and terrible confrontation between the heroine and a herd of malignant horses. Huxley hardly ever does this kind of thing. Instead, his aim seems to be to bring everything into the foreground, to diminish the shadows by bathing human existence in as much light as possible. In the useful terminology employed by Erich Auerbach in *Mimesis,* Huxley is a hypertactic writer, Lawrence a paratactic one; Huxley is the Hellene who must see and elaborate all the connections which go to make up an experience, Lawrence the Hebrew who intimates and suggests rather than states; Huxley is the Platonic rationalist who finally prefers history to fiction, Lawrence the Aristotelian who knows that art can be truer than life.

Not that the one is wrong and the other right. They are merely different, with each having his particular virtues and concomitant vices. And surely it is good that it should be so, that there should be many great traditions and not merely a single exclusive (not to say, narrow-minded) one. If the bent of the modern mind is still more toward an appreciation of the paratactic or "congenital" type of novelist, this should not mean that its sympathies might not extend occasionally to writers of the opposite kind. Or as Huxley himself once wrote of another author, thinking no doubt of his own predicament as he did so: "It is foolish as well as ungrateful to criticize an author for what he has failed to achieve. The reader's business is with what the writer has done, not with what he has left undone."[3]

CHAPTER I

The Defeat of Youth and the Victory of Age

IN RECENT years the Huxley name has become a kind of patent of intellectual nobility. One is reminded of the genealogies of royal houses or — since the Huxley achievement is primarily internal — of those great Roman families who seemed to specialize in producing generations with the same characteristic virtue — or characteristic vice. The Huxleys are probably the only fully, or almost fully, documented case (and this surely would have pleased T. H. Huxley) of natural selection along intellectual lines: a living proof of the theories of the great progenitor.

Not long ago Ronald Clark set about tracing the Huxley tree in all its multifoliate intellectual splendor, and in the process produced what seems to be a new type of biography: the intellectual life history not of a man but of a family, spanning centuries and not decades, to which the conclusion has not yet been and may never be written.[1] This unanimistic life of the Huxleys reads like a happy *Buddenbrooks,* where the trade in the goods of the mind always flourishes, where new markets are continually being opened up, and where the consuls of the spirit appear unfailingly on time, ever ready to transform the republic into an empire. In fact, thinking of the remarkable heritage of the Huxleys, one is sometimes tempted to cry out, "Huxley is dead, long live Huxley!"

Still, after the death of this last great Huxley, no matter what new scion next opens the doors of perception, there probably will never again be anything resembling the old satirical-mystical management. Aldous Huxley was not merely an extraordinary man in an extraordinary family, distinguished as that was and is; he was someone for whom that tradition and almost every other tradition was too narrow. His life, so richly variegated, so filled with public cynicism and private warmth, so dramatic in its continual search for the answer to what it all means, resembles more the lives of those men who came to fascinate him in later life than it does that of any other member of his family: for example, the Abbé Surin in the *Devils of Loudun* or the Capuchin monk in *Grey Eminence*. For he was himself, with his gaunt tallness and shyness of fame, a kind of grey eminence, and toward the end of his life he also became a genuinely religious man who nonetheless continued to attempt to resolve the practical problems of the world of appearances. And like still another of his favorite subjects (and occasional victims), St. Francis, Huxley was a man who gave up several possible and eminently worthy lives to choose finally one that seemed foolish to most of his contemporaries. He was a man of great complexity and deep simplicity; a man accused of changing his opinions at the drop of an idea, but who demonstrably pursued, with different means, a single and almost invariable end throughout his entire life; a practically blind man who saw further and more acutely because he possessed the art of seeing, because he possessed something rare even among Huxleys: genius.

A critical study of a writer's work is not always the proper place to practice biography, but in Huxley's case, with his habit of transforming life into fiction, of producing stories and novels *à clef,* a certain amount of knowledge about his life is necessary, particularly during its early stages. Until quite recently, very little was publicly known about Huxley's life, because he almost

invariably displayed a marked reluctance to discuss with interviewers any matters but those of strictly intellectual or literary
interest; about his personal life he could only "tolerate reticence,"
as he once told a prying interviewer.[2] But now with the publication of Ronald Clark's *The Huxleys* and Laura Archera Huxley's
This Timeless Moment,[3] the massive and yet incomplete *Letters*
compiled by Grover Smith,* as well as the promise of an official
biography by Sybille Bedford, there will soon be sufficient material on Huxley to establish in detail the relation between
Dichtung and *Wahrheit*.

One may wonder if all this is necessarily a good thing, if
the vision raised by an admiring memorialist, of "hundreds and
perhaps thousands of writers and scholars" accumulating more
and more bits of information, is altogether attractive, but it is
almost certainly inevitable.[4] In any case, what Lawrence Clark
Powell terms the "abhorrence of personal publicity," which, for
example, prevented Huxley from being a witness in the *Tropic
of Cancer* trial, did largely succeed in forcing those who insisted
on criticizing him during his lifetime to do so on intellectual
rather than personal grounds.[5] However, a less happy consequence was to force this urge for the personal fallacy into different channels, distorting what little critics did know about Hux-

*In his brief introduction Smith speculates that during Huxley's life-
time "he perhaps wrote at least ten thousand letters" (3). Of the twenty-five
hundred which passed through Smith's hands, only about nine hundred were
actually published. Some important letters — those to his first wife and possibly a few to D. H. Lawrence — perished in the disastrous fire of 1961 which
destroyed his entire collection of books and manuscripts; some, notably those
to Lady Ottoline Morrell, were withheld from publication.

The published letters make for rather disappointing reading. They
reveal that Huxley was no congenital letter writer. With the exception of a
few high-spirited letters from his Oxford and Garsington periods, as well as
his correspondence with Robert Nichols, Huxley reserved his wit and charm
for his essays and fiction. By and large, he seems to have written letters hur-
riedly and with a desire to get on to more interesting and profitable things.
Perhaps the real problem with the *Letters*, as Huxley himself was well aware,
is that he was not a writer who creates "in first fine careless raptures, but in
a series of second and third thoughts" (879). As anyone who has examined
the manuscript of one of his novels can testify, Huxley knew what he was
talking about. But even so the *Letters* is of course absolutely essential to any
student of Huxley's life and work.

ley's life into absurd pseudo-Darwinian speculations on the relative importance of the biological and intellectual inheritance
from T. H. Huxley (grandfather) and Matthew Arnold (great-
uncle), or into smug censures of his supposed inability to follow
his first "master," D. H. Lawrence, properly, or his presumed
penchant for following his second, Gerald Heard, too well.

The salient known facts of Huxley's early life are as follows.
He was born in the small village of Godalming in Surrey, England, on July 26, 1894, the third and last son of Leonard Huxley
and Julia Arnold (there was also a younger daughter). He first
attended a variety of private schools near Godalming, then went
on to Eton on a scholarship intending to prepare himself for a
career in biology. But at sixteen he was struck down by total
blindness (*keratitis punctata*) which forced him to withdraw from
school and which only gradually began to improve after several
operations, though even these left him practically blind in one
eye and with severely impaired vision in the other. Huxley, however, did not give himself up to despair. He went to Marburg to
study German; he learned Braille; and he occupied himself by
writing a full-length novel of which the manuscript has unfortunately been lost. There is little likelihood now of its ever being
recovered, so we probably will never know just what this work
was about, but it is not too difficult to imagine that its contents
were as dark as the world around him had become and was to
continue to be for some time. For physical blindness was not the
only personal tragedy he experienced during this dark period:
two years earlier his mother, to whom Huxley, as the youngest
son, had been particularly close, had died of cancer, and four
years later his brother Trevenen committed suicide. And behind
all these personal darknesses was the vaster, impersonal darkness
of the threat and then the reality of the Great War.

The outbreak of hostilities found Huxley ready to start his
second year at Balliol College, Oxford, where he was studying
(under Sir Walter Raleigh, among others) for a degree in English.
Like almost all of his contemporaries, he seems to have reacted
with a rush of patriotism to the news of war — the famous en-

thusiasm of the August days — but all his efforts at enlistment were rendered futile by his poor eyesight. Later, he probably had reason to thank his bad eyes for saving his life — as Philip Quarles and Anthony Beavis, the semiautobiographical heroes of *Point Counter Point* and *Eyeless in Gaza* were to thank their crippled legs for the same reason. Only a short time passed before the casualty lists began to make him aware that many of his friends and acquaintances would never return to Oxford. From a jingoistic desire "to extirpate the vipers," expressed in a letter to his brother Julian on February 1, 1915 (L66),* he gradually moved to a point of almost total disillusionment with the war, which he voiced in a letter to Julian about a year later: "At the beginning I shd. have liked very much to fight: but now, if I could (having seen the results), I think I'd be a conscientious objector, or nearly so" (L97). His taste in poetry underwent a similar change, progressing from an emotional admiration for Rupert Brooke and Walter de la Mare to a more sober and intellectual appreciation of Laforgue and Villiers de l'Isle-Adam, whom he considered "the greatest satirist of the nineteenth century" (L96), and T. S. Eliot, whom he first met and read in the fall of 1916.

His initial inability and later reluctance to join in the patriotic rush to slaughter did not prevent him from seeking distinction in other, less martial ways. During his first two years at college his rooms became, according to his cousin Gervas Huxley, "the centre where the *élite* of our year gathered, drawn by the magnet of his mind, the curiosity of his catholic tastes, and his unassuming friendliness."[6] It was at this time as well that Huxley began publishing his first poems and stories in undergraduate magazines like *The Palatine Review* and *The Varsity*, which was edited by his friend Thomas Earp, with whom he was later to share briefly an apartment in London (along with Russell Green and Roy Campbell). The poet L. A. G. Strong was

---

*Sources of Huxley quotations are indicated by page numbers which, unless otherwise specified, refer to the Chatto and Windus *Collected Works Edition*. Page numbers preceded by an "L" signify that the quotation is taken from the *Letters of Aldous Huxley*, ed. Grover Smith (London, 1969).

later to recall how Earp made him "a member of a group which met once a week to read aloud what they had been writing, and exchange criticisms. Foremost in this group was Aldous Huxley, shy, myopic, the astringent ferocity of his writing contradicted by the gentleness of his manner. He was contributing regularly to *The Varsity* under the pseudonym of Aloysius Whalebelly, and writing other things beyond the scope of that lively journal. He seemed in these early years less well-defined in appearance, less clear-cut in feature, his tall, angular frame amorphous beneath jacket and trousers, his face half-hidden behind large, thick lenses and long unruly hair. He read extremely well, and everyone of the company treated him with extreme deference."[7]

Another literary inhabitant of this wartime Oxford, A. E. Coppard, occasionally accompanied this "most formidable undergraduate" to the movies (where he had to use opera glasses to see the figures on the screen) and was struck by his love for out-of-the-way language. "Even while an undergraduate," Coppard later wrote in his autobiography, "Aldous Huxley was a highly regarded personality, whose esoteric utterances impressed me as he trotted out so casually the obscure words and the most unusual epithets for the most ordinary objects. One of his verses circulating at the time encased the shattering word 'amphisboena'; it may have been indigenously used, on the other hand it could have come from Donne."[8] It may indeed have come from Donne, for Huxley's interests at this time included the metaphysicals and poets like Fulke Greville, who exercised a considerable fascination on him during his Oxford years and about whom Sir Walter Raleigh even suggested he write a thesis. And a few years later, while teaching at Eton, Huxley turned both David Cecil and Harold Acton into readers of Donne. Donne et al. were unquestionably in the Oxford air and did not really need an Eliot to pull them out of it. Still, Huxley's love for strange language is almost certainly not derived directly from Donne; rather, it was probably Donne's similar taste for odd sounds and surprising substances that made him seem so attractive. Even during the years of his own schooling at Eton, Huxley's cousin Lawrence

Collier observed, "Aldous seemed to cherish words as things in themselves and almost regardless of their meaning."[9]

Frank Swinnerton, who met Huxley immediately after the war, was, like Coppard, struck by his odd vocabulary but, unlike Coppard, saw his use of it as strictly "indigenous": "Years ago, I asked Huxley why he wore such a very large-brimmed hat; and he answered: 'Because if I don't I look microcephalous.' He added that as it was the little boys at Hampstead used to call out to him: 'Cole up there, guvnor?' Thinking over this remark, I realized that in his place I should not have used the word 'microcephalous' but should have said 'my head would look like a dot.' And this led me to understand that Huxley's vocabulary, which some readers find pretentious and others impressive, was as natural to him as simpler words must be to others."[10] Huxley's native penchant for collecting words as if they were rare and valuable coins — to be spent only in the right place — explains a good deal of his fondness for English "nonsense" poets like Edward Lear or French symbolists like Mallarmé, whose "L'Après-midi d'un faune" he translated. But this love was not limited merely to the sound or the strangeness of the word; it extended to the oddness of the thing, which led to his adopting the *Encyclopaedia Britannica* as a constant travel companion, and to his introducing such topics into conversation as the amorous habits of crayfish — to the delight of Osbert and Edith Sitwell and to the disgust of Roy Campbell. As Arnold Bennett was to observe, the word "fantastic" was one of the leitmotivs of Huxley's talk; astonishment was obviously the only possible reaction to the strangeness of the world.

With all this interest in the peculiarities of language and life, Huxley was no doubt fated to make the customary assault on Parnassus, and in 1916 and 1917 he published his first two "slim" volumes of verse, *The Burning Wheel* and *Jonah,* both of which passed almost unreviewed and unnoticed in the world outside Oxford. And though the rumblings of verbal wheels or whalebelly palpitations might be pleasant to the mind, they were inadequate when it came to silencing the grumblings of his

stomach.* Thus, when he graduated from Oxford, he seems to
have been obliged (for want of anything more interesting or
profitable) to take a job at Garsington, doing "odd jobs, such as
cutting down trees."[11] Fortunately, however, his activities were
not to be confined to this kind of rustic exercise.

Garsington Manor was and is a Tudor estate near the village
of Garsington, some five miles southeast of Oxford. A treelined
avenue leads up to the main entrance of the house which lies a
little off the road; behind it a beautifully manicured lawn slopes
gently down to a rectangular pool in the center of a garden
punctuated by tall hedges and statuary. Sir Philip and Lady Ottoline Morrell owned the manor during the war and the years
immediately following, at which time it came close to being the
intellectual and literary center of England. Sir Philip was one
of the very few members of Parliament who had opposed Bri-
tain's entry into the war, and Lady Ottoline was a fervent sup-
porter of Bertrand Russell's pacifists (she had also been, Russell
was to reveal half a century later, his mistress). As the war pro-
gressed, Garsington became both a haven for conscientious ob-
jectors, like Clive Bell, who occupied themselves with farm
chores, and a focal point for opposition to the war. It was here
that Huxley first met the great figures of his age as they dropped
by for tea or came to stay the weekend: Bertrand Russell, Osbert
and the other Sitwells, Robert Graves on leave from the front, D.
H. Lawrence full of wild ideas about a Utopia in Florida, the
painter Mark Gertler, Lytton Strachey and all the rest of the
Bloomsburies.† It was this stay of a few months at Garsington

*Huxley's early letters, particularly those to his father, reveal how
straitened his financial circumstances were. His poor eyesight may have kept
him out of the war, but it also hindered his efforts at getting a job which
would give him some security. It was only after the publication of *Crome
Yellow* in 1921 that money ceased to be a full-time worry.

†Huxley's response to Lawrence's invitation to join him there was
guarded but not antagonistic. Writing about it to Julian in December 1915,
he thought he would very likely visit this "novelist and poet and
genius . . . this good man, who impresses me as a good man more than
most" and "spend, perhaps, a little while in his eremitic colony" (L88).
Nearly forty years later, while participating in a "D. H. Lawrence Round-
Table Conference" sponsored by the Friends of the UCLA Library, Huxley

and frequent visits to it afterward that probably made Huxley aware for the first time of the full horrors of war, and gave him a sense of how unusual and precious a place Garsington was: an island of light in a vast sea of darkness, a Red Indian Reservation of reason and civilization surrounded by the savages of democracy and hysteria. It was at Garsington too that Huxley met, among the Belgian refugees who were staying there, his future wife, Maria Nys, an attractive young girl who had already aroused the amorous interest of Lytton Strachey.[12]

Nonetheless, despite the influence of Garsington, what little remained of Huxley's patriotism impelled him to try to do something for his country. But here again the attempt was unsuccessful: the massive amount of paper work connected with the administrative position he accepted with the Air Board was simply too much for his eyes. He left to take on teaching duties at Eton where, though he personally considered himself a failure, his influence was sufficiently beneficial to make at least one pupil, Harold Acton, deeply, if indirectly, indebted to him.*[13]

During these final years of the war, Huxley was also engaged in establishing and furthering his reputation as a poet. In the autumn of 1917 we hear of him reading his poetry at a gathering organized by Edmund Gosse, and featuring such other partici-

remarked that "I was very lucky it didn't take place . . . To Florida of all places" (March 7, 1952, from a tape in the possession of the UCLA Library, Special Collections). Huxley's first novel, *Crome Yellow*, is, as we shall see, based on Garsington, the Morrells, and some of their distinguished hangers-on, including Huxley himself. Another rather less humorous portrayal of this place and some of the same characters is contained in D. H. Lawrence's *Women in Love* (1920).

*Lord David Cecil, Brian Howard, and Christopher Hollis were other Etonians of the period who have testified to Huxley's impact. Perhaps an important reason for his success was his guiding principle to "do my best to make my boys have no respect for me whatever" (L143). Among other signs of Huxley's unconventionality, the *Letters* tells of his having long discussions on theosophy with his students, as well as helping them found a political society and the *Eton Review*. It may be that Huxley's feeling of inadequacy (aside from pure modesty) derives from his performance in the more public context of the classroom. It was not until rather late in life that Huxley altogether overcame his antipathy toward appearing in public. The story of how this happened is told in the guise of Anthony Beavis in *Eyeless in Gaza*.

pants as Robert Graves, T. S. Eliot, and the three Sitwells.[14] In
May of the same year, Lady Ottoline had written to introduce
him to Edward Marsh, the uncrowned monarch of *Georgian
Poetry*, but Huxley was the "first to decline a place among the
Georgians" because his appearance in the Sitwells' *Wheels* had
already "become a habit" that he did not care to break.[15] The
following year saw the publication of his third volume of poems,
The Defeat of Youth, which — in part because of an unsigned
review by Virginia Woolf in the *TLS*[16] — began to make him
known to a larger, though still very small, public. One young
Etonian member of this audience tells of reading these poems
one by one each time he went to Spottiswoode's, where the book
was displayed in the window, until he finally bought it.[17] The
poet who looked like a juvenile giraffe and wore a conspicuous
orange scarf trailing behind him, as Acton described the Huxley
who stalked absentmindedly and nearsightedly about the Eton
landscape, was finding a voice to which the young, whether
defeated or not, were eager to listen and respond. When his
fourth collection, *Leda*, appeared in 1920 and was greeted in
some quarters as the new hope for English poetry, Huxley the
poet seemed to have come into his own.

Although his literary position was now what is usually
termed promising, the same could not be said of his financial
situation. Masterships at Eton were (and probably are) not particularly well paid, nor do slim volumes make fat poets. To be
sure, a relatively small amount of money would have been
enough to keep him in orange scarves, in food and lodging; but
Huxley was no longer interested in supporting merely himself
alone: he desperately needed money to marry Maria Nys who,
after the war ended, had gone off to live with her mother in Italy.
It was very likely at this moment that Huxley first conceived of
the idea of Gumbril's patent small clothes, the financial liberator
of the Etonian master and hero of *Antic Hay*.

In real life, financial salvation came from quite another
quarter: in the spring of 1919 Middleton Murry, then a young,
imaginative critic and journalist who enjoyed (and sometimes

disliked and was disliked by) a wide literary acquaintance, offered Huxley the place of second assistant editor (J. W. N. Sullivan was the assistant editor) on *The Athenaeum* which had just been bought by Arthur Rowntree and which Murry had been asked to reorganize and edit.[18] During the following two years this journal was to become the most brilliant literary review in England, publishing not only regular contributions by Huxley, Murry, and Murry's wife, Katherine Mansfield, but fiction and essays by such people as D. H. Lawrence, the "Woolves" (Virginia and Leonard), the brothers Strachey, T. S. Eliot, George Santayana, Paul Valéry, Clive Bell, Roger Fry, and E. M. Forster. Huxley, besides doing editorial work and writing a weekly column "Marginalia" under the pseudonym "Autolycus," also did a very considerable amount of largely unsigned reviewing.*

His salary at *The Athenaeum,* though rather less than the £500 T. S. Eliot had stipulated and failed to receive when offered the same position, was enough to enable him to marry and settle down, first in Hampstead and later in Westbourne Terrace. There, with occasional intervals of leisure and travel, Huxley produced in the next few years an astonishing amount of astonishingly varied writing. Naturally a large proportion of his work was "journalism," but even this was frequently of a sufficiently high quality to ensure publication in book form, as in the case of *On the Margin* (1923), a selection from his "Marginalia" column.† At this time, Huxley was also continuing his more "serious" work: poems, stories, and a novel, as well as working part time at the Chelsea Book Club, collaborating on a play with Lewis Gielgud, and helping to edit *Coterie.* Then in 1920, after

---

*The Autolycus of Shakespeare's *Winter's Tale* is a rogue and "snapperup of unconsidered trifles," whose main source of revenue is "the silly cheat." In Greek mythology, Autolycus was a famous thief and swindler who had the gift of transforming everything that was touched by his hands.

†Two decades later Richard Aldington was to observe that the journalist Huxley helped to hold the line against those who wanted to do completely away with the artistic heritage of the prewar world: "However much Aldous Huxley may now laugh at his experience on the Athenaeum, he and Murry also did useful work in maintaining standards." *Life for Life's Sake* (New York, 1941), p. 218. The "also" refers to T. S. Eliot, whose essays of this period Aldington particularly admired.

some dissension with Murry, he added to this already massive
burden the job of drama critic with the *Westminster Gazette*.
All this, we should remember, was performed by a man who had
to do his reading with only one eye and the aid of a magnifying
glass, and who was convinced that "all writing is a torment."[19]
Small wonder, then, that looking back at this period some ten
years later, Huxley was to observe that he had "nearly killed
[himself] with overwork."[20]

But strenuous as they may have been, these years of journalistic apprenticeship probably served to temper Huxley. They
certainly gave him confidence, sometimes too much confidence,
as when he remarked that he was prepared to write convincingly
on any subject, given half an hour in the British Museum. They
introduced him to the art of the informal essay, something which,
with his initial bent for poetry, he would perhaps in the normal
course of events have turned to only much later, and they gave
him sufficient practice in this art form so that he eventually
honed it to perfection, to the point where some critics were
subsequently to refuse to recognize him as anything else. These
years also gave him experience, both in his writing and in his
nonliterary life, in dealing with people and situations, often
very complex ones, and this experience was to prove invaluable
for his fiction. They forced him to be "readable," to appeal to
the large masses rather than the cultured few, and they afforded
him a portion of the "vulgarity" which, as he was later to con-
tend, is an essential component of every great writer. In short,
they made a professional out of an accomplished amateur, a
man of the world out of a potential academic recluse.

These years of intensive and extensive exposure to a society
and an art that was still struggling to be reborn after four years
of bloody labor also served to force Huxley into thinking deeply
about social and cultural problems and led him to become increasingly disgusted with the course modern culture and society
were taking. Publicly his insights and disgust precipitated in the
stories and novels that were to make him famous while the
century and he were still in their twenties; privately they took

the form of a desire to withdraw from the pointless activity of that society and culture (while still commenting on it) and to travel to other countries and to study other societies and other cultures, past and present.

In a sense, Huxley's life really begins here, with the defeated youth refusing to accept his defeat, with the perennial voyage of the mind in search of meaning, with the desperate urge to put a positive point against a great many negative counterpoints and thereby perhaps establish a harmony. It is the persistence and uncompromising nature of this attempt that explains why Huxley took up and expounded so many out-of-the-way ideas and philosophies, only to abandon them later, thereby leaving his readers and would-be followers in hopeless confusion. As Huxley was to observe in an interview with J. W. N. Sullivan sometime in the early thirties, his "chief motive in writing . . . has been to express a point of view . . . [to make] clear a certain outlook on life . . . My books represent different stages in my progress towards such an outlook. Each book is an attempt to make things clear to myself so far as I had gone at the time it was written. In that sense they are all provisional."[21] But confusing and provisional as this progress may have been then, at least in hindsight it now becomes clear that it was not a random progress. For Huxley was basically — though this is something that always surprises critics who approach him with prejudices and planned witticisms about mystics — an empiricist. In this respect he remained, like his grandfather, in the most characteristic tradition of English thought, although he differed from most self-proclaimed empiricists by taking his empiricism seriously. For if empirically he saw that the intellectual emperor had no clothes (even if the emperor happened to come from Bloomsbury), he did not hesitate to say so, uncomprisingly and therefore un-Britishly. This subsequently earned him the epithet of inhumanity and the displeasure of such critics as David Daiches and Arnold Kettle.

With the publication of the mass of articles and reviews in *The Athenaeum* in 1919 and 1920, Huxley became a well-known and occasionally respected figure in English intellectual circles, and with the publication of *Leda* and *Limbo* (stories) in 1920 and *Crome Yellow* in the following year, he established a national reputation and the beginnings of an international one. Though, unlike Byron, he may not have awakened one morning to find himself famous (one wonders anyway if he ever slept at all during this period), it is certainly true, as Edwin Muir noted only a few years later, that "no other writer of our time has built up a serious reputation so rapidly and so surely."[22] In fact, by the early thirties, when he was only thirty-six, an American publisher had already brought out a volume of critical essays dealing exclusively with his literary achievement. And this, we should remember, was in the days before casebooks on practically anybody and everybody became a common occurrence.*

Huxley was now more or less a made man, and he used his new-found financial security to remove himself physically but not intellectually from England. In 1923 he went to Italy where, except for one trip around the world — with stops in India, the Dutch East Indies, and the United States, all vividly described in *Jesting Pilate* (1926) — and a great deal of traveling in Europe, he remained until 1930. This was the period of his greatest popular successes, of *Antic Hay, Those Barren Leaves,* and *Point Counter Point,* when the name of Huxley ceased to be attached in the popular mind to evolution and monkey trials, and came

*A good index to Huxley's international popularity is given by the enormous number of requests for permission to translate his works contained in the file kept on Huxley by his agents, Ralph and Eric Pinker, which is now in the possession of Stanford University. One begins to wonder, however, about the quality of the translations when one reads a letter like the following to Chatto and Windus, dated May 4, 1926, and signed by M. Ortega y Gasset: "Dear Sir, Wishing us to publish in Revista de Occidente the article 'The Monocle' [actually a short story] from Mr. Aldous, justly appeared in the first number of 'The Criterion' we would thanks you for making us know as soon as possible the translations rights of the mentioned work. Waiting for yours kind answer I remain yours very truly."

For a good discussion of the difficulties of translating Huxley into German, see Hans-Joachim Kann, *Übersetzungsprobleme in den deutschen Übersetzungen von drei anglo-amerikanischen Kurzgeschichten: Aldous Huxleys "Green Tunnels," Ernest Hemingways "The Killers," und "A Clean Well-Lighted Place,"* vol. 10 of the Mainzer Amerikanische Beiträge (Munich, 1968).

to be associated more and more with a fashionably modern disillusionment and a satirical iconoclasm of the idols of the tribe
and the elite. It was the time of his intellectual and personal
friendship with D. H. Lawrence, clearly a major phase in Huxley's development, about which a lot of nonsense has been written,* but which, it is hoped, will be elucidated when his official
biography is published.

The greater part of the early thirties Huxley spent in relative seclusion in his villa at Sanery-sur-Mer in southern France
along a coastline dotted with the homes of other British writers
in voluntary exile (because the climate and cost of living were
much more attractive there than in England). But he still continued to travel, including one extended trip to Central America
which resulted in what is perhaps one of the best travel books
ever written, *Beyond the Mexique Bay* (1934), and he of course
made frequent trips to London. During the mid-thirties, with the
threat of another world war growing increasingly ominous and
with an actual war going on in Spain, Huxley became more and
more concerned with *What Are You Going to Do about It?*
(1936), as the title of a pamphlet he wrote during this time
phrased the question (and which evoked from C. Day Lewis the
reply *We're Not Going to Do Nothing*). He joined Canon Sheppard's Peace Pledge Union, began to lecture on pacifism, conferred with Gerald Heard on practical ways and means of pre-
venting war, and in 1937 came out with *Ends and Means,* a closely reasoned, forceful analysis of the motives and futility of war.

In April of the same year Huxley left Europe for the United
States, first apparently intending only to visit, but gradually
arriving at a determination to stay, in part perhaps because there
seemed little prospect of derailing or diverting the European express train to doom, in part certainly because Huxley and his
wife came to love the desert of the American Far West. Besides,
there was the even more compelling reason that his vision was

*As well as, more recently, some sense, especially in "Huxley's Lawren-
tian Interlude," chap. 4 of Jerome Meckier's *Aldous Huxley, Satire and
Structure* (London, 1969).

rapidly deteriorating, and Southern California, where, as he himself said at the time, the "facilities for eye-training by the Bates
method are particularly good," seemed an especially propitious
place to be.[23] (In any case, his decision was probably not influ-
enced, as some British superpatriots would have us believe, by a
reluctance to face the battle he so clearly saw coming.) Under the
Bates regimen Huxley's vision began to show marked improvement, to the extent that he was able, for the first time since he
was sixteen, to see without glasses. Huxley expressed his grati-
tude not long afterward by extolling this unconventional method and detailing his own experiences with it in *The Art of
Seeing* (1942), a book which was to arouse the ire of scientifically
orthodox theoreticians, serving thereby only to strengthen his
empirical contempt for any theory which refused to examine all
the available evidence.

The thirties were also years in which Huxley, like most other
writers of the time, became increasingly *engagé*, convinced that
he could no longer be a detached and heckling observer standing
above the melee, that he had to try to do something meaningful
and constructive. The problem, of course, was to discover what
was indeed meaningful and constructive. The usual solutions —
communism or fascism — were out of the question because both
insisted on confusing the part with the whole, a fallacy shared,
though to a far lesser extent, by the Lawrentian "philosophy" he
had earlier believed in. There were, to be sure, relatively short-
range goals whose desirability seemed obvious, like that of stopping the onrushing war and doing so in a way that did not involve war itself. But more and more Huxley came to realize that
what was really needed was "some definitive and comprehensive
outlook," a system that would tie things together, *all things,* and
create order out of a seemingly chaotic world.* The first hints
that he had discovered such a system were to be found in *Eyeless
in Gaza, The Olive Tree and Other Essays* (both published in

---

*As he said to J. W. N. Sullivan and as he was to say again at much
greater length and with much more passion through Propter in *After Many
a Summer* (1939).

1936), and *Ends and Means.* The hints turned into lectures in
After Many a Summer (1939), into deeply perceptive psycho-
historical observations in *Grey Eminence* (1941), into visionary
dreams in *Time Must Have a Stop* (1944), and into a paradoxically fragmented but unified religion in *The Perennial Philosophy* (1945).

Huxley, it was abundantly clear, had arrived at the conclusion that mysticism was the only valid perspective on (but not
alternative to) reality. He did not, however, as is often asserted,
become a mystic; he never, at least in his writings, called himself
such, for that would have meant he had himself experienced the
mystical union perceived by genuine mystics. And even when he
did experience something analogous to it, like the telepathic
experience he mentions having undergone sometime before
1934,[24] or, more importantly, the visions induced by mescalin
and LSD — described in *The Doors of Perception* (1954) and *Heaven and Hell* (1956) — he never equated these in a simplified
way with the complexities of mysticism. This kind of sloppy
thinking and uncritical belief would have destroyed for him the
whole point of mysticism — namely, that it was true. True,
though this may seem paradoxical, in a scientific way: for, as
Huxley's examination of a mystic like Father Joseph in *Grey
Eminence* (1941) or of a supposed diabolic possession in *The
Devils of Loudun* (1952) reveals, he approached mysticism in a
pragmatic, empirical way, much as he had approached the Bates
eye-training method. He clearly understood that the mystics were
all, no matter of what time or what official or unofficial religion,
describing essentially similar experiences, that they were almost
always exceptionally sensitive and perceptive men, and that
logically it was impossible to explain this perennial phenomenon
as a mere delusion. Even if it was not sanctioned by twentieth-
century science, it had too much of the feel of reality to be dismissed in the way this positivistic science had dismissed it.

Mysticism, in both its theoretical and its practical aspects,
now became Huxley's prime subject of study — and single pillar
of wisdom — for the remainder of his life; at last he had found

the consolations of philosophy, consolations whose reality and effectiveness were to be tested and reaffirmed when he had to grapple once more with personal tragedy, first when his wife died of cancer in 1955, and later in his own protracted struggles against the same disease, to which he finally succumbed on November 22, 1963.

Huxley's concern with mysticism did not mean that he withdrew into seclusion; for him mysticism meant more rather than less. It was, after all, the one way of looking at life and the universe that embraced all significant material and spiritual manifestations (even those that did not seem to exist), and it did not commit the grave error, as Huxley thought other "systems" did, of accepting some truths to the exclusion of others, thereby producing the lie known as half-truth. It did not, for example, seem impossible to him to combine the world of Hollywood with the world of the Spirit; or to employ his time partly in writing scripts for various film studios (usually not produced or produced only after being unrecognizably revised, but very amply compensated), partly in studying and writing on mysticism, partly in demolishing satirically, as in *After Many a Summer* and the first section of *Ape and Essence* (1948), the people and mores of the "Joy City" which sustained him. As Ronald Clark points out, it may seem curious that Huxley should once have been hired by Walt Disney to work on the script of Lewis Carroll's *Alice in Wonderland,* but it seems much less curious when we realize that Huxley was composing fairy tales for a young niece at roughly the same time, one of which he wrote down and which has been published under the title *The Crows of Pear-blossom* (1967). And the paradox seems even less curious when we become aware that still later, after he had become further identified in the public mind with an ethereal mysticism, he had no qualms about publishing his articles in such unmystical magazines as *Esquire* and *Playboy.*

Mysticism was not merely for mystics, so much was evident to him. Mysticism was not even exclusively for the spirit, but for the body as well — witness the provisions for sexual satisfaction in his last completed novel, *Island* (1962), or the sensual appreciation of the life of the body expressed in some of the letters to his second wife published in *This Timeless Moment*. Moreover, a mystical understanding of the universe did not preclude his being intensely concerned with such pressing problems of the temporal world as overpopulation — a concern that led Huxley in the last year of his life to attend a conference of the United Nations Food and Agriculture Organization and help it in its Campaign against Hunger. And, finally, mysticism did not prevent Huxley from enjoying an active social life, from meeting new people, from pursuing his old love of travel, or from cultivating close friendships. During the last two decades of his life, we frequently hear of his hospitality and amiability to great (as well as ordinary) people of all kinds: conversations with Igor Stravinsky, walks with Thomas Mann, a drive with a juvenile delinquent, picnics with Anita Loos and Charlie Chaplin, lunch with Krishnamurti and the queen of Belgium. As the *Memorial Volume* (1965), edited by his brother Julian, testifies, the variety of Huxley's friends and acquaintances was equaled only by the variety of his mind.

But within that variety there was unity. Despite the frequent and dramatic demarcations of his life, there was only one Huxley, or more accurately, a single fundamental personality that was capable of expansion and inner transformation, but whose basic outlines always remained the same. Between the young Huxley and the old, between the satirical skeptic and the confident mystic, between the defeated youth and the victorious sage there is a direct and unbroken line. It is the beginning of this line, gradually discernible in some of his early poems and stories, that we shall examine in the following chapter.

CHAPTER II

Double War and Triune Peace

EXCEPT for the first years of his literary existence, Huxley never made much of a mark as a poet; even now, few people are aware that he ever wrote poetry. Only the testimony of library shelves, an occasional item in a new anthology, and a rare scholarly article serve to remind us of the fact.* The faint shadow of the poet clad in orange scarf, black cape, and broad-brimmed hat that first began to catch the imagination of his contemporaries has been replaced, probably permanently, by the equally surprising but more lasting image of the writer of prose and the proclaimer of Eastern wisdom.

In part, Huxley himself was responsible for this oblivion. After the initial spurt of four volumes of poetry in as many years, he allowed nine years to elapse before he published *Arabia Infelix* (1929), and another two before he brought out his last, *The Cicadas* (1931). So already in the twenties it seemed as if Huxley had given up poetry, and the two later volumes of verse were not enough (either in quantity or quality) to modify even partly the impression his novels and essays had already made on the public mind.

Perhaps this is not altogether regrettable, for Huxley's po-

*This situation may change with the recent publication of *The Collected Poetry of Aldous Huxley,* ed. Donald Watts (London, 1971).

etry is largely of the kind that "has some good things in it"
rather than being good throughout. And even where the poetry
is consistently good, as in the fairly well-known "Philosophers'
Songs," it is good in a way that has now come to seem less original and forceful than it once did, chiefly because of the vogue
of later poets like E. E. Cummings, Gregory Corso, or Lawrence
Ferlinghetti who managed the subtleties of the Laforguean and
Apollinairean ironic modes at least as well as Huxley and certainly much more popularly. Huxley's derivativeness did not
seem quite so clear in the teens and by 1920 he had attained considerable notability and notoriety as a radically modern poet,
particularly with the publication of *Leda.* Harold Monro, who
owned the Poetry Bookshop and was one of the poetical midwives
of the period, considered Huxley "among the most promising of
the youngest generation of contemporary poets,"* and Herbert
Gorman, reviewing *Leda* for the *New York Times,* recognized in
him a genius comparable only to T. S. Eliot. To be sure, there
were also other and harsher (and perhaps envious) voices, like
that of Middleton Murry, who dismissed the title poem as being
"without significance," and thought that "as for two-thirds of the
shorter pieces, we think he would have been well-advised never
to print them." Probably Desmond MacCarthy adopted the right
course — the usual middle one — in proposing that Huxley's poetry was good, but of a goodness chiefly suggestive of a "finer,
richer poet in the making."[1]

It is hard to say why Huxley never lived up to his early
promise as a poet — except to observe that he stopped writing
poetry, which only means throwing the question one step further
back and asking why he stopped doing so, particularly at a moment when he had achieved his first real poetical successes. Late
in life Huxley remarked in an interview that "I'm unfortunately
not writing any poetry because I find it just takes too much time.
I mean it's an entirely whole-time job, and then I'm not happy

*Reviewing the book in which Monro made his statement, Huxley
killed without any qualms the goose that laid the golden eggs. His verdict:
"Mr. Monro lays before us a volume of criticism in which there are no
ideas at all."

with the results. It just isn't good enough."[2] This turning away
from poetry of course does not imply that Huxley had lost faith
in its intrinsic value — only in his ability to produce it. And really
not even that. For *Island* contains a number of poetical fragments. When his house burned down and he lost his whole library, Huxley took up an offer to supply him with some replace-
ments by asking for "the poets, first of all" (L918), and going on
to draw up a list beginning with Shakespeare, Chaucer, Wordsworth, and Keats, and ending with Latin and medieval Latin
verse. And in a talk commemorating Dylan Thomas on September
20, 1954, Huxley sees the primary function of the poet as a puri-
fier of language and therefore of thought, and concludes with the
exclamation that "God help a generation that neglects to read its
poets."[3] If, for all intents and purposes, the mature Huxley had
stopped writing poetry, he never stopped reading it.

Naturally, these are not necessarily the reasons which impelled Huxley to abandon poetry in the early twenties. Just what
those reasons were is perhaps impossible to determine now. It
does seem clear, however, that Huxley, though no Rimbaud, had
reached a point about 1920 when he rather desperately needed
more money in order to support his growing family; in lieu of
gun running there was journalism, theater reviewing, and the
writing of short stories and eventually novels. It was probably
Huxley's enormous success in the latter genre that shunted his
poetical inclinations aside, and finally persuaded him to confine
his poetical imagination almost exclusively to novels and essays.
There is perhaps another reason as well — namely, that Huxley
had "ideas," something which few other English writers of his
generation seem to have had, judging by the inability of contemporary (and many succeeding) critics to forgive Huxley his intel-
lectuality. Possibly it was this un-Jamesian trait in Huxley's artistic temperament that led him away from a medium better suited
to the communication of emotion than ideas, or led him at any
rate to attempt to inject ideas into poetry, into choosing modes
and genres — like the mock epic or the long reflective poem —
that lend themselves more readily to an ironic intelligence.

Huxley's poetry is certainly an intellectual poetry — or an intellectual's poetry — though not in the same sense as, for example, Eliot's is. To be sure, the ingredients in Eliot's verse were quite similar to those that made up Huxley's: a dash of Laforgue, a pound of Donne (not the same pound, however), a sprinkling of symbolists, a spoonful or two of Dowson and the other Decadents — and some Browning. Nevertheless, the proportions were different. Furthermore, not only did Huxley take much larger doses of Laforgue and Dowson, but he also lacked Eliot's Jessie Weston and Sir James Frazer. Hence his poetry does not have the same density or breadth or obscurity as Eliot's. In compensation, it probably has a greater polish, a more pleasing surface, though one that hides the same ugly wasteland that Eliot charts so delphically and brilliantly. Huxley and Eliot, however, shared the conviction that what was wanted was a greater impersonality and "hardness" in poetry. This emerges clearly from a letter Huxley sent his father, dated November 12, 1917, which contains probably the closest thing to a poetical manifesto that he ever wrote: "I find that more and more I am unsatisfied with what is merely personal in poetry. What one wants, it seems to me, is this: first to receive one's impressions of outward things, then to form one's thoughts and judgments about them, and last to reobjectify those thoughts and judgments in a new world of fancy and imagination. The intermediate subjective stage must be cut away altogether" (L137).

The real difference between Eliot and Huxley, I suppose, lies in the difference in the bent of their minds: Eliot was continually in search of some ultimate objective correlative that would render his perceptions adequately — a correlative that in the end he probably found only in the thirty-nine articles of the Church of England. Huxley was not so much in search of a correlative, whether objective or otherwise, as in search of the thing itself: he was interested less in how to capture the elusive poetical emotion or intellectual insight alive than in how to dissect it — or vivisect it — and lay it out clear on the anatomical table.

Hence Huxley, even in his poetry, works more by the rational knife of argument than by way of symbolic nets. His most successful poems, the five "Philosophers' Songs" for example, do not drag us down into an Eliotesque whirlpool of bloody myth and dismembered tradition in the manner of "Sweeney among the Nightingales," but confront us rather with an ironical, syllogistic dead end. A good many of his poems — one with the unlikely title of "Crapulous Impression" springs to mind — are built up as arguments, even to the point of culminating with some kind of clincher. Perhaps the difference is best or at least most economically expressed if we remember that for Eliot the seventeenth century's murky metaphysical struggles between faith and reason seemed the most moving and relevant historical comparison, whereas for Huxley (of this period at any rate) it was the eighteenth century's brightly illuminated rationalistic acclamations or denunciations of the universe. It is symptomatic of this attitude that the vaguely autobiographical heroes of his first novella, "The Farcical History of Richard Greenow" (1920), and *Crome Yellow* both attack and condemn the universe from rationalistic points of view.

Shortly after the Second World War when Huxley's British publishers, Chatto and Windus, reprinted his poems for their collected edition of his works, Huxley seems to have balked at resurrecting them in their entirety. The volume which finally emerged from his pruning knife, *Verses and a Comedy* (1946), contains only a fraction of his total poetical output and is so short that, as can be seen from the title, it had to be rounded out by the inclusion of a play, *The World of Light* (1931). Of his early poems, Huxley judged only twenty-two fit for the eyes of posterity — almost literally, it appeared for a time, because the original editions of his poems have become so rare that relatively few libraries have complete sets. Now, of course, with the publication of Donald Watts's edition of the *Collected Poetry*, Huxley's reputation as a poet may undergo drastic reevaluation.

This study is not the place for a thorough discussion of Huxley's poetry — a subject which in any case will one day elicit its own monograph. What interests me most here about Huxley's poetry, particularly the early poetry, is the ideas it develops and the attitudes it characteristically takes. From this point of view, one of the most interesting of the early poems is a curious and in some respects rather juvenile but striking poem entitled "The Reef" (1918).

This poem begins with a description of an aquarium and its fish and continues through a series of aquatic metaphors to an imaginary reef set amid a broad expanse of ocean, the sky above filled with birds, the water below with fish that have now become "jewels" instead of the disgusting "phantom," "idiot" fish of the aquarium. Without undue strain, I think we can say that the stagnant aquarium is an image for a stagnant civilization, the harelipped fish metaphors for the people who inhabit it:

> I am grown less
> Than human, listless, aimless as the green
> Idiot fishes of my aquarium,
> Who loiter down their dim tunnels and come
> And look at me and drift away . . . (page 3).

Understandably enough, the speaker wants to escape this kind of mindless existence, wants to smash the green, slimy glass walls of his confinement, and escape into something purer, cleaner, better:

> these are the things
> I search for: — passion beyond the ken
> Of our foiled violences and, more swift
> Than any blow which man aims against time,
> The invulnerable, motion that shall rift
> All dimness with the lightning of a rhyme,
>
> Or note, or colour. And the body shall be
> Quick as the mind; and will shall find release
> From bondage to brute things; and joyously
> Soul, will and body, in the strength of triune peace,
> Shall live the perfect grace of power unwasted (pages 4–5).

At this point in the imaginary voyage to perfection, the poet

pauses to examine himself, to see if he is capable of making the
voyage in reality as well. The reply, one that was to become
habitual for the youthful Huxley and perhaps for an entire
generation of skeptical intellectuals, was ambiguous:

> They were strong and bold
> That thither came; and shall I dare to try? (page 5).

"The Reef" can usefully serve not only as a paradigm for
Huxley's career, but as a particularly effective intellectual guide
through his early poems and short stories. For the basic conception of this poem — the division between matter and spirit or,
put differently, the lack of inner balance — is the thematic heart
(usually broken, of course) of most of the young Huxley's poetry
and fiction. Time and again his readers are confronted with the
dilemma of a split personality, with the woeful discrepancy between illusion and reality, with the eternal ebb and flow of passion and reason, with the groans of the wearisome condition of
humanity which is wearisome precisely because it is able to
imagine other conditions that are not so.

Though the view from "The Reef" provides us, on an occasional clear day, with the prospect of a distant triune peace,
there are frequent storms and great drifts of fog when all is
obscured. A somewhat earlier poem already referred to, "Crapulous Impression" (1916), sees the spirit confined to the bottle
and life's meaning a meaningless chess game, where the only
victory is to savor the intense materiality of the pieces. This is
also true — or, if possible, even truer — of another poem from the
same year, "Mole." In this magnificently compact and sonorous
poem, Huxley describes how the mole of the title, an obvious
image for man, stupidly "tunnels on through ages of oblivion,"
blind and unaware of the light and beauty just above him until
he emerges by chance into the sunlight and is overcome by the
clear beauty of this new world. The Platonic mole realizes that
this world of light is incomparably superior to the dark world
which is his natural habitat. But, unfortunately, because it is his
natural habitat, he must inexorably return to it, he must "obey /

Necessity again and thrid / Close catacombs as erst he did"
(pages 26–27).

At least one of his first poems, "Topiary" (1918), goes beyond even this extreme point of satiric acerbity to a kind of
saeva indignatio approaching Swift's, though Huxley, perhaps
more rationally and consistently, lashes the cause and not merely
the effects. In this poem there is also an early example of what
later came to be called Huxley's penchant for disgusting physi-
ological imagery, a suspicious habit to critical minds joylessly
steeped in Freud. But here the lesson in physiology does not exist
for its own sake: Huxley does not savor necrophilously the human objects whose flesh looks like "carrion puffed with noisome
steam, / Fly-blown to the eye that looks on it, / Fly-blown to the
touch of a hand" (page 16). Nor does he, I think, particularly
enjoy the fact that there are "men without any legs, / Whizzing
along on little trollies / With long long arms like apes," (page 16).
It is, quite the contrary, Huxley's great indignation at the existence of such phenomena that provokes him into portraying
them so vividly and disgustingly. Because he is able to conceive
of God as a rational, beneficial "gardener," he is frustrated by
"God the Topiarist" who trains and carves and twists "Men's
bodies into such fantastic shapes" (page 16). Because life is so
unjust and irrational, he prefers, to quote the last line of the
poem, to be "very remote and happy, a great goggling fish."
Reason cannot be an adequate answer in such a predicament, for
it is precisely the light of reason that makes the deformity and
misery visible. Rationally, therefore, it is preferable to make a
rational abnegation, plunge into the darkness, and revert to
animalism: dive deeper into the slime of the aquarium, rather
than make a futile attempt to escape it.

Huxley's "Philosophers' Songs," first published in *Leda,*
also focus on much the same problem and reach analogous and
equally bitter conclusions. The "Second Philosopher's Song,"
for example, examines Pliny's proposition that a man when
drowned will float face down, but a woman face up. The final
stanza draws the following conclusion:

'Tis the Lord's doing. Marvellous is the plan
By which this best of worlds is wisely planned.
One law he made for woman, one for man:
We bow the head and do not understand (page 58).

The other "Philosophers' Songs" contemplate such subjects as
the mass extermination of millions of spermatozoa with the consequent elimination of possible Shakespeares, Newtons, or
Donnes; the lamentable umbilical connection between man and
monkey; and the enviable happiness of a God who absents himself from terrestrial misery while "the cancer gnaws our tissues, /
Stops to lick chops and then again devours" (page 59).

What all of these poems reveal — besides an obvious relish
for the odd subject and the odder word — is an intense concern
for humanity and an extensive search to find a remedy for its
present sad condition. His answers range from the hopeful balance of a triune peace in "The Reef" to the profoundly pessimistic recipe of prefrontal lobotomy in "Topiary," a spectrum
that is wide enough to indicate that Huxley himself was not yet
quite sure about the accuracy of his diagnosis. But meanwhile,
until such a diagnosis could be made, he would prescribe a mixture of both strong and weak medicines.

But strong or weak, the fundamental ingredient always remained satire. As Huxley was to observe in 1920, the year of his
first substantial successes (and first substantial satires), *Leda* and
Limbo, satire is, at least in one of its manifestations, practically
synonymous with truth. *Omnis satura divisa est in partes tres*,
said this theoretical Autolycus: the impulse toward the first and
most common type lay in the "sneaking Thersites" who lurks in
almost all of us and whose preference is for scrawling "ribald
sgraffiti on the base of statues of the gods." This apelike being is,
however, accompanied by two "more respectable and intelligent
partners — the solid earthly man who walks firmly on the ground
and feels no need of wings, who respects the gross truth as he sees
and comprehends it; and the clever man who is intelligent
enough to see that the world is infinitely obscure and compli-

cated, and despises those who take refuge from it in bright homemade universes of their own."[4]

It is this third person, this "clever man," who is the author
of almost all of Huxley's satires. It is he who perceives that the
"idiot fishes" of "The Reef" are idiotic precisely because they will
not or cannot take into account any aspect of existence but the
material, cannot, as the image he uses here and elsewhere has it,
escape the labyrinth of tunnels that governs all their movements.
So too with the man-mole, whose blindness is, however, extenu-
ated because God made him that way — which is why Huxley is
not so much satirical of the mole, as savagely indignant at a
universe that does not give the mole a chance to see. It is only in
poems like the "Ninth Philosopher's Song," where man apparently has some, though limited, choice, that Huxley attacks man
rather than the human condition. There the Ninth Philosopher
mocks all those for whom "Beauty provides an escape," or those
who mount up to some "better" world than this by way of "passion's all-too-transient kiss" (page 59). He ridicules them because
they concentrate too exclusively on one of the aspects of "The
Reef's" triune peace (which is the customarily unmentioned back-
drop before which all of Huxley's characters live their unbalanced and in that sense inhuman lives) — in this case either the
body or the soul — instead of focusing on the whole. They do not,
in short, take into account reality as it is perceived simultaneously from both the spiritual and the carnal viewpoints, but limit
themselves arbitrarily to one. They are satirized, in other words,
because they take refuge in "bright home-made universes of their
own" where, though they may in some sense be "happy" (for
example, as in *Brave New World*), they will be happy only at
the price of relinquishing their humanity, their ability to comprehend reality both spiritually and materially. It is from this
perspective, as we shall see in the novels, that Huxley surveys
and judges his characters and the world they inhabit. What he
is searching for from the very beginning is neither happiness nor
unhappiness — he is particularly suspicious of the former — but

awareness, a knowledge of and sympathy for the nature and circumstances of humankind.

As might be expected from the foregoing, the theme of Huxley's first significant short story is imbalance: it is the story of a character who not only inhabits but consciously constructs his own homemade universe.* Despite its intriguing title, "Eupompus Gave Splendour to Art by Numbers" is not especially good, at least by Huxley's later standards, but it does deserve some more than passing attention because of its position as a kind of signpost at the beginning of a distinguished career.[5] Briefly, the plot concerns a minor modern poet of considerable learning, a certain Emberlin, who becomes so intrigued with the history of an insane Alexandrian painter and would-be mathematician, Eupompus, that he falls into an abject imitation of him and begins compulsively and "Philarithmically" counting any and all objects, right down to the tiles in the narrator's bathroom.

The satire of this short story is clearly based on the imbalance of the two major characters, Eupompus and Emberlin. Both focus so exclusively on the analytic intellect as an instrument for discovering "true" reality that they completely lose contact with reality as it actually is. Because of their arbitrary selection of a part of reality (mathematics) and their confusion of that part with the whole, they are incapable of seeing other human beings except as numerical objects; and they themselves have lost their humanity, degrading themselves to the status of calculating machines. It is this type of imbalanced, arbitrary conception of reality and its concomitant isolation and inhumanity that form the basic subject of all of Huxley's future satire.

A secondary, but still quite important, satiric thrust in this story (and in Huxley's early fiction generally, but most notably in *Crome Yellow* and *Antic Hay*) is directed at what Huxley considered to be the excesses of modern art. (Here, if not elsewhere in Huxley's work, the customary assertion that satire is

*While at Oxford, Huxley had published two rather inconsequential stories, "The Chimney" and "The Death of Pellenore" (both 1916), which are probably earlier than this one.

essentially a conservative force is confirmed.) According to Huxley, art, like so much else in life, consists in a delicate balance of various elements, none of which can be disproportionately stressed without risking the destruction of the work of art as a whole. Huxley developed this idea in a number of reviews he wrote at roughly this time, as well as in his fiction — here and more memorably in Philip Quarles's notebook in *Point Counter Point*. And, of course, it was not merely an excess of intellect that was to be feared, but — and here Huxley's fears were prophetic of the course the novel was to take in the second half of the twentieth century — an excess of sensation as well.

From Huxley's rationalistic perspective, the whole basis of modern art seemed radically wrong; but this was a conviction which naturally and ironically did not prevent his becoming known during the twenties as one of the most avant-garde of the moderns. What disgusted him most was, rather typically, the contemporary mania for "primitivism," with its accompanying corollaries of art-for-art's-sake and the cult of the new. Not that he objected to the primitive as such. What rankled him was "the contemporary habit of emptying the primitives of their content and significance," to quote one of his fulminations from an essay published in 1925. The "obstreperously gross and blasphemous" novel *Ulysses* seemed to him simply the product of Joyce's reaction "against his medieval education." And as alternatives to such massive eructations there were only the vaporish effusions of Ronald Firbank and the Dadaists. All of this, Huxley paradoxically maintained, was not modern. What was really modern, what was really new, were intelligence, sensitivity, spirituality, tolerance. Hence, for him the most modern novelist was not Joyce or Gide or Cocteau, but Dostoevsky.[6]

Huxley, to be sure, never did become a Dostoevsky, though as time passed, he did come to share more and more of Dostoevsky's characteristics. Like the great Russian novelist, Huxley went through a period of doubt and search, and came out at the other end with a great urge to proselytize. Furthermore, both writers consciously went against the grain of their times and national-

ities; both were compulsive fabricators of fictions, and yet both
were interested not so much in the niceties of their craft as in
the effectiveness of their gospels. For that matter, even the notorious focusing on gruesome details in Huxley's fiction can be
derived from a similar trait in Dostoevsky, for example, in the
murder of the pawnbroker in *Crime and Punishment*. And, of
course, both had "ideas." Also, Huxley's first extensive published
work of fiction, the novella "Farcical History of Richard Greenow," a piece that deserves to be much better known than it is,*
is based on one of Dostoevsky's favorite structural and thematic
devices, the double.[7] This story, which is much too long and
complex to be adequately summarized here, concerns a young
intellectual who gradually grows to realize that he is at least a
spiritual, if not a biological hermaphrodite. After a series of
painful and painfully amusing attempts to assert herself — including a mawkish infatuation at the titular hero's public school —
the female alter ego establishes her identity firmly as a sentimental novelist, essayist, staunch patriot, and upholder of the
moral status quo. Richard, of course, is her conscious opposite:
sensitive where she is gross, skeptical where she is certain, intellectual where she is ignorant, pacifistic where she is bellicose.

As might be expected, this dual personality is too unstable
to cohabit the same body. The initial, orderly division of day-
time Richard and nighttime Pearl Bellairs becomes increasingly
unclear and confused until, shortly after the outbreak of the war,
the latter revolts against the former's opposition to violence, attempts to take over the whole personality, and lands them both
in a lunatic asylum where, in a magnificent final insane contrapuntal fugue on the futility of man and the horrors of the Hun,
they succumb to their inevitable fate.

This novella has some obvious parallels to Huxley's poetry
and the earlier "Eupompus Gave Splendour to Art by Numbers." One scene, in which Richard returns from a vacation in

*Cyril Connolly (sometime critic, parodist, and admirer of Huxley)
has done something to aid the cause by including "Richard Greenow" in his
collection *Great English Short Novels* (New York, 1953).

Scotland, stops in Glasgow, and gets his first good, close view of industrial laborers, is reminiscent of "Topiary." "Was it possible," Richard asks himself, "that there should be human beings so numerous and so uniformly hideous? Small, deformed, sallow, they seemed malignantly ugly, as if on purpose" (page 54). And of course its theme is fundamentally the same as that of "The Reef" or of "Eupompus"; for, like the main characters of that story, Richard suffers from a terrible imbalance, though here the imbalance is not merely in one direction, but in both. Richard's farcical tragedy is that he cannot modify and combine his excessively rational and emotional sides, or that fate formed him in such a way that he cannot. Therefore he is doomed to view reality successively from one of two homemade universes, from that of pure reason or that of pure emotion.

Paradoxically, however, because Richard is schizophrenic or "double-minded," he is saner than any of the "single-minded" characters of the story. His schizophrenia enables him (or forces him) to see a much larger spectrum of reality than do any of the others. In this he resembles the characters of the short play "Happy Families," which, like "Richard Greenow," was included in *Limbo*. The two protagonists of the play, one male and the other female, are each split up into three distinct personalities (or brothers and sisters as they are called) who also appear on the stage.* Each represents one aspect of human nature: reason, "humanity," pure animalism; and each understands only its own limited reality, each, as in Huxley's poem "Two Realities,"

Seizes the bun that he likes best
And passes over all the rest (*Verses and a Comedy*, page 27).

Moreover, the characters (or at least the two "human" ones) are almost incapable of communicating with each other directly; instead, they talk to each other by means of dummies that they hold in their hands.

What Huxley split up in the ironically happy families of

*A device Huxley borrowed from the Russian playwright Leonid Andreyev (L157).

the play, he combined but did not fuse in the ironically farcical "Richard Greenow." But, at any rate, these characters and Richard are exposed, though unable to adjust, to a series of realities and not merely a single reality. This is true in the novella even on a social level, but with somewhat different implications. In the first half of the story we see Richard growing up in the typical prewar upper-class surroundings of public school and Oxbridge college, a world suffused by the delicate aura of wealth and perfumed by a refined ennui. Richard resolves to be a voluntary exile from this world; prodded by his superior sensitivity and intelligence, he wants to do something for the downtrodden masses of the world. But when he catches an actual whiff of the nether regions, he begins to realize that an aristocratic limbo may be preferable to a lower- or middle-class hell, a realization not radically dissimilar to the one outlined by Huxley in 1920 in a discussion of Balzac's *Les Paysans*: "Balzac feared and hated democracy because he loved culture and art and grandeur and the other luxuries of the leisured rich. Culture and the beautiful amenities of civilization have always been paid for by slavery in one form or another . . . The aristocracy is a sort of Red Indian Reservation, where the savages of the mind are permitted to live in their own way, untroubled and relatively free from persecution. In a little while the advancing armies of democracy will sweep across their borders and these happy sanctuaries will be no more."[8] Here, then, on the plane of social action there is also imbalance; there are the savages of the mind and the barbarians of the body, neither of whom are really desirable. But given this choice — and no other — the former are infinitely preferable, as *Crome Yellow* goes on to show at some length and *Brave New World* in some depth.

From a purely artistic point of view, the idea that man and his society are fragmented and imbalanced carries with it certain dangers as well as a number of interesting possibilities. One of the more obvious and yet almost unavoidable dangers is that literary characters who are fragmentarily portrayed have a habit of being only fragmentarily real — that is, they degenerate into types. With the possible but rather doubtful exception of Richard, for example, all the characters of the novella are certainly types; their single-mindedness is what the eighteenth century would have called a ruling passion (which controls them as much as they control it). Richard's sister, Millicent, is and remains throughout the story the prototype of almost masculine efficiency, a primitive human form of a data-processing machine; his teacher, Skewbauld, is a monomaniacal prophet of paraffin, who sees all the world's problems rooted in the evil of inadequate bowel movements.*

In an obvious sense, these people are simply clichés which Huxley has captured, intensified, and set in motion. Nevertheless, they have an enormous amount of vitality which, though it may not be as officially "novelistic" as the minutely delineated pallor of Jamesian portraits, still has its own charm and credibility. It is in fact this very intensity of his characters' lifelikeness that lies, like some smoldering explosive charge, beneath the smoke and fire of Huxley's satire. If these types did not exist in reality, and if we did not recognize them as real beings, there would be little point and less effect in satirizing them.

The reasons for Huxley's success in creating lifelike type characters are manifold. In part it is probably his uncanny gift for brilliant and witty dialogue — much like that in the stories and plays of Oscar Wilde — that forces the reader to accept as real and vital a character whom, as the creation of a lesser author, he would reject out of hand. In addition, Huxley employs a whole arsenal of devices for characterization which it would be too tedious to catalogue here but which he gets progressively better and better at using with deadly effect. One of these, however, because it anticipates a structural device which Huxley came to be famous for later, deserves to be looked at somewhat more closely. Though at this stage of Huxley's development this technique had not yet reached the flexibility and range it later achieves in *Point Counter Point*, I think it can already appropriately be called the contrapuntal technique. Basically and in its

*Inspired perhaps by Huxley's own chronic difficulties with digestion.

simplest form, it consists of juxtaposing simultaneously two different points of view — that is, two different homemade universes or different conceptions of reality. This device enables Huxley to present various aspects of a problem or situation or character at the same time and thereby gain an astonishing series of kaleidoscopic perspectives on reality. And it also enables him to achieve some of his most brilliant satirical effects, as for example in the stories "Green Tunnels" and "Nuns at Luncheon" in *Mortal Coils* (1922), or in his early novels. The effect it aims at is a revelation of the impossibility of any significant contact between human beings because each human being is imprisoned like a fly in amber, in his own point of view, in his own homemade universe. It is as if two different radio transmitters were to continue broadcasting after the receivers had broken down. This is, of course, the basic situation underlying the whole of "Richard Greenow," as we see most clearly in its phantasmagoric concluding segment. Passion and reason, Pearl and Richard — self-division's cause — are continually transmitting and forever unable to receive; both, to borrow a phrase Huxley was to use a year later in his first novel, proceed along parallel lines to meet only in infinity.

A more prosaic but probably equally convincing reason why Huxley's characters are so successfully lifelike is that some of them at least are drawn from the life — a habit which, despite everything that was and could be said against it, Huxley never broke. Mrs. Cravister, for example, the eccentric but penetrating wife of Richard's headmaster at school, is a caricature of Mrs. Warre-Cornish, the wife of the vice-provost of Huxley's old school, Eton — a circumstance which caused the authorities there to seize the book. Hyman, sometime idealist and full-time opportunist, appears to be based in part on John Middleton Murry, and Richard's agricultural work at Crome (Garsington) may refer either to Huxley's own experience at "odd jobs, such as cutting down trees," or else to some conscientious objector's, like Clive Bell's, experience along similar lines. And the trial scene can be traced back to Lytton Strachey's well-known trial for avoiding conscription.

Amid all this hidden topical reference and technical complexity and ingenuity, it might be forgotten that a good deal of the appeal of this story lies in its humor (as distinct from its satire). The word "farcical" in the title — ironic though it may be — is surely a broad hint that the story is meant, at some level at any rate, to be funny. Certainly the farfetched idea of a schizophrenic, hermaphroditic combination of cultivated intellectual and semibarbaric woman journalist is at least partly farcical; it has that air of total improbability customarily associated with farce, as does the scene when Richard / Pearl tries to obtain "her" vote (under the new law enfranchising women) from the clerk of the Wibley town council: the whole thing is so improbably and yet so logically incongruous. Yet "Richard Greenow" is not merely farce — even here, at the very outset of his novelistic career, Huxley is able to pull out not just one, but an entire range of emotional and psychological stops. It is, after all, precisely this farcical scene that leads Richard to the madhouse and to a horrible death. Like Wycherly's farce, Huxley's has fangs, not just a toothless grin.

Huxley, as usual, seems to have been fully conscious of what he was trying to do when he began to combine the apparently disparate and certainly explosive elements of broad farce and profound satiric analysis. At least this is one of the conclusions to be drawn from an article on the Sitwells and "The Modern Spirit" which Huxley published in 1922.[9] After expounding on the destruction of the old world and all its values and traditions by the combined forces of war and the new psychology, Huxley notes that even the "last idol which we all tried so pathetically to keep standing," namely art, had now been attacked and demolished by Dada. Furthermore, anticipating the so-called death of tragedy by at least a quarter of a century, Huxley suggests that the "social tragedy of these last years has gone too far and in its nature and origin is too profoundly stupid to be represented tragically. And the same is true of the equally compli-

cated and devastating mental tragedy of the breakup of old traditions and values. The only possible synthesis is the enormous
farcical buffoonery of a Rabelais or an Aristophanes — a buffoonery which, it is important to note, is capable of being as beautiful
and grandiose as tragedy. For the great comics . . . are those
who, almost miraculously, combine the hugely, the earthily grotesque with the delicately and imaginatively beautiful." In a
world devoid of values, one's only recourse is laughter — the
laughter of an Aristophanes, of a Rabelais or a Swift.

Or of a Huxley. For, in "Richard Greenow," Huxley has
achieved this miraculous amalgamation of grotesque and beautiful: the beautifully delicate hues of prewar Eton and Oxford are
superimposed on the ugly townscapes of wartime Glasgow and
London; the sensitive beauty of Richard's mind is inescapably
bound to the gross vulgarity of Pearl's. And in this marriage of
opposites, Huxley's comic and satiric genius is actually much
closer to the writers named above, or to others like Laurence
Sterne, the early Dostoevsky, and E. T. A. Hoffmann, than he is
to either Thomas Love Peacock or Norman Douglas, who are
usually cited as his main models and influences. For, like Sterne
or Hoffmann, Huxley has a firm grasp on a total reality, both
ugly and beautiful, which is lacking in Peacock and, to a lesser
extent, in Douglas.

"Richard Greenow" is only one, though by far the longest, of
the stories in *Limbo,* Huxley's first collection of prose pieces.
The critical reaction to this collection — or to Huxley's shorter
narratives in general — has not been especially lively or penetrating. Still, the contemporary reviews do have a kind of archaeolog-
ical interest since a good many of the critical dicta which were
to haunt Huxley's reputation during the rest of his career had
already made their appearance here. The anonymous reviewer
for the *Spectator* is the first of a long line of critics to proclaim
Huxley's "inhumanity"; Virginia Woolf, in an unsigned review
for the *TLS,* found the stories "uninteresting" and went on to
note that Huxley was incapable of writing about anything he
believed in, or dealing effectively with the great human themes

of life and death. And thereby she opened another avenue subsequent critics have enjoyed exploring. Finally, as if to
prove that Huxley was to suffer as much at the hands of his
critical friends as his critical enemies, another reviewer saw
beneath the surface mockery of "Richard Greenow" a "seriousness indicative of that most tragical of causes of tragedy — social
ignorance."[10]

Ironically, "Richard Greenow" and *Limbo* as a whole almost really did become, though in a rather different sense, victims of social ignorance. Frank Swinnerton, who was a reader
for Chatto and Windus when Huxley submitted his manuscript
there, recounts in his *Autobiography* how the publisher was only
too delighted to receive a work from a grandson of his great idol
T. H. Huxley; so pleased, in fact, that he undertook to read
through a set of proofs himself. Delight turned to outrage and
he "refused absolutely to publish anything so appallingly gross,
blasphemous, and horrible. He was not, he said, squeamish;
but a line must be drawn, etc."[11] It was only after much diplo-
matic persuasion by Swinnerton (who, incidentally, later became
a good friend of Huxley's) that *Limbo,* shorn of only a very few
of its monstrous blasphemies, appeared in print. Mild as *Limbo*
may seem to us now, hardened as we have become by more
intense and more frequent psychosexual shocks, it clearly carried
something of a punch for most of its first readers. And *Limbo*
was to be only the beginning. For before ascending to the para-
diso, Huxley had arranged for his audience an extensive tour of
the inferno.

CHAPTER III

The Music of Pan
The Early Novels

IN MARCH 1920, not long after *Limbo* had shown definite signs of becoming a success, Huxley told one of his friends (and later critics), Raymond Weaver, that he was writing "a novel in the manner of Peacock."[1] He must already have been at work on it for some time because during that same spring he published in *Art and Letters* a short story entitled "One Sunday Morning," which deals with a fantastic sermon delivered by an equally fantastic clergyman named Bodiham on how Roman Catholicism caused the First World War.[2] That story, with some revisions and enlargements, later became chapter 9 of *Crome Yellow*. In the fall of the same year, Huxley published another short story, "A Country Walk,"[3] which, though not included in the novel, has perhaps an even more direct bearing on it.*

* Weaver's date for the letter may be wrong. March 1921 would seem more logical in view of the first mention of the novel in the *Letters*, when Huxley writes on June 28, 1921, to his father that he is "working hard at my Peacockian novel, which I have pledged myself to finish by the end of July" (L198). In his next letter, dated August 4, he reports its completion, adding that "practically, I have written the whole thing, some 60,000 words in the 2 months I have been here [in Italy]" (L199). The "practically," however covers a good deal of ground, since "A Country Walk" is certainly one of the

The central character of this very short story (as of the novel) is a young poet named Denis Stone. We meet him first as he walks toward Crome, musing on such questions as the probable effects on poetry and music of a humanity created with three legs instead of the usual two. These whimsical speculations are interrupted by a poor old deaf woman who complains to him about having to push her heavy cart. Denis, half sympathetic and half horrified and wholly embarrassed by this intrusion of an unpleasant reality, wonders if he should offer to help; he continues wondering and not helping while she starts telling him about her poverty-stricken family. Eventually they stop to rest and as she pulls out some bread to eat, he envisions her suddenly as one of those rustic Wordsworthian characters, like the Old Cumberland Beggar, whose function it is to arouse pleasurable feelings of sympathy in the beholder. But when she bares her rotten teeth, Wordsworth disappears and is replaced by a vision of a medieval deity reminiscent of "Topiary." The people of the Middle Ages, he reflects, "must have seen in their god a kind of Japanese gardener, snipping roots, paring twigs and buds, till he had made what should have been a tree into a wizened, twisted, fantastic thing, stunted and yet pitifully alive" (pages 72–73). Arriving at this point, Denis checks himself, lest he become too "cosmic" and forget that "at all costs one should live *terre-à-terre*" (page 73). But now he does help the old woman with the cart, even if only after a final reflection that all of human action simply consists in moving bits of matter from one place to another and that personally he would "very much rather sit still and read" (page 73).

"A Country Walk" was, it seems logical to conclude, written as a part of the projected *Crome Yellow*; surely it is more closely connected to the novel than is "One Sunday Morning." The

Crome Yellow episodes. Even if the earlier "One Sunday Morning" was not originally intended to be part of *Crome Yellow* — a good possibility — the publication date of the latter story (Autumn 1920) shows that Huxley must have planned and worked on the novel as early as the summer of 1920. Unless, of course, *Crome Yellow* was actually inspired by the short story, which seems unlikely if we take into account all the background information that is presupposed in "A Country Walk."

name and character of the protagonist, the mention of Crome,
and the time of publication all point to this conclusion. And yet
Huxley excluded it from the novel as it was finally published.
One can hardly help asking why. Leaving aside the possibility
that he rejected this story because it was not good enough (a not
very likely inference since Huxley, after all, did have it printed
elsewhere and it certainly is at least as good as the story he did
include), I would say he probably dropped it because it is based
on a very clear-cut satiric juxtaposition of the upper and lower
classes. In *Crome Yellow* there is no corresponding juxtaposition,
at least in correspondingly forceful terms. It has none of the
socially dark underside of "Richard Greenow," of the later
"Fard" (1922), or of the subsequent novels. Hence it is, I think,
reasonable to speculate that Huxley felt the realistic treatment
of social issues in "A Country Walk" was not suited to the lighter
mood of the Peacockian novel.

This story does, however, broach a theme of great importance in the novel: that is, the idea of the necessity and probable
futility of trying to bridge the gap between the individual homemade universes in which people live. Denis, for example, dwells
in a universe inhabited by ideas "of a purely speculative, unac-
tual nature" (page 69), and is so little aware of the general misery
of mankind that for him even the telegraph wires by the roadside
reveal "the glory of God to those who have eyes to see and ears
to hear" (page 69). His companion, however, is deaf both physically and spiritually, and is condemned to a homemade universe
as purely material as Denis's is intellectual.

Still, the story does present us with some possibility of escaping one's preconceptions. Looking at the old woman's foul
teeth, Denis can no longer dismiss her merely by allotting her a
place in a hygienic literary world. He is forced to recognize her
as a real and distinct human being, not just an imaginary one —
a rather painful process, for it is much easier, as Huxley insists in
Crome Yellow and elsewhere, to live in the world of ideas than
in the world of men. So painful does Denis find it, in fact, that
rather than be too "cosmic" or human or real, he prefers in the

end to pursue the "proper study of mankind . . . books" (page 73).

The Denis of the novel faces many of the same problems as the Denis of the short story and resolves them in much the same manner. He makes the attempt — dares to try, as "The Reef" has it — to achieve contact with another human being, though again in only an uncertain, halfhearted way. Yet, in making even this fumbling gesture, he differs from practically all the other characters in the novel. Although several of these characters, like Ivor or Gombauld, may be more agile in body, and others, like Wimbush or Scogan, more clever than he is, he alone is able to begin to act with soul, will, and body in some kind of harmonious combination.

The difficulty — one which plagued Huxley from the beginning to the end of his career — is that men of thought are rarely men of action, and vice versa.* As an early poem, "The Life Theoretic" (1917), has it, there are basically two types of men: (1) the theoretic ones, knowledgeable in matters of theology and books, but crumbling "to impotent dust before the struggling" and palsied by fear of women; and (2) another class who "have faces like battering rams," who "have been battling with the days" and "kissing the beautiful women."[4] The speaker, a self-styled member of the theoretic class, is unsure about which it is better to be: "But perhaps the battering-rams are in the right of it, / Perhaps, perhaps . . . God knows." In terms of this poem, Denis (at least for the greater part of the novel) falls into the theoretic category, whereas Ivor and Gombauld clearly belong to the battering rams — in fact, the identical image is used in the novel to describe the latter. But, suggestive as it is, the poem is ultimately inadequate as a guide to the novel. For, like "The Reef," *Crome Yellow* goes beyond this simple dualism to speculate on how to escape into a third category which is neither theoretic nor bestial.

---

*This is already implied in "Richard Greenow" where the title character comments on "the futility of action" and concludes that there is "nothing permanent, or decent, or worthwhile except thought." Probably Huxley's most thorough analysis of the problem is the brilliant historical study *Grey Eminence* (1941).

The only action the young Huxley seems to approve of
completely is that of the very simple, almost instinctive characters, like George in "Happily Ever After," or Irene and Hovenden in *Those Barren Leaves*. For a brief interval or so, to be
sure, they may fall under the spell of some other character's conception of reality, as Hovenden does under Falx's socialism, or
Irene under Mrs. Aldwinkle's pretensions to art, but, at the first
opportunity, they liberate themselves and revert to their prelapsarian state of ignorant bliss. They are able to achieve real contact with each other (even if only on a rather primitive level) because they are untrammeled by extraneous theories. However,
this kind of pure simplicity of action is impossible for the great
majority of Huxley's characters: impossible because most of them
have intelligence and have eaten of the tree of knowledge. Hence,
Mary Thriplow's conscious efforts in *Those Barren Leaves* to
achieve such simplicity are brutally satirized; for intelligence,
once possessed, cannot be denied. In the early Huxley, there is
no way back to paradise; yet a total denial of heaven leads to a
terrestrial hell, as it does for the diabolists Coleman in *Antic
Hay*, Chelifer in *Those Barren Leaves*, and Spandrell in *Point
Counter Point*. Mary Thriplow is satirized for the subversion of
her intelligence, the others for the perversion of theirs.

Denis Stone, like the speaker in "The Life Theoretic," recognizes his predicament and wants to escape it. The first and
most obvious strategy is, naturally, to become a "battering ram,"
a man of action who will not hesitate to smash the worlds of
other people in order to get his own way. At the beginning of
Crome Yellow, Denis, traveling on a slow local train, bemoans
the loss of two precious hours in which he might have done almost anything, "written the perfect poem, for example, or read
the one illuminating book" (page 1). When the train stops at
Camlet, the village nearest Crome, he rushes impatiently to the
baggage car to get his bicycle: " 'A bicycle, a bicycle!' he said
breathlessly to the guard. He felt himself a man of action" (page
2). But the guard, seemingly aware that Denis is really a man
theoretic, pays no attention to him and "Denis's man of action

collapsed, punctured" (page 2). Later on, his attempt to cut a fine conversational figure by relating a prepared account of his experiences in London is frustrated by the impervious monologues first of Priscilla Wimbush, then of her husband, Henry. Anne disconcerts him out of another proposed plan of action by remarking how "perfectly sweet" he looks in his white trousers, all of which finally leads him to break out in a tirade against the human condition in general and his own plight in particular. "One entered the world . . . having ready-made ideas about everything," Denis observes miserably. "One had a philosophy and tried to make life fit into it. One should have lived first and then made one's philosophy to fit life . . . Life, facts, things were horribly complicated, ideas, even the most difficult of them, deceptively simple. In the world of ideas everything was clear; in life all was obscure, embroiled. Was it surprising that one was miserable, horribly unhappy?" (page 24).

Some time later, sitting in the main hall of Crome and pretending to read while Gombauld and Anne are dancing to the music of a popular song, Denis gloomily pursues these reflections in a different key: " 'They're making a wild man of me.' The refrain sang itself over in Denis's mind. Yes, they were; damn them! A wild man, but not wild enough; that was the trouble. Wild inside; raging, writhing — yes, 'writhing' was the word, writhing with desire. But outwardly he was hopelessly tame; outwardly — baa, baa, baa" (page 64). He questions why the universal order of things demanded that he should be born with "a woolly face" and not one like those "old brazen rams that thumped against the walls of cities till they fell" (page 64). And why, he asks as he watches Ivor, Mary, and Anne exuberantly cavorting in the dark down the steep slope of the embankment, why did these people behave as they did? For, examining his own inner self, he could, to be sure, feel "a certain kittenishness sporting within him; but it was, like all his emotions, rather a theoretical feeling; it did not overmasteringly seek to express itself in a practical demonstration of kittenishness" (page 116). When Anne falls and sprains an ankle while running down the hill, Denis, for once, seems to have his wits about him and makes use of the opportunity by ministering, now shepherd and not sheep, to her needs; he even dares kiss her. Yet then he over-reaches himself; he offers to carry her, but when he tries to do so she proves too heavy and he ignominiously lets her drop. His man of action is punctured again.

So is his last endeavor to play the battering ram. Under the mistaken impression that Anne has given herself to Gombauld, Denis resolves to leave Crome by the ruse of having a telegram sent from London urging his immediate return. Happy in the cer-tainty of his decision, Denis reflects that "one is only happy in action" (page 215). But soon doubts assail him again; he wonders if he has not misjudged Anne, if he ought not to stay. His neme-sis, Mary, will not let him extricate himself so easily. Denis is trapped in his man of action and is completely miserable: "If only he'd just let things drift! . . . Never again, he said to him-self, never again would he do anything decisive" (page 218). That stone is happiest, we are seemingly led to conclude, which lets itself be impelled freely in a Newtonian vacuum of ideas, rather than tries to change its course by attaching itself to the influence of human beings.

In his attempts to become a man of action, Denis resembles the protagonist of Huxley's next novel, *Antic Hay*; but unlike the bestially active Complete Man, he does not yet fully appre-ciate that to be a battering ram is to be no more than a goat. Or, in other words, he does not comprehend — until the last chapter, at any rate — that the battering rams are as locked in their brazen homemade universes as he is in his pale theoretic one. None of the other characters seem any better off: not, cer-tainly, Mary Bracegirdle, who tries and fails so dismally and farcically to apply to life what she has learned from the "most modern books"; and not Henry Wimbush, who has changed from a man of action into a kind of robot. As a young man, Wimbush had been involved in a series of the "most phantasmagorical in-trigues" which, however, seemed to him "no more or less exciting than any other incident of actual life." Climbing by night into a boudoir in Toledo, he has come to realize, is just as dull as "catching the 8.52 from Surbiton to go to business on a Monday morning" (page 206). Hence, he now prefers to spend his time reading and writing about past actions rather than performing any himself. In fact, he looks forward to a time when machines will have reached a point of perfection, thereby making it possible "for those who, like myself, desire it, to live in a dignified seclusion, surrounded by the delicate attentions of silent and graceful machines, and entirely secure from any human intrusion" (page 204). The views of Scogan, Wimbush's old school friend, are basically similar. For him (and incidentally for Huxley as well) action is performed primarily by madmen. Men of reason get nowhere because they appeal to a superficial faculty in man, whereas the madmen appeal to what is fundamental: to passion and to the instincts. His solution, like Wimbush's, is in some respects prophetic of *Brave New World*. The intelligent men are to combine, seize power, and "found the rational state" (page 163). The difficulty with this state, according to Scogan, is that it is completely mad and cruel — which merely reveals that Scogan's law of action and madness is proved in this hypothetical case by using himself as the standard.

The only characters in the novel (besides Denis) who come to grips with this problem in even remotely satisfactory ways are, interestingly enough, the central characters of the two interpolated stories. The first, the dwarf Sir Hercules Lapith, has been forced to withdraw from the ordinary world, but by the strength of his will, the beauty of his body, and the grandeur of his soul he manages to create a world of his own.* He marries a beautiful dwarf from the Venetian aristocracy, has furniture specially made to suit his needs, hires other dwarfs as his servants, and hunts rabbits with pugs while mounted on a pony. For a time, Sir Hercules succeeds in doing what both Wimbush and Scogan desire but fail to do — namely, make reality conform to his own desires. Sir Hercules's fortune, however, lasts only

---

*The fairly obvious origin of this character in "The Voyage to Brobdingnag," bk. II of *Gulliver's Travels*, shows that even here Huxley was working in the tradition of Swiftian, and not merely Peacockian, satire.

for a time, since the same cosmic joke practiced at his birth on his father is now played on him at his own expense. His son, on whom he had based his hopes for founding a "more delicate race," grows up to normal size and abnormal oafishness. In the end, rather than live in a mad world that has passed beyond his control, he commits suicide.

The second fable from Henry Wimbush's "History of Crome" deals with the same problem (obviously a recurrent one at Crome), but in this case the outcome is happier. Actually, except for the successful conclusion, the plot of this story is by and large a mirror for the novel proper. George Wimbush, though less intelligent and more bourgeois than Denis, resembles him in his weakness, his lack of self-assurance, and his reluctance to act. Like Denis he is afraid of the woman he loves and uncertain about how to approach her; but unlike him — perhaps because he is less intellectual and more bourgeois — when he sees his opportunity, he is capable of seizing it wholeheartedly. Because he is much more realistic than Denis, he can break through the artificial homemade universe in which his beloved Georgiana Lapith lives, the universe of the Rousseauistic sensitive soul, where eating is a base concession to the body and true love can only be consummated in imaginary aery spheres. Once he becomes aware that Georgiana is secretly stuffing herself with ham and chicken, he does the "ungentlemanly, horribly underbred" (page 141) thing and blackmails her into marriage.

Sir Hercules Lapith and George Wimbush, different as they are, resemble each other in being able to make their imaginary worlds match their real worlds: Sir Hercules on a scale inversely proportional to his size and with a nobility unique to the entire novel, tinged with ridiculousness and doomed to failure though it is; and George by a kind of down-to-earth appreciation of life and human nature that enables him to make the right decisions and act on them. These glimpses into the Cromean past seem to show that a meaningful relation between the ideal and the real once existed, even if it exists no longer. And they prove too that the colors of that earlier Crome were less monochromatic, brighter than they are now; that the "chrome yellow" to which the title refers is not the original color of this great Tudor mansion, but the color age has left it.*

Although these two interpolated fables serve to place present-day Crome in perspective and allow us to see Denis's problem as partly a problem of his age, they represent a rather odd and antiquated convention in a supposedly "modern" novel. They are much more reminiscent of novels like *Tom Jones* or *Pickwick Papers* than of *Ulysses* or *To the Lighthouse*. And with good reason. For what Huxley is portraying here (as in the first part of "Richard Greenow") is the last gasp of the past, not the frantic pullulations of the present; the few remaining aristocratic savages on their Reservation, not the democratic hordes in their slums.

In this respect, *Crome Yellow* is unique among Huxley's novels, and probably consciously so, if we recollect the exclusion of "A Country Walk." It is really only to *Crome Yellow* that Scogan's famous remarks on the nonexistent "Tales of Knockespotch" apply — those tales full of strange adventures, extraordinary speculations, and fabulous characters, where, moving to the music of an incessant wit, immense erudition, fancy, intelligence, and emotion perform their intricate and subtle dances. Only *Crome Yellow* is really like this, with its odd assortment of fabulous characters, its strange adventures, both past and present, and its delicate humor and erudite monologues. For even if Huxley's later novels sometimes do resemble it, they never again achieve an atmosphere so utterly fantastic or so exclusively civilized.

Perhaps one of the reasons why *Crome Yellow* is so uniform-

*And surely not a color inspired by "yellow journalism," as one Spanish critic, overly mindful of the events of 1898, suggested.[5] Yet probably the fact that the color "yellow" was the hallmark of the decadents does serve to indicate further that Crome is in decay. Also, though Huxley clearly had Garsington in mind, he may have used a name like Crome to divert attention to Frome, an ancient and picturesque town in Somersetshire whose "atmosphere" in many ways evokes that of "historic" Crome. Even more speculatively, Huxley may be alluding to John Crome (1768–1821), noted British landscape painter who is usually referred to as "Old Crome" and who, like Crome itself, could be viewed as the representative of a happier age.

ly Knockespotchian is that (again, unlike any of Huxley's other novels), it seems really to be made up of "tales"; it reads almost as if it had been composed of separate stories rather than separate chapters. The existence of "A Country Walk," "One Sunday Morning," and the fables of Sir Hercules Lapith and George Wimbush indicate that Huxley originally may have planned a series of stories to follow up *Limbo* and only gradually arrived at the conclusion that their similar themes might lend themselves well to the episodic format of a Peacockian novel.

This supposition, if true, would also help to explain why Denis, though indubitably the central character of the novel, occupies a less than customarily important place in it. It is almost as if Denis's story were the frame around which a series of other and equally interesting stories were hung. Whatever the reason, however, the so-called weak or "vanishing" hero (in Sean O'Faolain's phrase) was to become one of the hallmarks of Huxley's fiction. Huxley seems never to have wanted (or been able) to create a literary hero with whom one could wholly identify — a Frederick Henry or Paul Morel or Stephen Dedalus — perhaps because he still lacked a sufficient dose of that vulgarity which, in his own view, every great novelist must have.

But Huxley did have the vulgarity, or audacity, to do again in *Crome Yellow* what he had dared to do in "Richard Greenow" — namely, take real people as the models for his characters (one of the classic traits, by the way, of the novels of Peacock and Douglas). According to the annotations made by T. S. Eliot in his copy of *Crome Yellow*, Denis is Huxley himself and Scogan is "Russell" (presumably Bertrand), though in his *Paris Review* interview Huxley explicitly stated that Scogan's character was based on Norman Douglas.[6] Eliot also identifies Gombauld with the painter Mark Gertler, a frequent visitor at Garsington, and Henry Wimbush, as might be expected, with Sir Philip Morrell, owner of the estate.* But his final equation of Priscilla Wimbush

---

*In part confirmed by a letter of August 7, 1916, in which Huxley writes from Garsington about "sleeping out on the roof in company with an artistic young woman in short hair and purple pyjamas . . . spending most of the night in conversation or in singing folk-songs and rag-time to the

with Lady Ida Sitwell is rather puzzling, since it was notorious in the twenties that Huxley intended her to be a caricature of Lady Ottoline Morrell, something that Peter Quennell was later to affirm explicitly in an article commemorating her death.[7]

Crome Yellow, then, is clearly a roman à clef, an intentionally if not maliciously personal satire. But to read it only as such would be to understand only one aspect of the novel and its satire. For Huxley is interested not so much in his characters as personal caricatures as he is in their representing certain attitudes toward life and reality. As Grant Overton remarked, "Mr. Huxley is not so much engaged in hitting heads as in hitting what is in the heads."[8] It is Huxley's concentration on and analysis of his characters' psychology that forms the real satiric core of the book.

Denis, for example, is, as he himself admits, continually

stars . . . while early in the morning we would be wakened by a gorgeous great peacock howling like a damned soul or woman wailing for her demon lover, while he stalked about the tiles showing off his plumage to the sunrise" (L109). The peacock reappears in *Crome Yellow* at the end of chapter 19 when Ivor plucks one of his feathers as a trophy for Mary Bracegirdle, the "artistic young woman" identified by Grover Smith as Dorothy Carrington (L108n). On the same roof Denis somewhat later in the story (chap. 29) mildly contemplates suicide and converses with Mary. For more on the relation between Carrington and Huxley see Dora Carrington's *Letters and Extracts from Her Diaries,* ed. David Garnett (London, 1970).

In *The Huxleys* (London, 1968), p. 224, Ronald Clark asserts that Russell very definitely saw himself as the real-life original for Scogan and objected that the fictional character was made "to put forward seriously the very ideas which he, Russell, had discussed as a joke at one of Lady Ottoline's house-parties."

The name Gombauld is taken from the French seventeenth-century poet Jean Ogier de Gombauld. What Huxley means to suggest by doing so is not entirely clear. In *Texts and Pretexts* Huxley quotes twice from his verse, first under the heading "Self Torture," later under "Distractions." Possibly Huxley's painter, like the French poet, believes "que le vautour est doux à Prométhée, / Et que les Ixion se plaisent aux Enfers" (*Texts and Pretexts,* p. 88). He too persists in seeking out the self-torture of repeated frustration in his amours with Anne. The affair between Anne and Gombauld strikingly resembles in some respects that of Mark Gertler and Dora Carrington, as recounted in Michael Holroyd's *Lytton Strachey: A Critical Biography,* vol. 2, *The Years of Achievement* (New York, 1968), especially pp. 186–223. However, Carrington's erratic behavior and tomboyish appearance make her a much more likely Mary Bracegirdle than Anne Wimbush. Huxley seems here to be combining and redistributing characteristics of various people rather than trying to draw from the life.

laboring under the weight of the "twenty tons of ratiocination" his education has imposed on him. His problem is not, as one critic has explained, that he has no prepared attitude toward reality and life, but, on the contrary, that he has far too much — by about twenty tons. Like the Denis of "A Country Walk," this Denis inhabits a world of words and poetical speculations far removed from reality. At the beginning of the novel, on the way to Crome on his bicycle, he concentrates so exclusively on finding the mot juste for the beautiful landscape around him that, feeling for the word, he makes a gesture and almost falls off the bicycle. Denis is continually almost falling off something or other as his world of words keeps colliding with the world of things. So, for example, his frustrated love for the word "carminative." For years, Denis confesses, he had treasured the word because of its sound and the associations he had built up around it. Finally he finds the perfect opportunity to use it in a poem: "And passion carminative as wine . . ." Then it occurs to him to check its meaning in the only immediately available dictionary, an English-German one, where he discovers to his horror that carminative means *windtreibend*. As Denis is himself aware (and in this respect he differs from the other characters), for as long as he continues to live in his homemade universe, he is doomed to repeat these frustrating and humiliating experiences. But try as he may, he simply cannot change, and at the end of the novel he is no better off than he was at the beginning. The great illumination is still to come.

The other characters share Denis's problem, though often in cruder forms. Priscilla Wimbush and her horoscope, Barbecue-Smith and his pipeline to the infinite, and Bodiham and his mad prophecies are essentially three birds of a feather: *rarae aves* enmeshed in the snares of a superreality supposedly determined for their own private benefit by certain "Higher Forces." In a more subtle and frightening way, Henry Wimbush who, as we have seen, succeeds so well in living either in the past or the future that his physical appearance resembles either a corpse or a robot. And Scogan, who aptly characterizes himself as *vox et praeterea nihil,* is, as the train of imagery that pursues him throughout the novel suggests, a diabolical reptile: the dry voice of intellectual sin incapable of conceiving love.

The same holds true of the "battering rams" Ivor and Gombauld, the modern flapper Mary Bracegirdle, and, most obviously, Jenny Mullion who literally confirms Denis's assertion that "our minds are sealed books only occasionally opened to the outside world" (page 178). Literally and literarily — because Jenny's conception of reality is, in fact, confided only to her "sealed" and secret notebook, and because, with her deafness, she is inevitably removed from real contact with any other character in the novel. Coming down to breakfast and finding her alone at the table, Denis suddenly realizes that Jenny's plight is symbolic of the plight of all the others: " 'I hope you slept well,' he said. 'Yes, isn't it lovely?' Jenny replied, giving two rapid little nods. 'But we had such awful thunderstorms last week.' Parallel straight lines, Denis reflected, meet only in infinity. He might talk forever of care-charmer sleep and she of meteorology till the end of time. Did one ever establish contact with anyone? We are all parallel straight lines. Jenny was only a little more parallel than most" (pages 20–21). In short, all the characters of the novel are isolated in their private worlds, and Jenny only differs from the rest in that her isolation is a little more obvious.

The one possible exception is Anne, who has been called the only "normal" character in the novel.[9] But her "normality" is questionable, at the very least, for certainly the absolute detachment she preserves toward both Denis and Gombauld is not entirely normal, particularly since at times she seems to be leading them on. There is something of the later Myra Viveash in her: if she is not continually "expiring" like Myra, she does seem to be continually "languishing," drooped, lazily graceful, in some chair, waiting for something to happen, for something to interrupt the boredom of her existence. But, of course, since she insists on being detached and in control, nothing ever does. She rejects Denis because a love affair between them would not be their "stunt." Though she thinks him "sweet," she never makes his difficulties any easier, and she becomes quite indignant when Gombauld points out to her that she is "playing the same game" (page 156) with Denis as she is with him. Like the heroines of the Restoration comedies from whom she appears to be derived, she enjoys being surrounded, pursued, and flattered by her lovers, but does not want to give anything herself, does not want to get "involved." In this reluctance, she resembles her uncle, Henry Wimbush, whose expressionless, masklike face she, appropriately enough, has inherited.

Anne's attitude toward life may be described as a kind of educated, "civilized" hedonism; or, at least, this is what she thinks it is. In reply to Denis's complaint about having to carry around his twenty tons of ratiocination, Anne asks him, " 'Why can't you just take things for granted and as they are? . . . It's so much simpler . . . I've always taken things as they come . . . It seems so obvious. One enjoys the pleasant things, avoids the nasty ones. There's nothing more to be said' " (page 25). Certainly, in her amused detachment, Anne manages on the whole to avoid the "nasty" things; but does she really enjoy the "pleasant" ones? After all, how is one to tell, unless one is involved in an experience, if it is going to turn out "nasty" or "pleasant," or more of one than the other? And Anne does not want to be involved, which is probably why she becomes "somewhat pensive" as she begins to examine even a little her real feelings toward Denis. She seems to grow remotely conscious that through her deliberate avoidance of everything "nasty," she may have missed something very "pleasant" indeed. So that, in the end, because of her desire to remove herself from certain aspects of human existence, she has ceased to be entirely human.

Crome Yellow was an immediate critical and popular success. Almost overnight Huxley became an internationally famous literary figure. F. Scott Fitzgerald hailed the novel as "the highest point so far attained by Anglo-Saxon sophistication," and H. L. Mencken echoed these sentiments. In fact, the only openly hostile reaction came from Bloomsbury. Writing in *The Dial*, Raymond Mortimer sneered at *Crome Yellow* as "a desperately clever novel" with characters that are mere *"fantoches"* with gutta-percha entrails.* Huxley's problem, he noted, was that he was incapable of describing "direct and simple beauty," and that he really was no writer of stories at all. Like an earlier review emanating from Bloomsbury, he closed with a word of advice to the apprentice writer: he should try to be more "serious."[10]

Even if we do not see here, as Frank Swinnerton did,[11] an attempt by Bloomsbury to get its revenge on Huxley for daring to laugh at "first rate people," it still seems that, instead of asking Huxley to be more serious, Mortimer might have acted more wisely by taking himself less seriously. For surely a good deal of the charm of the novel lies in its very lack of heavy seriousness, its delicate farce and gentle caricature. Critically speaking, it seems absurd to want to deprive the reader of these qualities. But even on his own terms, Mortimer is wrong. For, as Scogan indicates in one of his many monologues, the inhabitants of Crome, given the proper, or rather, improper circumstances, could have been very serious people indeed. In his view, all human beings resemble the first six Caesars and, once placed in the appropriate "Caesarean environment," would inevitably develop as the corresponding Caesar did. The nineteenth century — and Crome is an isolated remnant of that age — did not permit the creation of such an environment, but the twentieth with its massive social changes and holocaustic great war does. What once would have astonished and aroused the indignation of the public now hardly causes a stir. Black and Tans can harry the Irish, Poles can molest the Silesians, Fascisti can slaughter their countrymen almost unhindered by civilized opinion. From this analysis Scogan goes on to portray the misery and horror that is the daily fare of the majority of mankind. And paradoxically, he observes, the misery and horror are tolerable only because each human being is alone in his own private universe. "If one had," he suggests, "an imagination vivid enough and a sympathy sufficiently sensitive really to comprehend and to feel the sufferings

*Ironically, it was by way of Huxley's introduction that Mortimer was launched as a second-generation Bloomsbury. See Clive Bell, *Old Friends* (London, 1956), p. 131n.

of other people, one would never have a moment's peace of
mind . . . One is always alone in suffering; the fact is depress-
ing when one happens to be the sufferer, but it makes pleasure
possible for the rest of the world" (pages 111–112). These remarks alone should have been enough to make Mortimer and
Bloomsbury realize that Huxley was not being altogether flighty
in this novel. And whatever justification their complaint may
have had for *Crome Yellow* was certainly to vanish with the publication of Huxley's next novel, *Antic Hay.*

In *Antic Hay* Huxley makes his first extensive foray into the
"real world" beyond the borders of the civilized Red Indian
Reservation. His hero, Theodore Gumbril, Jr., fed up with his
position as history master at a public school, decides to chuck
safety, learning, and boredom, and head for London where he
thinks the action is. There he hopes to gain wealth and happiness by marketing his patent small clothes, the inflatable underwear he invented while sitting on the cold hard benches of the
school chapel.* Gumbril's first stop in this pilgrimage is at his
philosophical tailor's to be measured for a prototype. Bojanus
the tailor, a kind of cross between Thoreau, Marx, and Emily
Post, proceeds to deliver a lengthy disquisition on human nature,
social revolution, and freedom, in which he implicitly questions
Gumbril's aims. Liberty, he observes in his makeshift Cockney
accent, does not really exist: certainly not for the great mass of

*The place is probably Eton, where Huxley taught for about a year
and a half near the end of the war. Like Gumbril, Huxley, occasionally tired
of correcting papers on historical subjects. Writing to his friend Lewis Gielgud on September 30, 1917, he remarks: "I don't know whether to advise
you to become a pedagogue: it has its pleasant side to be sure but also its
tediousnesses . . . for instance I have spent the morning in correcting twenty
eight essays on the possibility and desirability of a League of Nations, and
with such few exceptions they are all stupid."
The idea for the inflated trousers may have come from an incident in
the wartime trial of Lytton Strachey. Robert Graves writes of the "extraordinary impression caused by an air-cushion which he inflated in Court as
a protest against the hardness of the benches" (*Good-bye to All That* [Gar-
den City, N.Y., 1957], p. 249). But according to Michael Holroyd, *Lytton
Strachey,* vol. 2, pp. 178–179, this was merely a practical measure to alleviate
his suffering from piles. In any event, Huxley may simply have drawn on his
own ample experience of hard Etonian benches.

people because they would simply be lost in a waste of leisure time. And even those who would not — the so-called "Best People" — are at best confined to sexual freedom: "And sexual freedom — what's that? . . . You and I, Mr. Gumbril . . . we know. It's an 'orrible, 'ideous slavery. That's what it is. Or am I wrong, Mr. Gumbril?" (page 35).

Gumbril politely agrees with Bojanus's observations, but is not convinced. He is eager to lead the life of action, full of faith that it will grant him freedom, sexual and otherwise. It takes him the rest of the novel to find out differently and discover that old Bojanus was right.

Gumbril's next step in accommodating himself to the ways of the world is to tailor himself into a man of action, or what he calls a "Complete Man." When one of his friends tells him that men with beards seduce more women, he orders a false one made. As he tries it on, he finds that his mild and melancholy self has vanished completely, that instead he has become "a massive Rabelaisian man, broad and powerful and exuberant with vitality and hair" (page 94). In this new disguise, he ventures forth into the London streets, a modern Don Quixote in reverse, in search of adventure. After a brief interval of speculation about the millions of ravishing and ravishable women in the world, the Complete Man succeeds in picking up one of these "only possible soul-mates" (page 96), smiling to himself as he imagines how his former mild and melancholy self would have behaved. The introductory chat concluded, she invites him to tea at her home in the suburbs, and there he makes love to her. During the formal introductions that follow, he is, however, somewhat taken aback by her name. Quite possibly, it occurs to him, Rosie Shearwater may be the wife of one of his friends. And so she is, for just as he goes out the door he hears Shearwater's voice floating up the stairwell.* Suppressing his first impulse to run and hide (Complete Men, after all, do not hide), he strides

---

*In *JBS: The Life and Work of J. B. S. Haldane* (London, 1968), p. 57, Ronald Clark quotes briefly from the draft autobiography of this original for Shearwater. Among other supposed errors in Huxley's portrait, Haldane objects to being made to fall hopelessly in love with Myra Viveash. "Now

confidently past his friend, adding injury to insult by stepping on his toe.

But sexual success does not exhaust his repertoire of complete actions and freedoms. Having arranged with an entrepreneur named Boldero to manufacture his small clothes, Gumbril is surprised and outraged when he receives a letter offering ludicrous terms. Boldero had reckoned with the old, mild, and melancholy Gumbril, not the new one. When the hirsute Complete Man suddenly appears before him and pounds on his desk, Boldero succumbs immediately, wondering how he could have misjudged this man so badly.

But, as Huxley himself was fond of saying, nothing fails like success. What Gumbril the battering ram achieves, Gumbril the man theoretic pays for. For Gumbril, like Richard Greenow, cannot successfully integrate two such disparate personalities; he can only be one or the other, not both at the same time. He must either be the man of action and lust, or the man of reflection and love. Huxley's rigid dualism will allow him no other alternative. This is illustrated graphically in his encounter with a young woman named Emily. After having tried the Complete approach on her and failed, he barely manages to persuade her to see him again by almost breaking down in tears. At their next meeting he leaves his false beard and alternate personality behind, and arrives in his native guise of Mild and Melancholy One. In that form, Emily likes him much better. Together they walk out into Kew Gardens and the silence and the fresh greenness of spring. There, remote from complete men and their brutal and mechanical activity, Gumbril tells her of the "crystal world." It is the world, he says, that lies behind the jazz and the shouting, a world one becomes aware of sometimes at the still point of night, while lying in bed and waiting for sleep: a beau-

in 1919," he says, "Aldous Huxley observed me making advances, which he doubtless considered rather cumbrous, to a lady of his acquaintance. So many of the 'highbrows' of that day boasted of their amorous conquests, real or imagined, that he regarded such behavior as universal. It is not. Indeed, had the lady in question not been dead for many years, I should not even now venture to suggest that Shearwater may have known when to hold his tongue."

tiful and at the same time terrifying world that grows within one like a crystal, where one feels absolutely alone and where none of the distractions and trivialities of the outer world can save one from the pure center of silence. And if one should ever touch that center, then "one would have to begin living arduously in the quiet, arduously in some strange unheard-of manner" (page 147). But Gumbril is afraid to "touch" because it would require too much effort, it would — in Denis's words — be too cosmic.

Still, as Gumbril comes to realize that Emily is "native to that crystal world" (page 148), he tries to move into it with her: first by listening to the crystalline music of Mozart, then by taking her to his rooms where — through love, not just sexual attraction — they are enveloped by silence: "For them there were no more minutes . . . there was no need to think of anything but the moment. The past was forgotten, the future abolished. There was only this secret room and the candlelight and the unreal, impossible happiness of being two" (pages 154–155). But it is not a world of long duration, despite the intimations of eternity. Gumbril smashes the crystal he had constructed so arduously. On his way to join Emily in a cottage in the country, he meets a bored Myra Viveash who persuades him to postpone his trip and have lunch with her. Gumbril grudgingly agrees and stands by unheeding as the lunch turns into a prolonged "good time" lasting late into the night. Then he finally smashes the remaining fragments into little bits. He first tells Myra about Emily in veiled and mocking terms, then later in his own rooms, drunk himself, he tells his drunken friends the whole story in detail. He does exactly what he had earlier told Emily one should not do; terrified, he has withdrawn back into the "real" world: "Well, let everything go. Into the Mud. Leave it there, and let the dogs lift their hind legs over it as they pass" (page 186).

The next morning he awakes to the full realization of what he has done; a letter from Emily announces her departure to points unknown. After looking for her without success he resolves to leave England on the morrow. He spends the last evening with Myra trying to gather enough of their so-called friends for a farewell dinner. In a kind of "Last Ride Together," they drive from one end of London to the other, at Myra's request always passing through the brightly illuminated Piccadilly Circus. This circular ride through London and around the Circus becomes a symbol of the futility of action, at least as conceived and practiced by the Complete Man. The same symbol recurs even more strikingly at the end of the novel, when Shearwater vainly pedals his stationary bicycle, imagining he can escape reality and Myra Viveash.

And it occurs also and perhaps most prominently in the title of the novel, derived, as the epigraph tells us, from Marlowe:

> My men like satyrs grazing on the lawns
> Shall with their goat-feet dance the antic hay.
> *Edward II,* Act I, Scene 2

The word *hay* in this context refers to an Elizabethan (and probably pre-Elizabethan) ring dance which Marlowe qualifies with the adjective *antic,* meaning in Elizabethan times *foolish* or *idiotic.* It rather neatly describes the activities of almost all of the characters of the novel who move in rings and circles, and who, as satyrs or complete men, dance to the music of Pan — which is why they get nowhere. Throughout *Antic Hay,* there are hints that if they had danced to the music of Mozart instead, as Gumbril briefly did, they might have gotten somewhere. But they do not.

As satyrs, they are of course really Incomplete Men (and women), lacking the balance necessary for an arduous triune peace. At best (with one or perhaps two important exceptions), they combine intelligence with sensuality, not intelligence with strength of will and emotion. Hence they dance the dance of bestiality, not of humanity, as we can see not just from the epigraph but also from Gumbril and Myra's last dance together. The Negro jazz band plays a popular tune:

> "What's he to Hecuba?
> Nothing at all.

    That's why there'll be no wedding on Wednesday week,
    Way down in old Bengal."

"What unspeakable sadness," said Gumbril, as he stepped, stepped
through the intricacies of the trot. "Eternal passion, eternal pain
. . . Rum-tiddle-um-tum, pom-pom. Amen. What's he to Hecuba?
Nothing at all. Nothing, mark you. Nothing, nothing."
    "Nothing," repeated Mrs. Viveash. "I know all about that."
She sighed.
    "I am nothing to you," said Gumbril, gliding with skill be-
tween the wall and the Charybdis of a couple dangerously experi-
menting with a new step. "You are nothing to me. Thank God.
And yet here we are, two bodies with but a single thought, a beast
with two backs, a perfectly united centaur trotting, trotting"
(pages 168–169).

And on they trot.

    Centaur or satyr, but not human, they both continue danc-
ing to the music of the senses, where, by the very essence of such a
dance, he can never mean anything to Hecuba, nor Hecuba anything to him. Like Shakespeare's player (*Hamlet,* Act II, Scene 2),
they are simply going through the external motions which,
though they seem real enough, never touch any inner depth of
feeling. For the participants of the antic hay forever face each
other from behind the protection of their masks, in this instance
those of Complete Man and Complete Woman. Hence the only
significant distinctions in this sort of world are the type of mask
and the consciousness of it. Gumbril knows the part he is playing; Lypiatt, until very nearly the end, does not; and others never
do. Gumbril, as Huxley was later to say of Hamlet in chapter 11
of *Eyeless in Gaza,* knows too much to have a personality, knows
too much to allow himself to be deceived into believing that he
has a single, fixed, definable, and delimited psyche.
    The echo from *Hamlet* has other overtones as well. Both
Shakespeare and Hamlet's protagonists share an analogous skepticism about female virtue and romantic love, or, for that matter,
about the possibility of meaningful relations among human beings in general. And both works concentrate with bitter irony

on the plight of the intellectual in a time that is out of joint. Hamlet's mask of madness is only a more human solution than Gumbril's beard and goat's foot. The parallel comes closest to the surface in the "play within the play" which is an important feature of both works, providing in each case a mirror in which to see a caricature of the main plot. Furthermore, Gumbril, like Hamlet before him, idealizes his father and the world his father stands for, and yet cannot bring himself to support that world with more than words. *Meliora video,* as so often in Huxley's novels, but *deteriora sequor.*

In the goatish, brazen world of Complete Men, Huxley suggests, there is no room for any more significant kind of relationship. Except for the brief interlude with Emily, Gumbril is, as we have seen, both spiritually and physically bound by his transformation into a man of action. Myra Viveash, with her face always "agonizing," her voice either "expiring" or "dying," is, like Henry Wimbush, practically a corpse. When she lives at all, she lives in the past, mourning her Tony Lamb who was prevented by the slaughter of the war from turning into a sheep (or goat). But even this emotion is neither strong nor lasting; none of her emotions are. She is like a zombie, languishing about and waiting to be galvanized back into life.

The same is true of most of the other characters in the novel. For example, Lypiatt, the would-be great artist who succeeds only in being a great big bag of air, refuses to recognize that he is a clever but otherwise undistinguished hack.* Like Denis's world of words, Lypiatt's imaginary world of art keeps colliding with the world of things. When he finally realizes the truth in a moment of tragicomic awakening, he, like Sir Hercules Lapith, can resolve the dilemma only by suicide. Too long accustomed to one world, he cannot live in another. But Lypiatt at least becomes aware of the problem, even if too late to do anything constructive about it. Not so Mercaptan, the cultivated author on "mid-

---

*This character is probably based on the Romantic painter Benjamin Haydon. In 1926 Huxley published an interesting introduction for a new edition of Haydon's *Autobiography.*

dles," the polite hedonist. He continues to exist in his own private version of the eighteenth century, polishing his "exquisitely delicious" prose, and reclining occasionally on "Crébillon" (his sofa) to partake of some more immediately sensual pleasure. And not so Coleman, who likes to play Baudelaire and Mephistopheles, and is motivated by a fashionably black despair about the nonvalue of all values.* Though convinced that humanity is nothing but a vile pack of animals, he still spends a great deal of energy exhorting them blasphemously: "O all ye Beasts and Cattle, curse ye the Lord: curse and vilify him forever" (page 57). Coleman, like his spiritual cousins Chelifer and Spandrell in later Huxley novels, simply enjoys his own brutal existence too much to try to change it.

The only major character of the novel who consistently does not dance to the music of Pan is Gumbril's father.† Unlike the others, he does not need the crowd, the heat and proximity of other bodies to reassure him of his own existence; he is not afraid to be alone. In fact, he enjoys solitude and claims that he is

*According to Jocelyn Brooke, Coleman is modeled on the composer Philip Heseltine (*Aldous Huxley* [London, 1958], p. 15). Heseltine was also the original for the bohemian Halliday in Lawrence's *Women in Love* (see H. T. Moore, "Who's Who in the Lawrence Letters," in his edition of *The Collected Letters of D. H. Lawrence* [New York, 1962], p. xl). Cecil Gray tells of going drinking at Verrey's in the summer of 1922 with Heseltine, Huxley, and Eugene Goossens, and hearing Heseltine make "a witty and brilliant speech of which the essence is reproduced in the book." Quoted in Ronald Clark, *The Huxleys*, p. 224.

†Whoever might have been the prototype for this character, it certainly was not Huxley's own father. After reading the novel he testified to his outrage at his son's supposed "botanizing on his mother's grave." Just where this grave was to be found in the novel is not clear, since mothers are notably absent in *Antic Hay*. Huxley repudiated the charge in one of the few letters in the entire collection which might be classified as unfriendly (L224). He was more amused when his cousin, Arnold Ward, threatened to "take his trousers off and leave him" in Piccadilly for having maligned his ancestors in *Antic Hay* (L233). How scandalous, even in a less familial context, Huxley's novel was thought to be at the time emerges from the American publisher George H. Doran about it. Doran, who himself was exceedingly anxious that Huxley should not be "classed among the degenerating influences of his day," was quick to conform to the New York district attorney's stipulation that the publicity for the book should not "stress the pornographic aspect." See *Chronicles of Barabbas, 1884–1934* (New York, 1952), p. 174.

"not good at people. Most of them I don't like at all, not at all" (page 27). Nevertheless, when he must, he can be very good at people indeed, much better than anyone else. To save an old friend from bankruptcy, he sells his own most precious possession, a scale model of Wren's proposed reconstruction of London. By the very fact of his ability to be alone with himself, he is able to be with others in a more than merely physical sense.

Gumbril senior is like the vast old decaying eighteenth-century house he lives in: an antiquated but still vital remnant of an earlier and better age, he is a truly complete man, not simply bestial and derivative like the others. Inhabiting an Apollonian world of solitude, silence, and beauty, he dances, if he dances at all, to the music of Mozart, as his son realizes when he discovers what his father has done for his friend. Man is no longer just an earwig, as he had thought before, not merely beyond or below good and evil: "Beyond good and evil? Below good and evil? The name of earwig . . . The twelfth Sonata of Mozart was insecticide; no earwigs could crawl through that music. Emily's breasts were firm and pointed and she had slept at last without a tremor. In the starlight, good, true and beautiful became one" (page 247). Gumbril senior's crystal world is similar to the world Calamy, in Huxley's next novel, tries to enter, but Gumbril does not have to climb a mountain and contemplate his navel to do so; he simply steps out onto the balcony and watches and listens raptly to the birds that, strangely, settle only on his trees, though there are other, larger and more pleasant gardens nearby. His accord with these birds is almost mystical. Quietly he waits for them to break into their sudden bursts of song: "At these moments Mr. Gumbril would lean forward, would strain his eyes and his ears in the hope of seeing, of hearing something — something significant, explanatory, satisfying" (pages 243–244). This hope is never fulfilled, but that in no way lessens his happiness. He feels, as he explains to Myra, that the birds commune with each other by some kind of telepathy, a faculty he suspects man of having too. Sometimes he can even feel their thoughts striking against his own; and sometimes he inexplicably knows a moment beforehand when they are going to wake up. Trying to show this to Myra, he fails; but a little later when the birds do suddenly break into song, he listens enchanted, and "his face, as he turned back towards the light, revealed itself all smiles. His hair seemed to have blown loose of its own accord, from within, so to speak" (page 446).

Old Gumbril's life is organized around the principles of proportion and balance, the basic principles of his architectural profession. Unfortunately, these principles cannot be extended much beyond himself, for, as he recognizes, most men are little more than animals and therefore incapable of appreciating beauty and harmony. Wren serves as a sufficient example. After the great fire, he had offered to rebuild London "for the imagination and the ambitious spirit of man, so that even the most bestial, vaguely and remotely, as they walked those streets, might feel that they were of the same race — or very nearly — as Michelangelo" (page 135). But the Londoners preferred their former squalor, dirt, and ugliness, so much so in fact that the one street, Regent Street, "that was really like a symphony by Mozart" was in the process of being torn down.

The proportions of humanity and the modern world are wrong — or merely superficially right, as in the mask of the Complete Man. The novel's most concentrated expression of this falsity is the play that Gumbril and Myra watch. Its main character, simply and suggestively called "The Monster," seeks something that is not monstrous, crying out that "somewhere there must be love like music. Love harmonious and ordered; two spirits, two bodies moving contrapuntally together. Somewhere, the stupid brutish act must be made sense, must be enriched, must be made significant" (page 179). But the Monster finds only "monstrous" love — only the beast with two backs. Such is the fate also of Gumbril junior's friend Shearwater, who while madly pedaling his stationary bicycle, is haunted by two opposing images: the first of Myra Viveash walking among the ruins of the world she has destroyed, the second of old Gumbril, clutching his beard and crying out to him to rebuild his world "with proportion." However, the times are out of joint, and worlds are not put up as easily as pulled down.

Like *Crome Yellow*, *Antic Hay* directs the main thrust of its satiric attack against a disproportional, imbalanced humanity, or to revise its own phrase, against an incomplete mankind. It is an incompleteness that is felt all the more agonizingly by those, like the younger Gumbril and the Monster, who are sensitive enough to perceive it because somewhere a completeness does or did exist: in Wren, in the author of the Diabelli variations, in Mozart, in the quiet, proportional world of old Gumbril (the world he characteristically gave away only to gain it all the more certainly). It is by these hints and intimations of a true humanity that the extent of the false one's perversion can be gauged.

The results of incompleteness and imbalance are strewn all over the modern world. In education, where an elegant literary training is indiscriminately stuffed down the throats of all comers without regard for the fact that some of them, at least, would have been much happier apprenticed to a useful trade. In art and art criticism, where one critic demands "civilization," another "feeling," a third "knowledge," but none (except the artistically impotent Lypiatt) all three in harmonious combination. In advertising, which conditions men to new and more horrible imbalances and inanities. And in the organization of society, which arbitrarily divides people up into the "best" and the "worst," and does its best (or worst) to ignore all visible and audible signs of poverty and disease.

This emerges clearly during one of the central scenes of the novel when a number of the more important characters are taking a late-evening postprandial walk somewhere near Hyde Park Corner. By chance they run across Myra Viveash and one of her escorts, Bruin Opps, who is the epitome of the so-called Best People. Off to one side, some poor people are talking, and Bruin launches into a tirade against the lower classes, loudly proclaiming that he loathes them, wishing someone would invent servants with internal combustion engines, and quoting with great relish some lines from a song his grandfather used to sing during the

Reform Law days: "Rot the People, blast the People, damn the Lower Classes" (page 62). While this is going on, Gumbril becomes aware of a few adjoining members of the lower classes in the process of betraying their humanity. They are grouped in a circle around a man and a woman, who are sitting "like a limp bundle tied up in black cotton and machintosh" (page 62). With one ear attuned to his friends, the other to the miserable story of these two people, Gumbril forms a momentary bridge between two social classes. While Myra is busy extracting Shearwater's theories on love, the poor man tells his audience how he has lost his job, that his wife is pregnant, and that he has no money at all. As he listens, Gumbril becomes more and more disturbed, until he finally interrupts his friends and persuades them to donate some money. Still, his conscience is not easy. Like Denis in "A Country Walk," he has become directly (and not just theoretically) aware of a larger and uglier reality; he has been forced into seeing how horrible the human condition is and made to wonder if he really has a right to his comfortable existence. Yet, like Denis again, he answers these questions by eluding them: escaping not into a homemade world of books, but into an equally limited one of flesh.

The conversational counterpoint Huxley uses in this scene is repeated later for more obviously satirical purposes. The occasion is the play within the novel. There the Monster sees a lovely Young Lady and immediately proceeds to fall in love with her. He looks at her from his window and starts to describe her in words reminiscent of the Song of Solomon, but while he does so the Young Lady is wondering whether she ought to buy some new underwear, since her boyfriend's "hand already . . ." At this point the Monster interrupts her thoughts by shouting that he loves her, and their two parallel internal monologues meet, but only briefly, for the Young Lady explodes into noisily derisive laughter. The Monster's world of love, analogous to Gumbril's crystal world, is shattered by the intrusion of a gross reality. Nevertheless, like Gumbril the satyr, he is a monster only externally and artificially; he continues to hope that his ideal world of balance and harmony does exist, and that he, like some of the slimy fish of the aquarium, can manage to make it to the reef: "Somewhere there must be men, however. The variations on Diabelli prove it. Brunelleschi's dome is more than the magnification of Cléo de Mérode's breast" (page 181). Trying to find this somewhere, the Monster climbs up the back of his chair, falls off, and dies.

Like "Richard Greenow" and the Sir Hercules Lapith episode in *Crome Yellow* (which also feature monstrous protagonists), this play is a kind of tragic farce. And it is farcical, moreover, in ways not unlike other parts of *Antic Hay*: the adventures of the monstrous Complete Man, for example, or the confusion of Rosie Shearwater's airs and amours. But it is also tragic — as are the other incidents and characters, from their point of view, as Lypiatt carefully points out; tragic because there is some nobility in the Monster's refusal to accept the reality of the senses and in his attempt to impose his own ideal in the very sharp teeth of that reality. Because of that refusal, the Monster, like Richard Greenow, becomes a kind of everyman, a symbol for the tragicomical existence of all men. Evelyn Waugh was later to do much the same sort of thing in novels like *A Handful of Dust,* a circumstance that makes his remark (of some twenty years later) that *Antic Hay* is a "happy" book all the more surprising.[12]

Indeed, *A Handful of Dust* seems to represent a conscious attempt on Waugh's part to reconsider in a more orthodox religious framework the problem posed by Huxley ten years earlier in *Antic Hay,* namely, how to live in a world which has lost all meaning. (Though the most obvious model and the one Waugh would have been first to acknowledge is T. S. Eliot's *Waste Land,* from which, among other things, Waugh took his title.) Like Huxley, Waugh fixes a great gulf between the "complete" man of the world, and the man who withdraws from the world, who has some aim in life beyond mere gratification of the senses or making his way up the social ladder. In both novels, the reader is made painfully aware that significant action is not possible

in the modern world: Gumbril senior's model of Wren's London
will forever remain only a model, and Tony Last's — the protagonist of *A Handful of Dust* — beloved Victorian architectural
pile seems destined to decay progressively as it is handed down
the generations of last men. Eventually, one suspects, there is no
escape from the omniverous Mrs. Beaver's urge to gut the great
houses of England and chrome plate them, or turn them into
one-bedroom flats with running water. Also, in Waugh's novel
the possibility of inhabiting permanently a "crystal world" of romantic love is denied even more emphatically than it is in *Antic
Hay*. Tony Last learns to his own great dismay that crystal makes
a very poor foundation for building anything.* To be sure, in
Huxley's novel this conclusion is not underscored quite so firmly:
genuine romantic love and a cottage for two in the country seem
a desirable and perhaps feasible alternative to the antic hay.
However, even there the real answer to the problem seems to lie
more in Gumbril senior than in his son, who, despite his central
position is only a compromise between his father and the rest of
the world. A permanently satisfactory approach to life can be
found only in solitude and in one's self. Huxley's first three
novels, viewed from this perspective, reveal a progressive withdrawal from romantic love as a valid and realistic ideal. In
Crome Yellow, beneath the Restoration farce and wit, we sense
in Denis and in Anne the love that might have been. In *Antic
Hay*, though we are the astonished witnesses of a brief expedition into the world of crystal, its consequent shattering (echoing
the earlier breakage of the similar world of Myra Viveash and
Tony Lamb) indicates how essentially fragile a response to life
this ideal is. By the time we get to *Those Barren Leaves*, the
whole notion of a woman coming to live with him and being his
love seems utterly absurd to the disillusioned and experienced
Francis Chelifer, one of the many masks for Aldous Huxley.

Since most of the characters in *Antic Hay* are subhuman,
they are of course largely caricatures and types. Only when they

*There is even a verbal echo in Thérèse de Vitré, the name of the girl
with whom Tony has a brief idyllic love affair. *Vitré* is French for glass.

begin to face the truth about themselves and their environment
do they gradually evolve into humanity. The fact that so few of
them make it simply reflects Huxley's idea that very few truly
human beings exist.* Evolution into humanity is a long and arduous process, and some, like Lypiatt, prefer to kill themselves
once they have been forced to emerge from their pleasant co-
coons of private universes, and others, like Myra Viveash, paralyze
themselves into a state of living death. Suicide is, after all, in a
physical sense the logical finale of the antic hay, which in the
end becomes indistinguishable from the dance of death.

From this perspective we can see how irrelevant a certain
kind of criticism of Huxley's work really is. Edwin Muir, for
example, professes to feel sorry for Lypiatt — as most readers no
doubt would anyway — because Huxley is a "rather blind and
ignorant writer" who does not understand Lypiatt.[18] Muir objects to the crudity and superficiality of a satire that does not
allow for any humanity, any variety of "masks," or any past to
explain them. This is like criticizing Chaucer for not writing a
Bildungsroman about the Pardoner, instead of satirizing him as
he did. The point of course is that Lypiatt is satirized, just as
the Pardoner was, precisely because he is not a "human" being.
Huxley understands perfectly that he would be a completely
different character if examined from his own point of view (or in
the mode of the traditional novel); Lypiatt says as much himself
in his last letter to Myra Viveash.

This lack of humanity on the part of most characters in
the novel also occasions the strong current of animal imagery
throughout. Myra Viveash, when not expiring, is a tigress (whose
first victim, appropriately, is a Lamb). Lancing, Shearwater's
assistant, is a dog, and Shearwater himself, depending on the circumstances, either a cow or a whale. Most of the time Gumbril
thinks of himself (and the rest of mankind) as earwigs, very much

---

*In the story "Young Archimedes" (1924), a brilliant portrait of the
genius as a young man, Huxley suggests that "men of genius are the only
true men" and that only a few thousand "real men" have existed "in all the
history of the race."

as his father sees them as dogs, the Monster as apes, asses, and dogs, and Coleman as beasts and cattle.

Some characters (often the same) even go one step further and become things.* This is what happens, for example, to Albemarle, the owner of the art gallery where Lypiatt has his exhibition. Albemarle is first described as a "round, smooth, little man with a head like an egg" (page 39). A little later he becomes "egg-headed Albemarle," and finally he is completely transformed and is simply "nodding the egg." Something of the same sort is implied in the names of a few of the characters. Myra Viveash is obviously and appropriately "living ashes"; Mercaptan, according to *Webster's Unabridged,* is a colorless liquid "having a strong, repulsive, garlic odor." Gumbril may be a combination of gum and brill, the latter a turbotlike fish as rubbery and shapeless as his mask of the Complete Man and as idiotic as the fish of "The Reef."† Lypiatt, on the other hand, is perhaps an elaboration of the verb "to lib," meaning to castrate: hence a "libate," a castrato insofar as he is unable to carry out in practice what he wants to do in theory.

The culmination of this process of satirically brutalizing or materializing humanity is the visit Gumbril and Myra pay to Shearwater's laboratory. Lancing, his "doggy" assistant, shows them his collection of living experiments: the cock on whom Shearwater has grafted an ovary and who has grown unsure about whether he should crow or cluck; the rats to whom he had fed milk produced in London and who are starving to death, and the rat on a diet of country milk who is thriving — but only

---

*In Henri Bergson's view, "Les attitudes, gestes et mouvements du corps humain sont risibles dans l'exacte mesure or ce corps nous fait penser à une simple mécanique" (*Le Rire* [Paris, 1900], p. 30). Arthur Koestler claims Bergson's analysis is simply part of a larger process he calls "bisociation." Basically this involves "the abrupt transfer of a train of thought from one operative field to another," which then "leads to its separation from its original emotional charge . . . This sudden dissociation of intellectual and emotional states, the rupture between knowing and feeling, is a fundamental characteristic of the comic" (*Insight and Outlook* [New York, 1949], pp. 41 and 65).

†The name also evokes words like "gambrel," the hock of a horse or similar animal, or — more likely — "gomeril," a simpleton, fool, or dolt.

momentarily, since next week "the fates were plotting to give him diabetes artificially" (page 253); and finally the rejuvenated old monkey, placed behind bars but able to see his mate, gnashing his teeth with lust. Among these animals, Shearwater is a kind of topiarist god, but the half-human satyrs who watch are only dimly aware that they may be victims themselves of a more powerful but equally arbitrary god.

In the laboratory, there are two sets of windows. The one set faces a huge hospital where "men and women were ceasing to be themselves, or were struggling to remain themselves," just as the animals in the laboratory were. The other set faces Wren's beautifully proportioned dome of St. Paul's reflected in the moonlit Thames. In words recalling the earlier vision of the crystal world, Huxley describes Gumbril and Myra looking out this second set of windows: "Like time the river flowed, stanchlessly, as though from a wound in the world's side. For a long time they were silent. They looked out without speaking, across the flow of time, at the human symbol hanging miraculously in the moonlight" (page 253). The final choice is at least symbolically clear: through one set of windows, subman and the antic hay; through the other, proportion, humanity, and the crystal world.

Those Barren Leaves is usually thought of as the second of Huxley's "house party" novels in the manner of Peacock, and with good reason, for some of the parallels to Peacock and more particularly to *Crome Yellow* are striking.* There is the repeated focus on a great mansion and its resident Red Indians,

*The germ for the story is probably to be found in Huxley's plan, outlined almost at the moment he had finished *Crome Yellow*, "to do a gigantic Peacock in an Italian scene. An incredibly large castle — like the Sitwells' at Monte Gufone [Montegufoni], the most amazing place I have ever seen in my life — divided up, as Monte Gufone was divided till recently, into scores of separate habitations, which will be occupied, for the purposes of my story, by the most improbable people of every species and nationality. Here one has the essential Peacockian datum — a houseful of oddities . . . I am giving Realismus a little holiday: these descriptions of middle class homes are really too unspeakably boring" (L202).

Of course, *Those Barren Leaves* does not fit this description in detail. But the "essential Peacockian datum" remains identical in both cases.

this time located in northern Italy and therefore apparently even further removed from possible invading "colonials." There is a great deal of talk, some adventure, a strong current of ideas — occasionally the same talk, adventure, and ideas. Even the beginnings of the two novels are remarkably alike; there is the same opening scene with someone approaching the palace by bicycle, then Calamy's arrival, like Denis's, at an almost deserted house, and then the conversation of the new arrival with the sole occupant.

Still, as its title suggests, the later novel is rather less Knockespotchian than the earlier. The youthful sparkle and tartness have been replaced by an older, heavier, and more bitter spirit — which reflects, as Huxley wrote to his father while working on the novel, that "the mere business of telling a story interests me less and less" (L288). The palace of the Cybo Malaspina, with its background of gradual and uniform degeneracy, affords little opportunity for anything but gloomy reflections on the nature of inherited power, so that here we find no startling historical frescoes on the model of Sir Hercules Lapith or George Wimbush. Instead, we have the tragicomic betrothal of one of the house guests to an idiot, a variety of other more or less comical love affairs, some serious attempts to answer serious questions, and, for the first time in a Huxley novel, a certain amount of exploration of the historical development of one of the main characters.

The gathering at Mrs. Aldwinkle's both resembles and differs from that at Henry Wimbush's. Cardan takes up with more than equal volubility and dialectic skill the slot Scogan had filled so devilishly well at Crome. Mary Thriplow is a Mary Bracegirdle who has grown up and resents it; Calamy a fairly stable mixture of Gombauld and Denis, battering ram and man theoretic; and Mrs. Aldwinkle a more expansive and pitiable Patricia Wimbush. Here the similarities end. The palace of the Cybo Malaspina hosts no Anne, no Henry Wimbush, and no Denis, but in compensation does have two specimens of charming prelapsarian bliss, Irene and Hovenden, one example of miserable con-

genital idiocy, Grace Elver, and a superbly delineated member
of that distinctively Huxleyan species, *genius in vacuo*, Francis
Chelifer.

Like *Crome Yellow*, this novel has virtually no plot, though
it does have a kind of development: not that the characters —
with one notable exception — grow and expand, but that the basic themes of the novel gather momentum and finally achieve a
dubious yet still satisfying climax. It also has, despite its tight
thematic unity, the same episodic quality which *Crome Yellow*
reveals, though for somewhat different reasons. One of these is
that the Italian house party includes a guest who keeps a detailed journal into which we gain — unlike Jenny Mullion's satirical diary in the earlier novel — extensive insight. Another is
that, even more systematically than in the earlier novel, this
novel has its characters grouped in pairs, or would-be pairs, each
with its own more or less short story and all of them adding up
to the ironical happy or unhappy sum of being two.

In this sense, this novel is probably even more of a "love
story" than *Crome Yellow* is. In fact, one could look at it as an
almost scientific investigation into the varieties of amatory experience, human, subhuman, and divine; though, as might be
expected, almost all of these loves do not, for reasons already
suggested in the earlier novels and stories, get very much beyond
the self.

Mary Thriplow, a fairly young, attractive, and intelligent
psychological novelist of some reputation, is one of these
wretched solipsists. She suffers acutely from the disease endemic
to almost all Huxley characters — namely, Bovarism, the attempt
to assume a personality or mask (like that of the Complete Man)
not one's own. In Mary's case, it is the mask of the sweetly inno-
cent, prattling child/woman, a mask she only very occasionally
and briefly becomes aware of herself. One of these moments occurs shortly after Calamy's arrival and her inner debate about
what kind of man he might be and what kind of woman he
might like. Having given him a short and unsuccessful introductory dose of sophisticated charm, she immediately and quite con-

sciously reverts to her "real" simple self. But as with Denis's or Lypiatt's imaginary worlds, her role of Little Red Riding Hood is better suited to fiction than to life, where tangible realities have a habit of making unexpected and unpleasant intrusions.

When Mary opposes her sweet little child to Cardan's far more skillfully handled wise old man, she makes the first of a great many mistakes. He listens calmly to her description of an epiphany with a simple bus driver and the attractions of an uncomplicated life, "so easy to live well, even if it is a hard one" (pages 211–212). But when he makes her enter a butcher's shop filled with the basic odors of life and death, she needs a perfumed handkerchief for her squeamish nose.* And when the simple butcher is finally exposed as a complicated crook who cheats his customers, she regrets ever having opened her mouth.

But Mary is determined to withstand all attacks on her homemade universe. Thinking about her dead brother and her love for him, she manages to work herself up into a frenzy of grief — all the while registering her emotions in a secret notebook. When the cold voice of her alter ego guiltily suggests that she may be using her grief to exercise her prose, she indignantly tries to suppress it, as Burlap later does with his "devil" in *Point Counter Point*. The same is true of her relationship with Calamy, with whom she falls in love because she needs some "deep" emotions for her new novel to squelch the prevailing critical opinion that her writing is cold and hard. Of course Mary does not conduct this affair in an openly hypocritical way. She is not insensitive; on the contrary, she is sincerely convinced that she loves Calamy. Therefore, she is hurt when he decides to leave her and the life of the senses to seek solitary bliss in the higher spheres. In her own way she tries to imitate him, but not before she is sure that Calamy is written up in her diary and "safely laid down in pickle, waiting to be consumed whenever she should be short of fictional provisions" (page 359).

If Mary finds her chosen simple role difficult to perform, her hostess, Mrs. Aldwinkle, has one that is nearly impossible.

*Like Helen Amberley in *Eyeless in Gaza*.

Though deep in middle age, she desperately insists on being young, spending vast amounts of time on preening herself, emitting a smile of "chiefly historical" interest, and covering all of her many banalities with a thick layer of sentiment. When her more rational alter ego, like Mary's, objects to such behavior, she does her best to push it out of her consciousness, but with only temporary success. Her most difficult scene, the almost forcible attempted rape of Chelifer's affections, turns into a painful and painfully amusing fiasco. Mrs. Aldwinkle's private universe is simply too remote from any acceptable reality to make anything but a comical reaction possible.

Cardan, the "funny man" in Mrs. Aldwinkle's Italian ménage, is untroubled by such sentimental problems. Like his predecessor, Scogan, he is a simple materialist without much feeling but with a great deal of charm and wit. Despite occasional bilious premonitions of age, he accepts a Michelin three-star meal as an adequate answer to the main problems of life. When, for example, Calamy complains that there is no meaning in a life of the senses, Cardan diagnoses him as suffering from a case of inadequate sexual exercise or possibly a "catarrh in the bile ducts" (page 67). Though he is immensely well informed about art, his main interest is in what he can get out of it: either by talking wittily about it in his self-confessed role of parasite, or else by finding some objet d'art to smuggle out of the country and selling it at a high markup. Cardan is a successful entrepreneur of the spirit who appropriately nearly bankrupts himself in trying to cash in on the idiocy of Grace Elver.

By a series of adventures too involved to go into here, Cardan meets Grace, a retarded but happy and very wealthy young girl, and her quasi-homicidal brother. A man of action as soon as he scents money in the wind, Cardan wastes little time removing her from her brother's keeping and proposing to marry her. Elated at the prospect of unlimited cigars and good dinners, he suppresses all earlier moments of doubt and openly sings the praises of the hedonistic philosophy. But very soon the memories flood back, when a few lunches, dinners, cigars, much conversation, and one very bad fish later, Grace Elver, still unmarried, dies of food poisoning.

Sitting alone at sunset with her body in the chapel, he is overwhelmed by thoughts of death and mutability. He counts the few years, the few remaining millennia of days before "the end of everything, [when] the tunneling worms" (page 333) will have a good dinner at his expense. And he reflects that the tragedy of the body is dull and degrading, that it can ennoble neither the sufferer nor the spectator. Only the tragedy of the spirit is capable of significance, but even that, he concludes, is ultimately meaningless: "The tragedies of the spirit are mere struttings and posturings on the margin of life, and the spirit itself is only an accidental exuberance, the product of spare vital energy, like the feathers on the head of a hoopoo or the innumerable populations of useless and foredoomed spermatozoa. The spirit has no significance; there is only the body" (page 334). Life, he decides in the wake of a number of earlier Huxley characters, is a hideous farce "in the worst of bad taste" (page 334). And as far as his materialistic homemade universe is concerned, he is right. When the priest and his retinue enter the chapel to sing the funeral mass, he sees them only as animals, and the words of the Latin ritual reach him as the bleatings of idiotic sheep: " 'Baa baba, baa baa, Boo-oo-Baa,' bleated the priest. 'Boooo-baa,' came back from the bawling flock" (page 337). Cardan contemplates this scene with increasing despair and disgust, until finally Grace's body is carried away. But even then his role in the hideous farce is not over, and he is made to settle the bill.

Francis Chelifer shares Cardan's conviction that reality is essentially materialistic, but his is an almost puritanical conviction. He hates the reality he thinks he sees and passionately wishes it might be otherwise. But despite the intensity of these wishes, he will not succumb to living in a never-never land of daydreams; he refuses to live in a homemade universe if he can possibly help it (but naturally he cannot). Man, he knows, must face the "truth" and make a point of living as close to the central sewage plant of reality as he can.

Chelifer's real reasons for wanting to do so are complex, but some insight into them is provided by the intermittent extracts from his journal. His main problem, as Calamy suggests rather bluntly at the end of the novel, is that he is an inverted (Rampion would have said perverted) idealist and sentimentalist.* Heavily indoctrinated with Wordsworthianism, pre-Raphaelitism, and vegetarianism in his youth, he is incapable of shedding his conditioning in maturity; he can only reject it by turning it around. The mysterious and sonorous reverberations of Wordsworth's rhythms, for example, cannot be merely forgotten; as they draw closer to "reality" they have to be transformed into meaningless "hiccoughs" (page 122).

Chelifer's experience is in many respects identical with Richard Greenow's, though he is not so obviously schizophrenic as the latter was. Still, his first and most profound encounter with "reality" comes, significantly, in the shape of a woman who turns out to be a more sophisticated and less literary version of Pearl Bellairs. Chelifer had originally met her while both were children, but at that time, typical Wordsworthian that he was, he had only dared worship from afar. When he meets her again during the war, when he speaks to her for the first time and discovers her vulgarity, he has horrible premonitions of great suffering. For he loves her deeply — or loves, rather, his mental image of her as some pure and spiritual Lucy-like waif, and not the physical tangibility of her beautiful body and definitely nonethereal mind. Nevertheless, he feels the attractions of her body very strongly and struggles desperately against giving way to his and her desires. When he inevitably yields to them, he generalizes his experience into a description of absolute reality: "It was then that I learned, since the future was always bound to be a painful repetition of what had happened before, never to look forward for comfort or justification, but to live now and here in the heart of human reality, in the very centre of the hot dark hive" (page 145). Appropriately enough, the hive is inhabited by subhuman

*The type of the inverted idealist is a permanent fixture in Huxley's novels, beginning here with Chelifer and ending with Bahu in *Island*.

creatures and therefore has no room for dreams of universal justice or "imaginations of a future earth peopled by human beings who should live according to reason" (page 149). There is no place in such a world for Wordsworthian idealism, as Chelifer, like Denis in "A Country Walk" or Spandrell in *Point Counter Point,* bitterly recognizes.

The dynamic principle of this new reality is stupidity. From it can be derived all the conventional virtues. Chelifer is aware that some few nonstupid men do exist or have existed, but he considers them rare exceptions and therefore not a part of the real world. To devote oneself to studying and appreciating these men and their works to the exclusion of all else would mean escaping reality and being a coward. Besides, it would be stupid because being comforted "by what is untrue or what is irrelevant to the world in which we live is stupid" (page 150). Consequently Chelifer makes no constructive use of his obvious artistic talent, but edits instead something called the "Rabbit Fanciers' Gazette," and lives in the petty bourgeois environment of a boardinghouse in Chelsea, refusing to accept any invitations from people he might find interesting.

Only once during the whole course of the novel does he manage to escape the limitations of his homemade reality, and, ironically, it happens at the exact moment when circumstances reduce him to absolute subhumanity. Floating peacefully in the waters off the northern Italian coast, he is accidentally hit by a sailboat and nearly drowned. At the moment before impact he feels himself suddenly seized by violent spasms of fear that reduce him to "no more than a startled and terrified beast" (page 153), but as he slowly regains consciousness on the beach a new and radiantly human world is revealed to him. Merely to breathe is an exquisite pleasure; the landscape and the people are transformed by a strange beauty; and, groping with his hand to find his heartbeat, he for once does not "try to interpret it" (page 158). Momentarily, he breaks down the shell of his self-imposed reality and spontaneously accepts the unmediated pulsations of life. But not for long. By the time he reaches Mrs. Aldwinkle's domain, the effects of the sea-change are wearing off and the walls of the hive close in on him again.

Calamy is the only major character in the novel who has some chance of escaping his private universe for more than a few moments. He is the only character capable of growth and development, the only one prepared to exist in a universe without prefabricated signposts. He does his best, for example, to grow out of his dependence on sexual successes of the Complete Man variety, for he doesn't want to be numbered among the "leather-faced ruffians and disgusting old satyrs" (page 68). That he *is* numbered among them is, as he very well knows, due to the lamentable regularity with which philosophy, quite capable of dealing with past or future temptations, always breaks down before present ones.

Calamy illustrates perfectly one of Huxley's favorite maxims, *video meliora proboque, deteriora sequor.* Still, he does not always follow the worse. Satiated after his seduction of Mary Thriplow, he returns to his earlier speculations on the nature of reality and the meaning of existence. What astonishes him most and keeps his mind increasingly preoccupied is the great variety of "modes of existence a thing has" (page 343), and the consequent inability to define and classify neatly what it is. Here in the philosophical murkiness of essence and existence, Calamy hopes to find an answer, but to do so, he concludes, one must first renounce all bodily attachments: "If one were free, he thought, one could go exploring into that darkness. But the flesh was weak; under the threat of that delicious torture it turned coward and traitor" (page 344). Like the hero of *Antic Hay,* he is aware of a reality beyond the senses, the existence of some sort of "crystal world," but he is afraid to leave the ease and clarity of his private world and step into the dark, unexplored vastness outside. In the end he does decide to make the attempt and retires to solitary contemplation on a mountaintop. Like the old Gumbril, he discovers the truth of the paradox that only in solitude can one find an end to the spiritual loneliness which plagues the rest of mankind. Though he is not completely

certain that he will last the duration and is not even entirely
convinced that he may not be behaving like a fool, looking down
at the twilit world below, he still is "somehow reassured" (page
380) that he is not.*

It is with this reassurance that the novel concludes, and it is
to this reassurance that its title, among other things, refers. The
final stanza of the poem by Wordsworth from which it is taken,
"The Tables Turned," reads as follows:

> Enough of Science and of Art;
> Close up those barren leaves;
> Come forth, and bring with you a heart
> That watches and receives.[14]

Of all the major characters in the novel, only Calamy (with the
momentary exception of Chelifer) follows this advice; he closes
up the barren leaves of science by not accepting the materialistic
theories of Cardan and Chelifer, and the barren leaves of art by
not yielding to Mary's or Mrs. Aldwinkle's emotional and aesthetic onslaughts. And he differs from the former pair in not
being afraid to have a heart, and from the latter in having one
that does not merely receive but also watches. In other words,
he is not merely an animal or a machine, but a balanced human
being who approaches reality without trying beforehand (Denis's
complaint in *Crome Yellow*) to fit it into an arbitrary intellectual pattern. He knows, rather, in another phrase from the same
poem, that "Our meddling intellect / Mis-shapes the beauteous
forms of things: — / We murder to dissect."

By living according to their meddling intellectual and preconceived interpretations of reality, the characters of *Those*

---

*At roughly the same time (April 10, 1925), Huxley was endorsing a
similar solution to his friend the poet Robert Nichols: "Men are more solitary now than they ever were; all authority has gone; the tribe has disappeared and every at all conscious man stands alone, surrounded by other
solitary individuals and fragments of the old tribe, for which he feels no
respect. Obviously the only thing to be done is to go right through with the
process; to realize individuality to the full, the real individuality, Lao-
Tsz[u]'s individuality, the Yogi's individuality, and with it the oneness of
everything. Obviously! But the difficulty is huge" (L245). From this we can
see that Huxley was never really very much in doubt about the direction in
which salvation lay, only of the possibility of getting there.

Barren Leaves, like those of the two preceding novels, become subhuman. Because they do not try to break out of the limitations of their homemade universes, they are fair game for Huxley's satirical arsenal. Irene and Hovenden, for example, are subjected to satirical attack as long as they listen to the "meddling" interpretations of Mrs. Aldwinkle and Falx. Once they stop and approach each other with hearts duly watchful and receptive, they go free.

The same is true of Calamy. Because, in the words of "The Reef," he is "strong and bold," he may succeed in escaping the slimy aquarium and its idiotic fish; because he can and does act, he may achieve a "triune peace" and become truly human. This may be inferred even from the names used in the novel. Significantly, Calamy's name is the only one that refers directly to a human being or activity, specifically to a "calamist" or someone why plays a reed or a pipe — that is, a shepherd like the one in Huxley's early poem, "Song of Poplars" (1918), who knew how to tune his "music to the trees" and achieve harmony with nature. All the other names are strictly nonhuman or subhuman in their derivations. A chelifer, for example, is a book scorpion, a small insect found among books and papers, capable only of running sideways and backwards, and feeding on even smaller insects. Cardan's name apparently derives from the Greek *chartes,* meaning a leaf of paper or one of the barren leaves chelifers like to live near; it may also go back to the French *cardon,* a plant related to the artichoke and used in cooking and salads — more leaves, in this instance appropriately edible ones. Mrs. Aldwinkle is an *eald,* or old, winkle: any one of various marine gastropods. Like the aged winkle, her exterior may not be wholly unattractive but her insides are slimy and disgusting. Finally, Mary Thriplow may be a descendant of a "thrips," a woodworm or small insect that attacks useful plants; in this case, a parasite who converts the experience of others into novels and stories (like Miss Penny in "Nuns at Luncheon," or Philip Quarles in *Point Counter Point*).

Nomenclature, however, is only one method Huxley employs

to reveal the subhumanity and isolation of his characters. With the same end in mind, he uses the device of counterpoint, already briefly discussed with reference to the two earlier novels. Chelifer uses it self-consciously in reproducing the conversation at his boardinghouse, and Huxley makes it the structural basis for the whole third part of the novel. This section, entitled "The Loves of the Parallels," consists of four simultaneous conversations. While Cardan and Falx are talking inside the palace, Chelifer and Mrs. Aldwinkle are conversing on the terrace below; on the terrace below that, Calamy and Mary Thriplow are engaged in exploring the theory and practice of love, and out on the hills Irene and Hovenden are similarly occupied. Despite the great amount of talk, there is practically no communication, for the characters seem incapable of opening their mouths for anything shorter than a lecture. Cardan's discussion with Falx is symptomatic (though Irene and Hovenden, with their smaller vocabularies and preference for physical communication, are exceptions). Like Denis's attempt to strike up a conversation with Jenny in *Crome Yellow*, this conversation runs along parallel lines that never meet. Hence the title of the section, though it may also allude to Erasmus Darwin's "The Loves of the Plants" and its parody, "The Loves of the Triangles" — that is, anything but the loves of human beings. Cardan and Falx denounce each other windily until Cardan is provoked into an admission that he talks and argues for the sake of talking and arguing, not in order to communicate or learn anything. " 'You don't imagine,' " he inquires rhetorically, " 'I'd waste my time trying to persuade a full-grown man with fixed opinions of the truth of something he doesn't already believe?' " (page 189). None of the other characters are candid (or aware) enough to admit this, but their talk amounts to the same thing. When Cardan makes a crack about the lower classes, Falx, a homemade socialist, launches into a monologue of his own. Cardan reflects that this is only just: "For the last ten minutes he'd been boring poor old Mr. Falx. And now Mr. Falx had turned round and was paying him back with his own measure" (page 189). Bored now himself, he leans over the balustrade and wonders what the others are talking about. He need not wonder.

In *Those Barren Leaves,* as in the preceding novels, there is also some satire not directly related to the predominant theme of the awareness or lack of awareness of multiple levels of reality. Huxley, for example, at one point stops the action to deliver in his own person a tirade against the psychological interpretation of art, and occasionally he uses Irene and Hovenden as pegs on which to hang some observations about education (preliminary to their fuller development in *Proper Studies*). And there are, of course, some very apparent splotches of Knockespotchian high spirits, as in the incident of Mary's jewels or of Hovenden's mad drive around Lake Trasimene. In this novel, however, these secondary matters occupy a far less prominent position than they had before. The focus of the satiric vision here is almost exclusively concentrated on revealing the spiritual isolation of the characters. In this sense, G. U. Ellis is certainly right in calling *Those Barren Leaves* an artistically successful novel, even if equally wrong in calling it Huxley's only one.[15] In this sense also, it may surely be seen as a progression in the development of Huxley's art of satire. He has learned to limit the range of his attack; and for precisely that reason he can now direct his attack more effectively. It is a lesson whose benefits are even more obvious in his next, and perhaps best, satiric novel, *Point Counter Point.**

*Huxley himself, however, soon grew disillusioned with *Those Barren Leaves*. Thanking Naomi Mitchison on February 25, 1925, for her kind words about the book, he goes on to remark that it is "all right, certainly; tremendously accomplished, but in a queer way, I now feel, jejune and shallow and off the point." We begin to realize how ready Huxley was to fall under the influence of someone like Lawrence when he adds in the next sentence that "all I've written so far has been off the point" (L242).

That this is not false modesty is clear from the way Huxley had answered earlier and was to answer later compliments to his work — usually by admitting that he was rather pleased himself with what he had done.

CHAPTER IV

The Music of Humanity
Point Counter Point

POINT COUNTER POINT is probably Huxley's most important and most controversial novel.* It has been variously and savagely denounced as inept, puerile, misanthropic, mechanical, raw, unreadable, false, purposeless, inorganic, unoriginal, journalistic, and inartistic.[1] It has also, but far less frequently and much less impassionedly, been defended as a successful work of art. At the same time it has continued to be widely and generally read, and is even taught in some universities. In the collected works edition alone, *Point Counter Point* has been reprinted at least four times since 1947, and a number of other editions (both hard-cover and paperback) have appeared. Its importance remains undeniable, despite the regrets of the majority of the critics.

*Huxley had thought of changing the title to *Diverse Laws,* a phrase from the Fulke Greville epigraph to the novel (L296). However, as a letter dated June 19, 1928 (in the Stanford Manuscript Collection), from C. H. C. Prentice of Chatto and Windus to Huxley's agent, Ralph Pinker, indicates, the change, already made in the English proofs, was finally decided against because of objections from G. H. Doran, Huxley's American publisher. Earlier, because Doran had felt nothing with Mexico in the title would sell in America, Huxley's collection of short stories *Little Mexican* (1924) was called *Young Archimedes* in the American edition.

Of course, popular and artistic success are not necessarily synonymous. The mass of Huxley's readers may, it is possible, simply be a vulgar, tasteless lot. Huxley himself once implied as much in one of his more autobiographical short stories, "After the Fireworks," (*Brief Candles*, pages 170–172). Still, if a considerable number of readers did not turn to him primarily for aesthetic reasons, one can certainly infer from the well-publicized subject matter of *The Sun Also Rises* and from the equally well-publicized *Ulysses* obscenity trial that the same could be said of many readers of Hemingway and Joyce. To be sure, Hemingway and Joyce have received a favorable critical and academic press. They are officially recognized "classics," though perhaps not yet, in Huxley's phrase, "fossilized classics." *Point Counter Point* on the other hand, has not received any such official stamp of approval — fortunately, perhaps, or so Huxley would think, declaiming any desire to be fossilized. But decidedly unfortunate in that this has prevented a truly open-minded reading of the work, thereby perpetuating its misinterpretation.*

Much has been written about the narrative method of this novel, a method to which its title explicitly calls attention, and which is in part outlined by the novelist within the novel, Philip Quarles. Quarles calls this method the "musicalization of fiction," and a number of critics have gone to the trouble of attempting to read the score with varying degrees of success. The substance of most of their criticisms, with some important exceptions, is that the complex structure and the musical analogy of this novel serve no discernible purpose, and are therefore gratuitous and pretentious. David Daiches, for example, writes: "The musical analogy in *Point Counter Point* is quite false and the tampering with chronology there is quite purposeless."[2] Moreover, even sympathetic critics rarely do more than take the book through its paces and show more or less how Quarles's literary theory matches Huxley's literary practice; what they do not seem to be able to explain convincingly is *why* Huxley used the method in

*Since this was written, a number of good analyses of the novel have appeared, notably that of Peter Bowering's *Aldous Huxley* (New York, 1969), pp. 77–97.

the first place (except as a demonstration of technical virtuosity) and *how* that method is related to the thematic content of the book.[3] But it is clear that no matter how virtuosic, no work of fiction whose form and content are not directly and organically related can be considered a major work of art, which one instinctively feels this novel is.

Point Counter Point is not the first novel in which Huxley makes use of a contrapuntal technique. He had used it in the three preceding novels, primarily in order to expose the isolation of the characters, to indicate, in other words, the lack of any kind of communication among them. One recalls in this connection Denis Stone's conversation with deaf Jenny Mullion in *Crome Yellow*. In that conversation, as Denis himself remarks, their thoughts run along parallel lines with no possibility of ever meeting (except perhaps in infinity) — and the same thought in similar circumstances and identical phraseology occurs to Eleanor in *Point Counter Point*. For all it matters, they might as well be talking to themselves. Or, in terms of the musical analogy, their conversation is counterpointed, with Denis's point of view in one register and Jenny's in another. Like the parallel lines, the two registers never meet; they are scored simultaneously, but the parts remain separate. The essential characteristic, consequently, of this type of counterpoint is that it is disharmonious. However, because the purpose of musical counterpoint is obviously to achieve harmony, Huxley's literary counterpoint is therefore a misnomer, though from the point of view of satire the name is most appropriate, since it is precisely out of the dissonance that the satire arises: where there ought to be harmony and significant contact, there is only discord and meaningless noise. To reveal this discord and noise is one of the basic functions of this technique in the early novels.*

*It is this satirical, disharmonious dimension of Huxley's use of literary counterpoint that is usually overlooked. So, for example, Theodore Ziolkowski in *The Novels of Hermann Hesse* (Princeton, 1965), p. 198, can praise Hesse's contrapuntal technique at the expense of Huxley and Gide. But is the revelation of nearly universal dissonance to be equated with the revelation of universal harmony?

Another, and closely related, purpose is to achieve an accurate portrayal of reality and of various conceptions of reality. Evidently, if one could counterpoint the homemade universes of a sufficiently large number of characters, one could thereby attain a kind of *Gesamtbild* of reality itself, with each character contributing his fragmentary vision to form a complete picture of the human condition. In the conversation between Denis and Jenny this was possible only to a very limited extent, since only two characters and two points of view were counterpointed. It was a very simple form of counterpoint, with only two instruments making the "music." Even in *Antic Hay* only a few more instruments were added, as, for example, in the counterpointing of the conversations of Gumbril's friends with the account of the "black bundle's" and her husband's wretched existence. The same essentially holds true for *Those Barren Leaves,* though here there is already one section of the book which is structured according to this method (namely part III, "The Loves of the Parallels"). *Point Counter Point,* however, is a full orchestration, with an entire complement of instruments, which enables Huxley to present a more accurate and thorough transcription of his understanding of the human condition than was hitherto possible.

To arrive at an accurate portrayal of a manifold reality is also one of the fundamental reasons why Quarles wants to "musicalize" fiction. It is for this reason, certainly, that he plans to meditate on the example of Beethoven, who in his symphonies is able to alternate "majesty" and "joke," or, in other words, is able to present a complete picture of human existence and not merely a fragmentary one. Huxley explicitly raises the same problem — that of an artistic portrayal of the "whole truth" — in an essay published three years after *Point Counter Point* entitled "Tragedy and the Whole Truth" (1931). There he praises Homer and Fielding precisely because they were able to alternate majesty and joke, because they were willing to sacrifice what he calls "chemically pure art" for the (to him more worthwhile) purpose of achieving a total vision of reality. In an even earlier essay, originally an introduction to the younger Crébillon's *The*

Opportunities of a Night, Huxley indicates that he may have held this preference for *Wahrheit* to *Dichtung* as early as 1925. In this essay, while speaking of the tragedies of Crébillon père, Huxley comments in passing that Racine and Corneille — "chemically pure" artists if ever there were such — are of rather doubtful artistic interest. At the same time he quotes with evident relish Crébillon fils' confession "qu'il n'avait encore achevé la lecture des tragédies de son père, mais que cela viendrait. Il regardait la tragédie française comme la farce la plus complete qu'ait pu inventer l'esprit humain."[4] From these comments it may be inferred with considerable certainty that Huxley viewed with approval Philip Quarles's attempts to put the "whole truth" into a novel.*

It is an inference all the easier to make because this is in fact what Huxley does in *Point Counter Point.* Quarles's simultaneous hypothetical juxtaposition of Jones murdering his wife with Smith wheeling his perambulator in the park is, for example, matched by Huxley's simultaneous juxtaposition of Spandrell's suicide with Burlap and Beatrice Gilray's frolicking in the bathtub, or by Lord Edward Tantamount's† grafting tails on asymmetrical tadpoles with Lady Edward's and John Bidlake's remarks on "asymmetrical" human beings.

This simultaneous juxtaposition is, of course, not restricted merely to the alternatives of majesty and joke, for instance, to Spandrell's perverse nobility and Burlap's ludicrous asininity. Rather, it embraces a large number of variations between these two poles; it modulates, as Quarles observes, "not merely from one key to another, but from mood to mood" (page 408). To be sure, the number of themes that are (and can be) modulated in this way is limited; it would be clearly impossible to handle all the possible human themes in a novel even of the length of *Point*

---

*In a letter to Robert Nichols dated November 14, 1926, Huxley admits as much: "I work away on a long and complicated novel, which I want to make a picture of life in its different aspects, the synchronous portrait of the different things an individual simultaneously is — atoms, physiology, mystic, cog in the economic machine, lover, etc" (L276).

†Based, according to Ronald Clark, on John Scott Haldane. See his *JBS*, p. 57.

Counter Point. For this reason Quarles and Huxley limit their themes to the most basic ones, to "love, or dying, or praying in different ways" (page 408). The controlling themes of *Point Counter Point* are precisely these three, and every individual in the novel experiences them in one way or another, though never in the same way. Each character is like an instrument in an orchestra — an equation Huxley specifically makes — which takes up at various points one or another of these themes and "plays" it according to the properties peculiar to its construction, or, in different terms, according to the limitations of the character's own individual conception of reality.

There is no need to show in any great detail how these three main themes run through the novel — it should be obvious enough that all of the major and most of the minor characters represent variations on them. For example, the theme of death is stated and varied and modulated in the horrible and seemingly senseless death of little Philip Quarles, the murder of Everard Webley, the farcical pseudo death of the elder Quarles, Spandrell's climactic suicide, and John Bidlake's cancer. And, naturally, the deaths or dyings of these characters affect almost all the other people in the novel. The same holds true for the theme of religion: one need only think of Marjorie's vapid mysticism, Burlap's Jesus perversion, Rampion's Hellenism, Quarles's skepticism, Spandrell's diabolism; and the theme of love: Lucy and Walter, Walter and Marjorie, John Bidlake and virtually everybody, Spandrell and his mother, Philip and Eleanor, Eleanor and Webley, Rampion and Mary, Burlap and Beatrice. There is no need to continue the list; it should be sufficiently apparent already that Huxley has practically infinite possibilities for the statement and repetition of themes, for their variation in tragic and comic and tragicomic modes.

By means of the technique of counterpoint Huxley skillfully manages to weave all these themes together, thereby developing a variety of characters and giving the novel a solid structural and thematic unity. He uses the technique, however, for another purpose as well: to satirize the narrow conceptions of reality which isolate most of the characters in the novel. Huxley almost directly admits as much in at least two passages usually neglected by the critics. The first incident occurs during the party at Tantamount House. Huxley describes Pongileoni's playing of the flute part in Bach's B-minor suite, which is then repeated with variations by other instruments in the orchestra: "The parts live their separate lives; they touch, their paths cross, they combine for a moment to create a seemingly final and perfected harmony, only to break apart again. *Each is always alone and separate and individual.* 'I am I,' asserts the violin; 'the world revolves about me.' 'Round me,' calls the cello. 'Round me,' the flute insists. *And all are equally right and equally wrong; and none of them will listen to the others*" (page 32, my italics). In the next paragraph Huxley completes the identification. The individual is an instrument, humanity an orchestra: "In the human fugue there are eighteen hundred million parts" (page 32). Each character of the novel, consequently, like each instrument of the orchestra, has a different mode of seeing things, produces a different noise, and plays a different variation. Each character, like each instrument, is insulated in his own conception of reality, in his own kind of music. To be sure, as Huxley admits, it would be impossible to transcribe the score of the entire "human fugue." Eighteen hundred million parts are simply too many, and the artist must therefore necessarily select: "The resultant noise means something perhaps to the statistician, nothing to the artist. It is only by considering one or two parts at a time that the artist can understand anything" (page 32). This is precisely what Huxley does in the novel; he considers one or two parts at a time, has one or two characters (sometimes a few more) embody and vary one of the principal themes. It is for this reason — and not by analogy to cinematic technique as is sometimes thought — that *Point Counter Point* is broken up into what Frank Baldanza calls relatively short "scenes."[5] In this way, and perhaps in this way only, Huxley can impose an artistic order upon the great many characters and events in this work.

Somewhat later in the book, Huxley offers another impor-

tant statement on the isolation of his characters and its relation
to the technique of counterpoint. This comment is made, unlike
the previous one, through Philip Quarles. Quarles and his wife
are on board ship returning from India to England, and he is
telling her that he might like to use the situation of Walter Bidlake's amatory entanglements with Marjorie Carling and Lucy
Tantamount as the basis for a new novel. It would serve, he
thinks, as "a kind of excuse . . . for a new way of looking at
things" (page 265). While they are speaking, their conversation is
counterpointed with the conversations of several other passengers
on the ship. In one of them a Frenchwoman is talking of the
price of *camisoles en flanelle* at the Galeries Lafayette; in another
an English girl is telling her admirers of the "wonderful time"
she had at Gulmerg the previous summer; in still another two
women missionaries are discussing the number of Chinese and
Malays the bishop of Kuala Lumpur made deacons during the
year. Quarles seizes on the example of these conversations to illustrate his new method of seeing reality in fiction: " 'All these
camisoles en flanelle and pickled onions and bishops of cannibal
islands are really quite to the point. Because the essence of the
new way of looking is multiplicity. Multiplicity of eyes and multiplicity of aspects seen. For instance, one person interprets events
in terms of bishops; another in terms of the price of flannel
camisoles; another, like that young lady from Gulmerg . . .
thinks of it in terms of good times. And then there's the biologist,
the chemist, the physicist, the historian. Each sees, professionally,
a different aspect of the event, a different lay of reality. What I
want to do is to look with all those eyes at one. With religious
eyes, scientific eyes, *homme moyen sensuel* eyes . . .' " (page 266).
The result of such a new mode of novelistic point of view, Philip
concludes, would be "a very queer picture indeed." Throughout
the novel, Philip is preoccupied with trying to get at this "queer
picture": he reads Burtt's *Metaphysical Foundations of Modern
Science* during the sea voyage and, much later, Bastian's *On the
Brain,* while on the way to London. His purpose is to gather
material to document one of the multiple modes of seeing things;

in this case the scientific mode. It is the same desire to see things from a multiplicity of viewpoints that motivates him later to take an interest in the kitchen and cook of the Bidlake country estate, or in the different ways in which Everard Webley's political demonstration might be perceived. Even more important in this respect is the entry in Philip's notebook which immediately precedes his statement on the "musicalization" of fiction. There Philip explicitly returns once again to the plan to use the Walter Bidlake–Marjorie Carling–Lucy Tantamount situation as the basis for a novel. He plans to begin his story with Walter suddenly seeing Lucy's laughing mouth transformed into a gaping maw of a crocodile, thereby "striking the note of strangeness and fantasticality at once" (page 407); or, in other words, getting at the queer picture of reality through yet another point of view (in this sense, the title of the novel refers not only to the musical method, but also to the countering of one *point* of view against another). Somewhat later in this passage Quarles touches on the same idea again, and this time states it directly: "The novelist can assume the god-like creative privilege and simply elect to consider the events of the story in their various aspects — emotional, scientific, economic, religious, metaphysical, etc." Such a multiplicity of points of view, either on the part of the isolated characters of the novel, or on the part of the novelist within the novel, or on the part of the novelist himself — *or all three* — would, Philip realizes, necessarily involve the introduction of ideas. For, if the characters are to be isolated within their private conceptions of reality, they must, as a minimum, have the intelligence to formulate such conceptions, must, in short, have ideas. But this requirement, as Philip is perfectly aware, would exclude all but one tenth of one percent of humanity.*

*This exclusivity has always been considered one of the weak points of Huxley's fiction. In a different novel, and a different context, and wearing a different mask (that of Anthony Beavis), Huxley retorts that all fiction is necessarily exclusive. "Life's so ordinary that literature has to deal with the exceptional. Exceptional talent, power, social position, wealth. Hence those geniuses of fiction, those leaders and dukes and millionaires. People who are completely conditioned by circumstances — one can be desperately sorry for them; but one can't find their lives very dramatic. Drama begins where

Of course, all the characters in *Point Counter Point* have "ideas" or — like Quarles senior and Marjorie Carling — at least think they do. These ideas are not, however, presented primarily for their own sake, but, rather, to enable Huxley to portray a large spectrum of as many points of view as possible, and to enable him artistically to represent by means of the technique of counterpoint the isolation of his characters within their closed systems of thought.

These ideas also are included to enable him to represent that isolation satirically. This is clear from an essay in *Music at Night*, "And Wanton Optics Roll the Melting Eye," written three years after *Point Counter Point*. In this piece Huxley specifically comments on the method employed in this novel: "The facts and even the peculiar jargon of science can be of great service to the writer whose intention is mainly ironical. Juxtapose two accounts of the same human event, one in terms of pure science, the other in terms of religion, aesthetics, passion, even common sense; their discord will set up the most disquieting reverberations in the mind. Juxtapose, for example, physiology and mysticism (Mme. Guyon's ecstasies were most frequent and most spiritually significant in the fourth month of her pregnancies); juxtapose acoustics and the music of Bach (perhaps I may be permitted to refer to the simultaneously scientific and aesthetic account of a concert in my novel, *Point Counter Point*) . . ." (*Music at Night*, page 40). What Huxley is analyzing here is essentially the same technique which Philip Quarles discusses under the heading of the "musicalization of fiction," namely the alternation of majesty and joke, coupled with the technique of multiple points of view. It is the juxtaposition of different points of view that is stressed here, not merely the juxtaposition of scientific imagery with musical or mystical imagery. It is a juxtaposition of the scientific "slice" of reality with the other "slices" that produces the satire, not the imagery itself. That this is Huxley's meaning is plainly

there's freedom of choice. And freedom of choice begins when social or psychological conditions are exceptional. That's why the inhabitants of imaginative literature have always been recruited from the pages of *Who's Who*" (*Eyeless in Gaza*, p. 313).

apparent from the continuation of his analysis: "This list of prolonged incompatibles might be indefinitely prolonged. We live in a world of *non-sequiturs*. Or rather, we would live in such a world, if we were always conscious of all the aspects under which any event can be considered. But in practice we are almost never aware of more than one aspect at a time. Our life is spent first in one water-tight compartment of experience, then in another. The artist can, if he so desires, break down the bulkheads between the compartments and so give us a simultaneous view of two or more of them at a time. So seen, reality looks exceedingly queer. Which is how the ironist and the perplexed questioner desire it to look" (*Music at Night*, pages 40–41). What this analysis means is that the fragmentary conceptions or points of view of the individual characters add up to something approaching a total vision of reality, but that each fragmentary vision *is* fragmentary and must remain so, just as each instrument of the orchestra plays only a fragmentary portion of the total piece of music. The irony (and, to generalize, the satire) of this is, as Huxley here implies and as he directly states in *Point Counter Point,* that each instrument and each character thinks he is the total music and the total reality. The point of the satire is that each character is in fact isolated.*

In another essay, "Sermons in Cats," Huxley makes an even more direct and general statement on the isolation of man: "In spite of language, in spite of intelligence and intuition and sympathy, one can never really communicate anything to anybody.

*In his preface to *Art and Artists,* ed. Morris Philipson (New York, 1960), pp. 7–8, Huxley returns again to the question of literary counterpoint. Though he clearly admits that "there is no equivalent in literature of sustained counterpoint or the spatial unity of diverse elements brought together so that they can be perceived at one glance as a significant whole," he still sees the need for some way of rendering the experience of "falling perpetually between half a dozen stools." Since the writer cannot say "several different things at once, he must, willy-nilly, say them successively." This means that he must choose between a more or less straightforward mathematically progressive method, or a "kind of directional free association" which is more realistic but less well ordered. This latter type of "melodic modulation" is the one Huxley prefers, even though it is much more difficult. "Hence," he concludes, "the essentially unsystematic nature of most of what I've written."

The essential substance of every thought and feeling remains in-communicable, locked up in the impenetrable strong-room of the individual soul and body. Our life is a sentence of perpetual soli-tary confinement" (*Music at Night,* pages 267–268). It is this iso-lation which *Point Counter Point* attempts to represent. Each character is confined to his solitary cell and has only one window through which he may look out upon the outside world. What he sees from his limited vantage point he generalizes into a pic-ture of the whole of the external world, a picture which is almost always bound to be distorted and false.* It is a portrayal of the human condition similar to that described by Ortega y Gasset in *El tema de nuestro tiempo,* in which everything is relative and each man sees only a small slice of the totality of existence. Or, in Huxley's own words, everyone sees only the reality he likes best and passes over all the rest.

There are, however, in this novel at least two characters who do not pass over all the rest: Philip Quarles and Mark Rampion. Both of them realize that they are only individual instruments in the vast human fugue and that man's understanding of reality is usually limited and therefore untrue. Philip Quarles is aware that his window looks out on a reality that is too exclusively in-tellectual and that he in consequence neglects the emotional and sensual aspects of life.† Rampion, on the other hand, has con-sciously attempted to avoid seeing reality with only a part of his being. He wants to perceive as much of the totality of life as possible; he wants to become himself an instrument which would be a substitute for the whole orchestra, which could play the whole human fugue and not simply an isolated part. It is pre-cisely for this reason that Philip Quarles admires him: "He lives more satisfactorily, because he lives more realistically than other people. Rampion, it seems to me, takes into account all the facts

---

*The essay on El Greco in *Music at Night* is a detailed exposition of this insight.

†Quarles's name is apparently an esoteric and ironic allusion to a work attributed to Peter Longueville, *The English Hermit; or, Unparalleled sufferings, and surprizing adventures, of Mr. Philip Quarll. Who was lately discovered on an uninhabited island in the South-sea; where he had lived above fifty years, without any human assistance* (London, 1786).

(whereas other people hide from them or try to pretend that the ones they find unpleasant don't or shouldn't exist), and then proceeds to make his way of living fit the facts, and doesn't try to compel the facts to fit in with a preconceived idea of the right way of living (like these imbecile Christians and intellectuals and moralists and efficient business men)" (page 440).

Rampion does not commit the fatal error which Denis in *Crome Yellow* had complained of in almost the same terms as Philip Quarles's; Rampion suits his way of living to reality, not to a preconceived notion of reality. In short, he tries to achieve what Huxley in "The Reef" had called the "triune peace," the perfect harmony of "soul, will and body." Like Gumbril senior in *Antic Hay* and Calamy in *Those Barren Leaves,* he is the positive point set counter against a great many negative points. He wishes to transform the noisy discord which is the common music of humanity into an ideal harmony.

Rampion's ideal of "integral living," however, differs in at least one important respect from the ideals of the old Gumbril and Calamy. Both Gumbril's "crystal world" and Calamy's mysticism take only minimal cognizance of the importance of the life of the senses. Both, in fact, would seem to be proposed primarily as solutions to the dreariness and sterility of that life; and Calamy actually at one point in the novel states explicitly that sexual activity is not compatible with an attempt to see reality in all its facets. Rampion's solution, however, is solidly based on the inclusion of the life of the senses. To be sure, it is at the same time opposed to a life exclusively sensual, such as the sterile hedonism of Lucy Tantamount. It calls, rather, for a complete bodily harmony and postulates that only through such balance can a consequent spiritual harmony be achieved. Like Gumbril, Rampion demands proportion and balance, but unlike him, he does not demand a proportion and balance of the spirit alone. What Rampion strives for is, to use a phrase Huxley employed later in a direct exposition of this same philosophy, "a balance of excesses" (*Do What You Will*, page 279), a balance including both body and spirit. Only through this kind of harmony and

balance, Rampion asserts, can one escape the "wearisome condition of humanity" of which the epigraph to the novel speaks.
Man must no longer be self-divided between passion and reason
but combine both into a harmonious unit. Only if he succeeds
in this can he escape the isolation which is otherwise the wretched
lot of humanity.

Rampion's criticism of the other characters in the novel is
based on this perception. His pictures portray monsters with
heads of men, or bodies of men with monstrous heads; he focuses
his entire attack on what he sees as the perversion (only incidentally sexual) of the wholeness of man: hence he assails Burlap for
being a "Jesus pervert," Spandrell for being a "morality-philosophy pervert," and Quarles for being an "intellectual-aesthetic
pervert" (page 564). Still, though his criticism is — and is meant
to be — brutally and personally frank, it is directed not so much
at particular individuals as it is at the society which nurtured
and shaped them. Rampion's diagnosis of the disease of imbalance or perversion is that it is universal, an epidemic which
threatens to destroy all mankind.

But it is curable — or so Rampion thinks. Otherwise, why
his constant condemnation, why his own "pedagogue perversion"? If Rampion did not believe that individuals and society
could change or be made to change, there would surely be no
point in criticizing them so heatedly. And indeed his continual
harking back to Greece as an ideal society indicates that in
Greece his concept of balance demonstrably took on a real and
historical form. So that which was, may be again.

Rampion believes that man is master of his fate, believes it
implicitly, unquestioningly — so much so in fact that he never
bothers to defend or even articulate this position. His first line
of defense is several logical miles further on: at when and how,
not if. His success in argument, however, is — perhaps significantly — minimal, at least in this novel (that is, to the extent that he
is the fictional character Rampion and not merely a mask for
D. H. Lawrence). Though he speaks persuasively and "wins" most
of the arguments he takes part in, he and his wife, and to some

degree Quarles, are the only real believers. Rampion's optimism about amelioration and his struggle to effect it may be admirable, but the evidence of the novel does not suggest that he will be practically successful.

The negative, pessimistic point set counter to Rampion's positive, optimistic one is most clearly propounded by Spandrell, a character who seems consciously intended by Huxley to be a kind of foil to Rampion.* The fact that when we first encounter them they are together is perhaps an indication of this; certainly the final scene of the novel, with its confrontation of Spandrell and Rampion, shows that Huxley is consciously working out a contrast, leading up to some final resolution of opposites.

In Rampion's eyes, Spandrell is a "morality-philosophy pervert," though in spite of this he is still a person eminently worth saving. In his own terminology, Spandrell is an Augustinian; and, as every good Augustinian, ergo good determinist, must, he believes in the existence of a first cause, in God. Indeed, like Rampion and Rampion's balance, he is more concerned with proving the existence of God to others than with proving it to himself. More precisely, his primary preoccupation is not so much the fact of God's existence as the meaning of His creation.

The fullest account of Spandrell's philosophy is given at a lunch in Philip's club, where Rampion is pointedly absent. Here Spandrell maintains that "everything that has happened to [him] was somehow engineered in advance" (page 290), a perception that soon leads him to proclaim the correctness of "old Augustine's" understanding of life. The upshot of this is that Spandrell disclaims ultimate responsibility for what he is and does, and disclaims further any ability to change, to become anything other than what he is. Indeed, all of Spandrell's life — or rather all that portion of it following his mother's marriage to the mustachioed

*Just as Rampion's name suggests a bridging of the gap between man and man, and man and nature, so Spandrell's evokes the "spandrel," which *Webster's* defines as "the triangular space between the outer curve of an arch and the rectangular figure formed by the mouldings or framework surrounding it." In short, where Rampion supports, Spandrell is useless ornament.

Major Knoyle — consists of a continual attempt (or series of experiments) to find out who God is. Spandrell tries to force God to come out of hiding, and reveal to him the meaning of his life. Hence he turns to the devil as the easiest way of coming into contact with God, for, as he perceives, an absolute quantity at one end of the scale posits another and opposite absolute on the other end; and further, an understanding of the one must eventually confer an understanding of the other.

Seen from this perspective, Rampion and Spandrell are the two poles within which *Point Counter Point* operates: the poles of Hellenic humanism and Christian diabolism. Put somewhat differently, Spandrell stands for the acceptance of the human condition as wearisome, for the inevitable duality or plurality of life and the inexorable separation of man from man, a condition that can only be transcended by death. Rampion, on the other hand, is the champion (Rampion/champion) of life, the bridge or "ramp" to the spiritual and social integration of man.* Rampion, unlike Spandrell, does not see man's nature as inherently double, that is, half body and half spirit, with the body evil and spirit good; he sees man as a continuum of bodily and spiritual elements which, when properly balanced, become a single unit, become that marvelous and rare thing, a human being.

The problem which the novel poses, when understood in this way, is: who is right, Spandrell or Rampion?

There are a good many overt indications in the novel that Rampion is right — or that we are meant to think so. For example, he is the one character (with the possible exception of Webley) who seems fully satisfied with what he has made of life. And Webley's satisfaction, interestingly enough, may be seen to arise from sources broadly similar to Rampion's: Webley, after all, seeks integration, not separation, though he seeks it on a social, not individual level. What Webley wants is the balance of society, the harmony of the social orders. This fact surely

*Specifically, however, a rampion is a European bellflower (*Campanula rapunculus*) whose roots are edible. Another hint that Rampion is rooted deeply to the earth?

serves, at least in part, to account for having Illidge participate in Webley's murder; for Illidge, the Marxist dialectician, the proponent of class warfare and social imbalance, stands in almost the same relation to Webley that Spandrell does to Rampion.

Furthermore, Rampion is at least respected, if not liked, by almost all the major characters of the novel — an indication surely that we are meant to respect him as well, a suspicion confirmed by Rampion's uniqueness in not being subjected to any sort of obvious satire. The fact that the author likes him seems to suggest that we should too, and that we should accept his philosophical position as the most correct one. Moreover, Rampion has an uncanny gift for perceiving what is wrong with the other characters in the novel — and subsequent events confirm the rightness of his diagnoses. Finally, of course, Huxley was advocating a philosophy remarkably like Rampion's — "the balance of excesses" — in a number of essays published at roughly the same time as *Point Counter Point.*

There are nonetheless signs (largely implicit to be sure) that Rampion/Lawrence's philosophy is not so wholeheartedly accepted in the novel as it is in the essays. The beginning of the novel is concerned with the fetal development of man, the progress of worm to fish to mammal and so on, something Rampion's static Hellenism is incapable of dealing with. Is it possible for an ex-fish to become a "balanced" human being? Such a question does not occur to Rampion, but Huxley, Lawrence or no, must still ask it. Rampion's philosophy cannot explain the curious and ironic twists — not of man — but of fate. Why, for example, should a cart have run over Philip's foot and maimed him — and maimed him not merely physically but emotionally as well? Only the Topiarist God of the early Huxley or the Augustinian determinism of Spandrell can interpret such happenings, certainly not Rampion's idea of a man-made and man-run universe. Neither can Rampion account — and, significantly, is not made to account — for the horrible and unexplained death of little Philip Quarles. Is it possible to achieve balance, or worthwhile to try to achieve it, if nature or God or fate can strike one down, maim or kill one at any moment? Rampion remains curiously silent.

Spandrell's moral-philosophical perversion, it is clear, cannot be dismissed from the novel as easily as it is from Rampion's mind. And it is consequently not at all coincidental that the story concludes with a final confrontation of Spandrell and Rampion: this is the culminating point of the novel. Just as it is no coincidence that the final scene but one opens with a recording of Beethoven's *Heiliger Dankgesang* which is described in the same duality of spiritual and material terms as the playing of the Bach B-minor suite at Tantamount House during the second scene of the novel. The two musical performances provide the frame for the novel, and their description provides also a symbol for the two primary ways of viewing life: Rampion's and Spandrell's. Rampion's: that the music is basically man's, hence fundamentally material and of this world. Spandrell's: that it is essentially spiritual, a revelation of God's existence in man; and that man perceives, not himself, but God in the beauty and harmony of the music, just as he perceives the devil, and not merely himself, in the ugliness and dissonance of life.

The conclusion of *Point Counter Point* seems on the more obvious level to confirm Rampion's position. In the silence following the shots, we no longer hear the music of divinity but only the music of the machine, the pointless scratchings of the needle on the inner grooves of the record. *Deus* has degenerated into *deus ex machina,* as from Rampion's intermediary human position, God inevitably must. Superhumanity and subhumanity are both enemies of humanity. The Spandrell who failed earlier in his attempts to become a devil by seducing virgins and murdering Edward Webley, now seems to have failed again in trying to become an angel by having himself killed — becoming to that high requiem a sod. Rampion is apparently right because he stands in between, because he balances, rather precariously to be sure, between God and devil, because he hears the music of neither divinity nor machine, but only of humanity.

Still, lurking doubts seem to remain in Huxley's mind, if

Rampion's humanity is in the final analysis a gift of the gods, or if its continued existence depends too heavily on such fortuitous matters as good health, a good wife, the absence of carts that run over one's feet or cancers that gnaw at one's stomach. Furthermore, the central, controlling image of the novel — that of the orchestra — seems at once to affirm and deny Rampion's position. For if, on the one hand, each individual man contains within himself all the instruments of the orchestra, then it is at least possible for him to achieve a harmony of the separate, individual parts. Therefore Rampion is right. But if, on the other hand — the hand Huxley implicitly shows us at the end of the novel — each man is not a sum of the musical instruments but merely a single, solitary instrument within the vast orchestra of humanity, then he will obviously only be able to play his own part and make his own noise; or rather not his own, but that which fate has noted down for him. And it will only be the conductor — God — who will be able to make sense out of the resulting noise.

If this is the case, then *Point Counter Point* ultimately returns full circle to the position Huxley enunciated in his early poems — despite all the affirmation of Rampion. For, though there may be a final harmony, perhaps like that which Claude Bernard saw as the guiding principle of the universe, or else the concordant interconnection of all aspects of life which Philip Quarles perceives, there still will be no harmony for man, at least for individual man. For the individual can be only a part, a very small part, of this greater harmony. In the final analysis, the achievement of harmony, as Rampion knows, depends on man's being God: only then can he be the whole musical score and not merely a fragment of it. But is man, is Rampion, a god? To himself and to his wife, perhaps; to his readers, whether in the guise of Rampion or of Lawrence, probably not.

This division of the novel — whether conscious or unconscious does not much matter — into one level of obvious affirmation and another of residual skepticism mirrors the other divisions that run, like great chasms, through the novel, beginning

with the epigraph from Fulke Greville and its vision of man
born to one law and bound to another. It is the "irony of being
two" all over again, but this time scored in many registers, with
multiple variations, played in many keys, and symphonically
orchestrated.

Nearly all the characters are plagued by this divisiveness
within their own personalities. All, with the exception of Rampion, are schizophrenic, split between the claims of the body and
those of the spirit; or else monomaniacs who have succeeded, for
the time being at any rate, in suppressing one half of themselves
in order to devote themselves entirely to the other. Only Rampion seems not to be content with a duality or moiety of self;
only he demands and achieves unity.

The division, too, runs in a rather different direction
through the novel as a separation between the real and the unreal. For this novel, like Huxley's earlier ones, only perhaps
more so, is autobiographical. Quarles, even without Huxley's
later explicit confession that he was "in part a portrait of me,"
clearly — to those who knew anything at all about Huxley — is
the author himself (with Spandrell possibly making up some of
the other parts of the self-portrait).[6] That Huxley does what
Quarles in his journal proposes to do should be a sufficient clue
that Huxley is here working out fictionally many of the problems, aesthetic, philosophical, personal, that concerned him in
actual life. And there is the further and by now notorious circumstance that both Rampion and Burlap are based on real people: the former on the man who in the years immediately preceding this novel had become Huxley's intimate and respected
friend, the latter on his old chief editor (and perhaps chief
enemy) at the *Athenaeum*, John Middleton Murry.*

*In *Figures in the Foreground, Literary Reminiscences, 1917–40* (London, 1963), p. 71, Frank Swinnerton feels compelled to "testify to Huxley's
laughing, disgusted perception that Murry was auto-intoxicated, and in the
habit of mystically identifying himself with whatever saint or genius was his
latest enthusiasm." Murry himself comments less enthusiastically on Huxley's
"distinctly pointed" portrait of himself in *Between Two Worlds: An Autobiography* (London, 1935), p. 438. According to F. A. Lea, *The Life of John
Middleton Murry* (London, 1959), pp. 115–116, the story of Burlap's involve-

Part of the sense of incompletion or division that one feels in reading this novel may arise from Huxley's attempt to transport these (and other) real beings into his fictional world. They — or at least Rampion — do not seem to have traveled well. Rampion does not fit in comfortably with the other inhabitants of Huxley's imagination, people whom we have met before, though bearing different names, in earlier works. Burlap is not nearly so much out of place, perhaps because he reminds us of similar characters like Barbecue-Smith in "The Farcical History of Richard Greenow," but also, I think, because he is somehow more acclimatized to the world of *Point Counter Point*. He is present there to the extent that he can *act* (in a double sense) in it, not merely talk in and about it like Rampion.

This distinction can be appreciated more fully if we compare Rampion with an earlier Huxley portrait of Lawrence, that of Kingham in the title story of *Two or Three Graces* (1926). There Kingham/Lawrence comes alive as Rampion/Lawrence never does in *Point Counter Point,* partly because Huxley is here poking fun at him ("King Ham"), partly because we are made more aware of his faults. The main point of difference, however, is that in Kingham/Lawrence (as in Burlap/Murry) Huxley is intent on transporting a personality from one realm of being to another; and he knows that to reassemble a personality in the realm of fiction one has to present it in action, not merely in contemplation or conversation. Kingham/Lawrence is alive because we see him act to become what he is at the end of the story;

ment with his secretary, Ethel Cobbett, is almost literally true, right down to her dismissal. Though Murry later pretended that Huxley's caricature had not wounded him, Lea reports that his first impulse was to challenge him to a duel — "a vision," as Lea says, "to which Max Beerbohm alone could do justice" (p. 159). That Huxley felt some real personal animosity against his former editor at the *Athenaeum* is clear from his reaction to Murry's biography of Lawrence, *Son of Woman*: "Murry's vindictive hagiography was pretty slimy — the slug's-eye view of poor L: and if you knew the intimate history of his relations with L and Mrs. L, you'd really shudder. One day it really ought to be published" (L352). Very likely a good deal of it had already been published in *Point Counter Point*. In a mellower mood, he later observed that "there is something of Murry in several of my characters, but I wouldn't say I'd put Murry in a book" *Writers at Work: The Paris Review Interviews*, 2nd ser. (New York, 1963), p. 210.

Rampion/Lawrence is dead (as a character) because he is fixed
and finished when he enters the story. There is no more growth
left in him — and the few flashbacks to his youth are not enough
to resuscitate him.

What Huxley has done in Rampion, in other words, is to
bring Lawrence's ideas across the gulf without bringing along
Lawrence's vitality and personality. Out of a man whose life con-
sisted of self-contradiction and growth and change, Huxley has
created a man who is incapable of any sort of change. Lawrence,
therefore, was certainly justified in criticizing Rampion as a "gas-
bag,"[7] though perhaps he should have remembered that at least
one aspect (and that not a minor one) of his own personality was
a profound windiness, as his autobiographical character Birkin
in *Women in Love* amply testifies. But even in *Women in Love*
we can discern that the difference between Birkin/Lawrence and
Rampion/Lawrence is not a difference in gases, either in kind
or volume (in both cases much the same and often equally inert)
but in the ability, shared by Birkin and Kingham but not by
Rampion, to drop the conversational bag and free their hands
for physical and emotional action.

To be sure, the gaseousness of Rampion ought not to be
exaggerated. Too often critics of *Point Counter Point* harp on
him and on his relation to Lawrence to the exclusion of all else.
They forget that Rampion actually appears only a few times in
the novel, even though his penchant for lecturing tends to make
him seem more prominent. Of course, *Point Counter Point* might
have been a more amusing and perhaps "better" novel if, as G.
U. Ellis suggests, Huxley had focused his satire on Burlap and
left Rampion out altogether.[8] By the same token, *David Cop-
perfield* would have been a much "better" book if Dickens had
left out the protagonist and focused his attention on Micawber.
But it would not have been the same book. It is futile to think
about what might have been. The point is that Huxley, beginning with this novel, has started to move, openly and consciously,
in the direction of constructive satire. He no longer lashes mankind simply for the painful pleasure of lashing it and hence him-

self; he now hopes to achieve a definite end through his satirical means (though how optimistic that hope is, the ambiguous figure of Spandrell is there to tell us). In practicing this new mode of explicitly constructive satire, Huxley runs certain risks — those, for example, that Fielding encountered in *Tom Jones*. There Allworthy is almost as much of a "gas-bag" as Rampion is here, but Allworthy cannot be removed without distorting the whole moral context of the novel. He must remain to provide at least the overt standard by which all the other characters are to be judged. And so must Rampion — though one might wish for a less obtrusive and more interesting standard.

Point Counter Point is doubtless marred by its "Rampionism," but it still remains the apex of Huxley's satirical achievement. It is his only novel (and one of the few novels *tout court*) which succeeds in portraying relatively succinctly and convincingly the main social and intellectual outlines of an era. In the manner of Stendhal's *The Red and the Black*, it could, without evoking undue surprise, have been subtitled "A Chronicle of 1928." Furthermore *Point Counter Point*, because of the possibilities of unity in diversity offered by its musical technique, focuses its satiric thrust in a way unprecedented by Huxley's earlier novels and perhaps equaled subsequently in the Huxley canon only by *Brave New World*. The whole force of the satire is now directed almost exclusively on an incisive exposition of the preconceptions of characters — even to the point even of extending, as we have seen, to the author himself.

This kind of self-satire, to bring up one of the perennial clichés about Huxley, is something he supposedly borrowed from Gide's *Les Faux Monnayeurs*. Perhaps he did, but not very likely. Huxley was well versed in French literature (well enough to translate a novel by Remy de Gourmont and Mallarmé's "L'Après-midi d'un faune"); he knew Gide personally, admired *The Counterfeiters*, but held certain reservations about him as man and artist, as Gide seems to have realized.*

*Huxley opens his review of *La Symphonie pastorale* for *The Athenaeum* (September 24, 1920), p. 422, with the observation that "Gide is one

Even in the early and mid-twenties, Huxley was by no means unknown in France: T. S. Eliot had written about him in the *Nouvelle Revue Française*; and Proust had mentioned him favorably — the only contemporary English novelist to be so honored — in *The Remembrance of Things Past*. Hence, to demonstrate or at least to suggest persuasively that Huxley's novel was a mere pastiche of Gide's would certainly have shed reflected glory on Gide's work in France and elsewhere, though Gide possibly did not intend his accusation to appear either so complete or so malicious. Still, he might have mentioned that Huxley had used the basic device of *The Counterfeiters*, the inclusion of a novelist within a novel, in a short story, "Nuns at Luncheon" (1922) and in *Those Barren Leaves* (1925), both published before Gide's novel. Furthermore, it is clear that Huxley uses this device in *Point Counter Point* primarily for satirical purposes, and in

of the problems of literature," and then proceeds to give a lengthy and biting answer to the question of how it is that "a man can possess so many of the qualities that go to make a great writer and yet be so definitely not an immortal, so certainly not great?" *The Counterfeiters* is the only novel of Gide that he liked. On January 18, 1927, he wrote to Robert Nichols: "Gide, as you say, is disappointing. He has a faculty for always touching on interesting subjects and never really getting hold of them. He attacks great moral problems and then, before the campaign has well started, beats an elegant, literary and genteel retreat. The only good book he has written is the last, *Les Faux Monnayeurs*, which is very interesting and in its way very good. It is good, I think, because it is the first book in which Gide has ventured to talk about the one thing in the world that really interests him — sentimental sodomy" (L281–282).

That Gide was by no means unaware of Huxley's opinion (or disposed to overlook it) emerges clearly from the account of a brief meeting with Gide in Clive Bell's *Old Friends* (London, 1956), p. 148. Sometime in the twenties, Bell was in a Paris restaurant dining alone when Gide came in with a large party, paused at Bell's table, and asked to join him later for coffee. His object was not small talk, but the answer to a very specific question. " 'Why does Aldous Huxley refer to me as a "faux grand ecrivain?" ' he demanded; adding traditionally 'I have never done him any harm.' I could not say; but we passed the five minutes he had to spare well enough, speaking ill of Aldous presumably. Later I asked Aldous whether he had said anything of the sort. Yes, he had — some twenty years earlier in a magazine, possibly an undergraduate magazine. But Gide had the eyes of a lynx and the memory of an elephant."

For an exhaustive (and at times exhausting) discussion of the influence, or lack of it, of *The Counterfeiters* on *Point Counter Point*, see Gerd Rohmann, *Aldous Huxley und die französische Literatur* (Marburg, 1968).

this respect imitates *The Counterfeiters* practically not at all. Ironically, Gide himself provides the best reply to those critics who would reduce literature to a game of who came first, when — appropriately in his *Journal des Faux-Monnayeurs* — he declaims against "cette manie moderne de voir influence (ou 'pastiche') à chaque ressemblance que l'on découvre, manie qui transforme la critique de certains universitaires en police et qui précipite tant d'artistes dans l'absurde par crainte d'être soupçonnés de pouvoir ressembler à quelqu'un."9 *

Point Counter Point, as far as the development of Huxley's satire is concerned, "points" in a new direction. It closes off the period of predominantly destructive satire, and begins the period of predominantly constructive satire. Huxley has now momentarily found — and not much later will permanently find — ideals which he considers both desirable and practical and which he hereafter expounds not merely novelistically but also essayistically. He begins to abandon that detachment which was by and large characteristic of the earlier novels and becomes *engagé*. Though never (with the possible exception of *Island*) mere *romans à thèse*, Huxley's later novels sometimes become so preoccupied with preaching the doctrine of humanity (or nonattachment or mysticism) that they become less than human. But even though the later Huxley turns to propaganda, he never loses his gift for brilliantly corrosive and destructive satire. All of the later novels are full of marvelously satirical parts, even if they now remain only parts and must alternate with extensive passages of almost direct exposition. With one notable exception, however: *Brave New World*.

*He declaims against "this modern mania of seeing influence (or 'pastiche') in every resemblance that one finds, a mania which transforms the criticism of certain academics into detective work, and which leads so many artists into the absurd, because they are afraid of being suspected of resembling somebody" (my translation).

CHAPTER V

The American Dream

Brave New World and *Ape and Essence*

IN 1932, almost as if bidding farewell to his own poetical vocation, Huxley published *Texts and Pretexts*, a personal anthology of favorite poets of the past (the texts), arranged thematically and accompanied by a series of descriptive, elaborative, often deeply perceptive comments (the pretexts). Huxley was to employ something of the same method more than a dozen years later in his attempt to prove that mysticism or the perennial philosophy (as the title of his book termed it) was always and everywhere the same, a timeless fixed point in a world of continual flux. The method was a good one, particularly effective because it was so empirical and therefore enabled Huxley to weave his web of persuasion around the solid structural supports of his selections. Here the accumulated thought and inspiration of the past shored up his indictment of the present and revealed, uncertainly and indirectly in the earlier case, confidently and explicitly in the later one, the direction in which salvation lay.

In the same year Huxley also published another work,

which achieved greater popularity than any other and (perhaps ironically) contributed considerably to his future financial se-curity.* Yet *Brave New World,* with its concentration on a remote future time (550 years distant) and its almost exclusively scientific and technological frame of reference, seems a far cry from the delicate poetic mosaic of *Texts and Pretexts,* a contrast reinforced by one of the more striking opening remarks in the latter work: "Personally, I must confess, I am more interested in what the world is now than in what it will be, or what it might be if improbable conditions were fulfilled" (page 6). Still, appearances apart, the two works are not really contradictory. Shakespeare — as we can see from the very title of the novel — invades the ironically brave new world, and science makes occa-sional textual as well as pretextual raids into the provinces of poetry. For to Huxley, as to his famous grandfather, it had long become obvious that literature and science, like matter and spirit, formed a continuum and not two sides of an unbridgeable gulf — a perception that, spurred on by the famous Snow contro-versy of the late fifties, was to form the substance of his last com-pleted book.

Equally important, especially for a proper understanding of *Brave New World,* Huxley almost certainly never intended his novel to be a satire of the future. For what, after all, is the good of satirizing the future? The only meaningful future is actually, as he observed in an essay published a year earlier, the future which already exists in the present. "O brave new world," let us remember, is what Miranda exclaims when she sees for the first time the as yet unredeemed inhabitants of the *old* world, an irony of which Huxley is fully aware. The present is what matters most in *Brave New World,* as it does in any good Utopia; and Huxley only uses the lens of future time (as preceding satirists

*Huxley's later attempt to make a film of the novel was frustrated by repeated difficulties with the holder of the rights. Another plan to make a musical of it seems to have foundered on his failure to find a suitable com-poser. One of the lyrics from the proposed libretto is quoted in a letter to his son, dated September 30, 1956 (L809).

had often resorted to geographical or past remoteness) in order to discover better the latent diseases of the here and now.*

Looking back at the novel after a lapse of fifteen years, Huxley once suggested (what should really be obvious to everyone and what differentiates this novel so radically from vaguely similar but inferior works by other authors) that the theme of the novel is "not the advancement of science as such; it is the advancement of science as it affects human individuals."[1] This is a problem which had been growing increasingly acute since the great scientific avalanche of the late nineteenth and early twentieth centuries (hence Helmholtz, Bernard, and Watson as names for some of the main characters in the novel), and which, after the First World War and the Soviet Revolution, had assumed ever more oppressive political and economic forms (therefore Lenina, Marx, and Mond).† Huxley had been charting the course of this sort of scientific progress for the last decade, particularly in its guises of psychology, political propaganda, and their popular corollary, advertising. In this sense, *Brave New World* is a direct descendant of *Antic Hay*. The world of A.F. 632 is simply the thoroughgoing realization of the ideal of the Complete Man, a never ending round of good times. Like the Complete Man's

---

*Another example of an anti-Utopia which uses a projection into the future to satirize the present is the Russian novelist Zamiatin's *We*. This work is occasionally mentioned as an influence on *Brave New World*, but Zamiatin's connection with *1984* seems more immediate.

In quite another, and rather more trivial, sense *Brave New World* is also an attack on the present's conception of the future. Specifically, it is a parody of H. G. Wells's optimistic fantasy of the future, *Men like Gods*. This is confirmed by Huxley in a letter dated May 18, 1931: "I am writing a novel about the future — on the horror of the Wellsian Utopia and a revolt against it" (L348). In *Private History* (London, 1960), p. 154, Derek Patmore relates how Wells reacted to this revolt: "Ever an ardent socialist, he was certain that social progress would cure the evils that men were so easily prone to, and when we discussed the works of such writers as Aldous Huxley he said to me savagely: '*Brave New World* was a great disappointment to me. A writer of the standing of Aldous Huxley has no right to betray the future as he did in that book. When thinking about the future, people seem to overlook the logical progress in education, in architecture, and science.' "

†Some of the future developments of science as presented in this novel, in particular the idea of the baby hatcheries, are derived from J. B. S. Haldane's *Daedalus, or Science and the Future* (London, 1924). For a discussion of this work, see Ronald Clark's *JBS*.

world, this world is basically materialistic and sensual — only
more so. The result of this intensification of "happiness" is that
there exists almost no possibility for the completer man to dis-
card his beard, listen to Mozart instead of the Sixteen Sexophon-
ists, or choose to enter a "crystal world" instead of an orgy-porgian Solidarity Service. In the name of a totally external happiness, any kind of significant internal life has been banished from
the Fordian world.

The intensity with which Huxley felt *Brave New World* to
be an attack on the present or on the present as contained in the
future can be seen from his repeated attempts to gauge the progress of the malady of dehumanization.* When he took its tem-
perature in an article written for *Life* magazine in 1948, the great
blights of fascism, the Second World War, and the atom bomb
had intervened to alter the condition of mankind and therefore
Huxley's diagnosis. Now he maintained that, instead of one, there
were two myths underlying the psyche and behavior of Western
man. To the myth of progress he added the myth of nationalism,
the former promulgated through the medium of advertising, the
latter through political propaganda and brainwashing.[2] From
this we can see — though Huxley did not explicitly make the
connection — that in the new world the myth of nationalism with
its accompanying propaganda has disappeared because of the
massive destruction of the Nine Years' War (as Mustapha Mond
instructs the Savage) and because the instruments of technological blandness have triumphed over those of nationalistic brutal-
ity; indeed, the plot of the novel (such as it is) consists of a re-
enactment of this triumph in miniature. On the other hand, in
Ape and Essence, which Huxley was working on as he wrote the
Life essay, it is apparent that the myth of progress has been dis-
placed by a religious variant of nationalism. The stupidity of
both of these myths, according to Huxley, is that they stress the
external aspects of life, not the internal. Their disciples, therefore, must inevitably "progress" to one or another kind of perdi-

*The most thorough reexamination is to be found in *Brave New World
Revisited* (London, 1959).

tion: the perdition of "heaven" or the perdition of hell. Hence, this kind of progress is really no progress at all. Real progress, in Huxley's terms, can only be defined as "personal progress," or "internal progress." It is only through this type of advancement that one can hope to create a "genuinely human society," and only such a society can assure the continued existence of genuine human individuals, not diabolically happy or diabolically unhappy animals.

The idea for the novel that was later to become *Brave New World* had germinated in Huxley's mind a decade earlier. In *Crome Yellow*, Scogan, a verbose and parasitical materialist, outlines for the benefit of Denis, the hero and something of a romantic idealist, his plan for the "Rational State." In this state, psychologists would examine all children and separate them into three distinct species: a small number of Directing Intelligences, a larger number of Men of Faith, and the vast mass of the Herd. The first class, the only one capable of thought and able to achieve even "a certain degree of freedom," would use the men of faith or action to govern the state and the herd. To ensure that this last class would carry out its appointed tasks dutifully and uncomplainingly, the Intelligences would devise and the Men of Faith would apply suitable mechanisms of conditioning: "In the upbringing of the Herd," Scogan almost ecstatically concludes, "humanity's almost boundless suggestibility will be scientifically exploited. Systematically, from earliest infancy, its members will be assured that there is no happiness to be found except in work and obedience; they will be made to believe that they are happy, that they are tremendously important beings, and that everything they do is noble and significant. For the lower species the earth will be restored to the centre of the universe and man to pre-eminence on the earth. Oh, I envy the lot of the commonalty in the Rational State! Working their eight hours a day, obeying their betters, convinced of their own grandeur and significance and immortality, they will be marvellously happy, happier than any race of men has ever been. They will go through life in a rosy state of intoxication, from which they will never awake. The Men of Faith will play the cupbearers at this lifelong bacchanal, filling and ever filling again with the warm liquor that the Intelligences, in sad and sober privacy behind the scenes, will brew for the intoxication of their subjects" (*Crome Yellow*, page 164).

After Scogan ends his hymn of praise to the bacchanalian Rational State, Denis naturally inquires what his place might be in the new order. The question is a difficult one for Scogan, but he answers it with admirable logic. Since Denis, a poet, would be unfit for manual labor, since he is clearly not a man of faith, and since he has not the "marvellously clear and merciless and penetrating" rational faculty of the Directing Intelligences, he would have to be consigned to the lethal chamber.

In this last respect, the Fordian world of the future is more humane than the world of Scogan's conception — but only because the quality of its mercy is not strained. As Mustapha Mond, a World Controller and the equivalent of a Directing Intelligence, admits, it is only because the earth happens to possess a considerable number of remote and relatively inaccessible islands that the sentence of extermination for Bernard Marx and Helmholtz Watson is commuted to one of exile. Even so, this avoidance of overt cruelty is symptomatic of the greater blandness of the new state and its deeper level of uniformity. For in the Fordian state, not only is the herd conditioned into an inescapable "happiness," but all the inhabitants — with the exception of a handful of World Controllers and a small number of malcontents like Marx and Watson — are forced to be "happy." To be sure, there are different classifications of people (Alpha, Beta, and so on) which echo the rigid stratification of the Rational State (or the triple order of Prospero, Ariel, and Caliban on Shakespeare's island), but for all practical purposes the brave new world is inhabited by only one species: *homo felix et stultus.* Alpha, Epsilon, and the whole range in between are alike artificially and scientifically prevented from experiencing any kind of unhappiness, or, for that matter, from experiencing any kind of real emotion whatsoever. All classes of men are fated to pass through life in a "somatic" cloud of greater or lesser density, fated even to die in that cloud, forever oblivious of any reality but the one imbued in them through their conditioning. That conditioning, as Mond remarks of the individual Epsilon in a passage of central importance, "has laid down rails along which he's got to run. He can't help himself; he's foredoomed. Even after decanting, he's still inside a bottle of infantile and embryonic fixations. Each one of us . . . *goes through life inside a bottle*" (page 182, my italics). The only difference between Alpha and Epsilon is the size of the confining bottle; each is in the end equally idiotically piscine in the aquarium of his biological and psychological conditioning, each equally the victim of the substitution of God the Bland Machinist for God the Cruel Topiarist.

Scogan's Rational State, despite its cruelty, still permitted a certain measure of freedom to an entire class of citizens. The intellectuals, within limits, could still be aware of reality and of themselves as individuals. Not so the citizens of the brave new world, for they are almost universally condemned to standardized thoughts and emotions. It is this difference which most clearly distinguishes the brave new world of A.D. 1932 (or A.F. 632) from the hypothetical Rational State of 1922 — and it is a difference which is due, apparently, to Huxley's intervening encounter with America and the "American Civilization."

In 1926 Huxley made a trip around the world, traveling eastward and stopping primarily in India, Burma, Malaya, and the United States, paying his bills by writing up his experiences for British and American papers. Later in the same year he collected these fragments and joined them together in *Jesting Pilate,* a fascinating travelogue of a man in search of the truth but too pressed to stay for a definite answer — but not too pressed to await and formulate provisional ones, such as the "truth" (which was later to become a massive lie for the author of *Island*) that the ways of the East were not noticeably superior to those of Europe, or the "truth" that Western culture in its westernmost or Californian manifestations boded ill for the future of mankind.

In a special section of *Jesting Pilate* entitled "Los Angeles.

A Rhapsody," Huxley records his impressions of the City of Dreadful Joy, or more briefly, the Joy City, with devastating irony. Los Angeles, as Huxley perceives it, is a city in which everybody is happy but no one is quite sure why, where there is hectic activity on all sides, with people rushing to and fro in their automobiles, bombarded by advertising and enticed by entertainment of every sort, from religious to alcoholic, but where there is hardly any trace of intellectual life or purpose. Here man, as in the brave new world, is created for the good time, not the good time for man, with the inescapable consequence that his soul and body become standardized. The women, for example, are "plumply ravishing" and give promise (as do their equivalents in the newer world) of an Eliotesque "pneumatic bliss" — "but of not much else, to judge by their faces. So curiously uniform, unindividual and blank" (*Jesting Pilate,* page 266). For Huxley, it is plain, there is no need to travel into the future to find the brave new world; it already exists, only too palpably, in the American Joy City, where the declaration of dependence begins and ends with the single-minded pursuit of happiness.

Typically "American," too, is the rejection of everything old. "History," Mustapha Mond remarks, citing one of the prime commandments of Our Ford, "is bunk." And not just written history or old books — Shakespeare and the Bible which have to be locked away in a safe — but all old ideas and institutions are bunk. The very concept of age is bunk for those who live modern in the soma generation. How horrified the orthodox Fordians are by the unexpected appearance of a woman who reveals her actual age in wrinkles, sagging breasts, and flabby flesh! How disgusted even that woman herself is by her own condition, exiled though she has been from earthly paradise for more than two decades!

In the new world, youth is not merely skin-deep. It penetrates far into the interior of the Fordian psyche, so far in fact that the lower orders have no choice but to be young. Heredity and conditioning will not permit them to think or act otherwise than in an infantile fashion. Only the Alphas, the managerial elite of the Fordian state, "do not *have* to be infantile in their emotional behavior." This, however, does not mean that they are freed from the obligation of maintaining "a proper standard of infantile decorum" (page 81), though to be sure a few Alphas like Bernard Marx or Helmholtz Watson do occasionally behave in indecorous adult ways. But their example can have no permanent effect, for the very simple reason that adults are removed at once from the society.

The only adults who are permitted to influence the Fordian state are the twelve so-called World Controllers, who function as a tiny priest class governing a vast population of blissfully ignorant babies. To judge by the example of Mustapha Mond, however, the World Controllers are a very sober and benevolent group who selflessly devote themselves to the welfare of their charges. Mond himself, as a former physicist of considerable promise, would have been happier pursuing his scientific researches undisturbed, but instead he chose the harder and less rewarding task of government. It is on his shoulders, and on those of his eleven peers, that the ultimate responsibility for the operation of the Fordian state rests.

Though there is no religion in the new world beyond the materialistically oriented orgy-porgy services — sustained youth, as Mond observes to the Savage, allows one to be independent of God — the World Controllers seem fairly clearly to be modeled on the pope and cardinals of the Church of Rome. Like these, Mond is a father to his "children," guarding them from the burden and temptations of excessive knowledge and filling their lives with time-consuming pomp and circumstance. The Fordian state — even phrases like "Our Ford" or "Ford's in his flivver" imply it — resembles nothing so much as a secular theocracy.

That Huxley is fully conscious of this dimension of his satirical parable is implicit in the extended dialogue between Mond and the Savage which occupies all of chapter 17. This chapter is a revision of the Grand Inquisitor episode in Dostoevsky's *Brothers Karamazov*, with the roles of the Inquisitor and Christ reversed. Here it is the Christ-Savage who is indignant at the behavior of the Inquisitor-Controller and his presumption that man can live by soma alone. To be sure, unlike Dostoevsky's Christ, Huxley's Controller does not maintain absolute silence in the face of his interlocutor's verbal onslaught, but he does the next best thing by seeking to overcome the Savage's objections through sweet reasonableness. Of course, like Christ he can afford to be tolerant, for he holds the supreme power in his hands: he rules over the godless utopia whose coming the Grand Inquisitor had foretold. That utopia exists — unlike Christ's heaven — not for the chosen few, who are in any event strong enough to help themselves, but for the masses of the weak and spineless, who don't know what to do with Christ's gift of freedom and who are only too pleased to rid themselves of the "terrible burden of that gift" in exchange for "being able to become a herd once again." The historical development of the Fordian world, as related by Mond, conforms strikingly to the pattern predicted by the Grand Inquisitor: "Oh, ages are yet to come of the confusion of free thought, of their science and cannibalism. For having begun to build their tower of Babel without us, they will end, of course with cannibalism. But then the beast will crawl to us and lick our feet and spatter them with tears of blood. . . . But then, and only then, the reign of peace and happiness will come for men. Thou art proud of Thine elect, but Thou hast only the elect, while we give rest to all. . . . With us all will be happy and will no more rebel nor destroy one another as under Thy freedom. Oh, we shall persuade them that they will only become free when they renounce their freedom to us and submit to us" (page 238).* In its essential outline, though not in its proportions and its technological details, the new world matches the Grand Inquisitor's vision: "And all will be happy, all the millions of creatures except for the hundred thousand who rule over them. For only we, we who guard the mystery, shall be unhappy. There will be thousands of millions of happy ones and

*Passages from *The Brothers Karamazov* are quoted from the New American Library edition, trans. Constance Garnett (New York, 1957).

a hundred thousand sufferers who have taken upon themselves the curse of the knowledge of good and evil" (page 239).

Against this enforced happiness, the Savage asserts the "right to be unhappy," the right to deformity, to disease and suffering of all kinds, the right to endure pain and to limit pleasure. To Mustapha Mond, as to the Grand Inquisitor, the desire for and the exercise of such a right seem the only evils of which they can conceive. In the end, as in Ivan Karamazov's tale, one or the other "right" must triumph, and the other vanish utterly. It must be either soul or stomach, the love of God or the love of man: there is no other alternative.

In the United States, especially in its westernmost parts, Huxley found incarnated most of the dream of the Grand Inquisitor, found the love of stomach and of mass man running rampant, and recognized that what confronted him here was the future of mankind. At the very beginning of "The Outlook for American Culture: Some Reflections in a Machine Age," an essay published in 1927, Huxley warned his readers that "speculating on the American future, we are speculating on the future of civilized man." One of the most ominous portents of the American way of life, Huxley went on to say, was that it embraced a large class of people who "do not want to be cultured, are not interested in the higher life. For these people existence on the lower, animal levels is perfectly satisfactory. Given food, drink, the company of their fellows, sexual enjoyment, and plenty of noisy distractions from without, they are happy." Furthermore, in America and the rest of the technologically advanced world, "all the resources of science are applied in order that imbecility may flourish and vulgarity cover the whole earth." The resources are so applied because quantity rather than quality is profitable for the capitalists involved: "The higher the degree of standardization in popular literature and art, the greater the profit for the manufacturer." All this mechanical and intellectual standardization, however, leads to the exaltation of the standardized man. It is this development which Huxley views with most concern: "This tendency to raise the ordinary, worldly man to the

level of the extraordinary and disinterested one seems to me entirely deplorable. The next step will be to exalt him above the
extraordinary man, who will be condemned and persecuted on
principle because he is not ordinary — for not to be ordinary will
be regarded as a crime. In this reversal of the old values I see a
real danger, a menace to all desirable progress."[3]

It is this "next step" that has been taken in the Fordian (that
is, American) world. For of all ideas, the idea of the extraordinary or individual can least be tolerated by the new world. Extraordinary or individual behavior is a punishable offense. That
is why the father of John the Savage, a Director of Hatcheries
and Conditioning, hastens to assure Bernard that he had had
"nothing emotional, nothing long-drawn" (page 80) to do with
the girl he had taken on a visit to a New Mexico Reservation;
that is, the girl who was accidentally left behind and thus gave
birth (another offense) to the Savage. This is also why he censures Bernard for suspected individualism, for not conforming to
the duty of all Alphas "to be infantile, even against their inclina-
tion" (page 81). The Alpha must inhibit his illicit desires for
adult behavior, must sacrifice his individuality for the sake of social solidarity and uniformity. But as the examples of Marx and
Watson reveal, not all Alphas do so.

Consequently, in spite of all the attempts of technology and
psychological conditioning to reduce man to an automaton, some
semblance of humanity and individuality still survives, even if
only accidentally. In this respect, *Brave New World* is not entirely the deeply pessimistic novel it is usually considered to be; the
hope for a continuation of humanity is not altogether extin-
guished. It is the same hope that Huxley offered to his contemporaries in an essay, "Foreheads Villainous Low" (a title also derived from *The Tempest*), published a year before the novel, at
a time when the gathering powers of fascism and economic depression inclined the majority of thinking men either to despair
or to desperate measures: "The new snobberies of stupidity and
ignorance are now strong enough to wage war at least on equal
terms with the old culture-snobbery. For still, an absurd anach-

ronism, the dear old culture-snobbery bravely survives. Will it
go down before its enemies? And, much more important, will the
culture it so heroically and ridiculously stands up for, also go
down? I hope, I even venture to think, it will not. There will
always be a few people for whom the things of the mind are so
vitally important that they will not, they simply cannot allow
them to be overwhelmed" (*Music at Night,* pages 208–209).

Yet, though the new world has its quota of individual survivors, the atmosphere of their environment is so oppressive that it
is nearly impossible for them to increase their awareness of themselves or each other. Bernard Marx has come to realize that he is
distinct from the mass of other Alphas only because too much
alcohol was accidentally added to his blood surrogate. Helmholtz
Watson has arrived at a similar perception by the more natural
but equally casual expedient of having been born too intelligent
to accept his conditioning uncritically. The two become friends
because they are aware of something in themselves that makes
them different, but their awareness is stifled at every turn. Their
surroundings offer them almost no opportunity to express themselves. Bernard struggles ineffectively to establish a human relationship with Lenina Crowne; Helmholtz Watson strives for the
poetical formulation of something he as yet only remotely understands. But only when they come into contact with the Savage, do
they finally become aware of the means for an expression of themselves.

The Savage is an individual. Nevertheless, though he comes
from a society which is in its externals totally different from that
of the Fordian world, he is, like Bernard, an individual merely
by accident. Because of his racial distinctness (and because of
what is considered the immorality of his mother), he is not accepted by the Indian society in which he grows up. Yet, again like
Bernard, he desperately wants to be a part of this society, wants
to belong; in other words, he has been conditioned, to use a word
Huxley employs in his later preface, to the "insane" behavior of
a "religion that is half fertility cult and half *Penitente* ferocity"
(page viii). He does eventually manage, however, to break partly

free from the vicious circle of his conditioning through the liberating influence of Shakespeare and the shock of his sudden encounter with the "lunacy" (to quote again from the same preface)
of the new world. For the brief period before his fated relapse
into insane *Penitente*-ism and his subsequent suicide, John is a
sane, human individual.

   As such, he rejects the lunacy of the new world and refuses
to accept as an ideal a happiness bought at the expense of a
total abandonment of humanity. He wants to feel *as* an individual *for* an individual, not as automaton for an automaton, as in
the orgy-porgian Solidarity Services. That is why he persists, in
face of the only too self-evident facts, in conceiving of Lenina as
an individual. He is not content with her merely as a "pneumatic" object for sexual satisfaction; he must love her as a human being or not at all. To love her as a human being, however,
as he gradually comes to realize, is impossible. To love her not
at all is not easy. Alone in his tower, haunted by the sensual
images of her body, he once more reverts to his former *Penitente*
conditioning. The ingrained idea of sin will not permit him to
think of sex as a normal human activity. For him it is evil and
must be punished: first by self-flagellation, later by suicide. He is
a male Miranda who, convinced he has found his Ferdinand, discovers to his horror that beneath the real morocco surrogate
clothing lurks none other than Caliban. In the end, exiled from
the vile old world and disgusted by the brave new one, he has no
place to go but into the desert.* Even there, however, he cannot
escape the power of Prospero-Mustapha's gray magic or the force
of his own primitive conditioning. The noble savage, the World
Controller's "experiment" finally demonstrates, can only exist
where there are opportunities to be both noble and savage. And
that is not Ford's world, where one can never be man or beast,
but only machine.

   The problem posed by the intrusion of the Savage is that in

---

   *Is there some autobiographical significance in Huxley's choice of a
tower not far from Godalming — his own birthplace — for the Savage to
commit suicide in?

neither society — the insane Indian or the lunatic Fordian — is there any provision for the human individual. Both societies have abolished individuality in order to become either subhumanly bestial or subhumanly mechanical. Both have paid far too high a price for social stability; and both, despite this stability, are consequently inferior to the unstable, unjust, unhappy, but still relatively human society of early twentieth-century Europe.

In the series of portraits of this twentieth-century society which Huxley satirically sketched in his earlier novels, the fatal flaw was always the isolation of the individual. He was alone, trapped in his own conception of reality. This is not the case with the society of the brave new world, or, to a lesser degree, with that of the Indian *Penitentes*. In these societies the individual is solidly integrated, to the point of becoming an almost indistinguishable part of the whole. Too solidly, too indistinguishably — that is what is wrong with them. The price of social solidarity is the loss of individual existence. This is the paradox at the very heart of the novel: to be individual is to be isolated and unhappy; to be integrated is to be "happy," but happy in an inhuman fashion. It is the happiness, in the words of one of Huxley's early poems, of a "great goggling fish," or that, as Mustapha Mond remarks, of being confined inside a bottle whose walls exclude any reality and any awareness but that which is allowed to filter through.

Huxley later came to consider the exclusion of no suitable alternative to piscine bliss or wretched individuality to be an artistic fault of the novel. In his view, *Brave New World* should have proposed another possibility, that of "sanity." In other words, it should have described a community where "economics would be decentralist and Henry-Georgian, politics Kropotkinesque and co-operative"; where man would not be the slave of science and technology; where his religion would be "the conscious and intelligent pursuit of man's Final End, the unitive knowledge of the Immanent Tao or Logos, the transcendent Godhead or Brahman"; and where the prevailing philosophy of life would be "a kind of Higher Utilitarianism, in which the

Greatest Happiness principle would be secondary to the Final End principle" (page ix).

Thirty years after *Brave New World*, Huxley fictionalized this third possibility at length and in detail in *Island*. But even in *Brave New World* itself some such possibility is already vaguely adumbrated in the happy-unhappy islands to which Bernard and Helmholtz are finally exiled.

The central problem of *Brave New World* could also be phrased in another way. The inhabitants of the Fordian state are aware (insomuch as they are aware of anything) of a reality which is totally "happy"; the inhabitants of the Indian Reservation (including, for the most part, the Savage), on the other hand, are aware only of a sinister, "unhappy" reality. In neither society is there an awareness of the whole truth, that is of all realities, sinister, "happy," and the multitude of intervening shadings; in fact, both are posited on a negation of this whole truth. Both societies, consequently — and the "individuals" they comprise — are imprisoned in their preconceptions of reality and are essentially unaware. But unawareness of the whole truth, as the novels up to and including *Point Counter Point* indicated, leads either to individual isolation or to the animality of the Complete Man; it does not lead to an integration commensurate with true humanity. And it is precisely because *Brave New World*, when measured against such a standard, is found sorely wanting that it is a bitterly destructive satire.

In *Ape and Essence* (1949) Huxley returns, after a disastrous war and the beginnings of an almost equally disastrous peace, to the basic question that had motivated his earlier anti-utopian satire: what is to become of man if he continues to live as he is living now? His answer, as might have been expected, was no more optimistic than it had been seventeen years earlier, but it was different.

This difference was striking but not radical. The constituent parts remained the same, only the proportions had changed. From a society of the distant future devoted to the exclusive pursuit of a merely mechanical happiness, Huxley shifted to a community of human beasts organized according to the Greatest Unhappiness Principle. Where he had earlier seen man doomed to blissful lunacy in the orgy-porgian embrace of science, he now saw him even more inevitably crushed by the cataclysmic collapse of that very same science.

Not that the collapse was any more accidental than the suffocating embrace: both were the result of refusing to look at the whole truth, of being either too apelike or too essential and not human enough. This is why the holocaust of atomic and biological warfare is precipitated by two Einsteins, controlled in each case by a hostile army of uniformed and bemedaled baboons bent on destroying the world.* Dying, the two Einsteins protest their innocence, rail against the injustice of punishing so terribly those who "lived only for the Truth." But that, of course, is the essential problem: truth divorced from the whole truth is no truth at all.

The situation presented by the novel — if that is the right word for this combination of film script and Hollywood vignette — recalls in a number of respects that of *Brave New World*. Aside from the Shakespearean title (taken from *Measure for Measure*, Act II, Scene 2), and the focus on the pernicious effects of natural science and unnatural technology, there is the same device of introducing and attempting to assimilate an outsider. In this instance, the intruder is very far removed from being a savage — but then the new society is mainly made up of such. Alfred Poole is a thirtyish, oldmaidenish, Britishy botanist from New Zealand, the only civilized country to survive the war unscathed.

*The idea for this scene and probably for the whole novel seems to have grown out of memories of the second voyage of Swift's Gulliver. Reacting to the recent atom bombing of Japan, Huxley writes on August 10, 1945: "I confess that I find a peace with atomic bombs hanging overhead a rather disquieting prospect. National states armed by science with superhuman military powers always remind me of Swift's description of Gulliver being carried up to the roof of the King of Brobdingnag's palace by a gigantic monkey: reason, human decency and spirituality, which are strictly individual matters, find themselves in the clutches of the collective will, which has the mentality of a delinquent boy of fourteen in conjunction with the physical power of a god" (L532).

Taking part in an expedition to rediscover America, he is captured by the new barbarians near Los Angeles and forced to do research in one of the old unused laboratories of the "Metrollopis." He is also, in a *Walpurgisnacht* of human slaughter and sexual indulgence, forced to admit to himself the existence inside his own body of a very powerful baboon.

But unlike his new companions, Poole does not worship the Beast (or Belial) in him. Rather, like his counterpart in *Brave New World*, he preserves his humanity by steadfastly keeping before his eyes an outstanding example of that humanity: Shelley. Yet he is a good deal more fortunate than John the Savage in that he receives considerable moral and emotional support from one of the female members of Belialdom. Loola, as her name suggests, is quite as pneumatic as the Fordian Lenina, but she has retained her ability to love by having been born into a tiny minority (of so-called "hots") who have remained sexually normal. Despite great danger and numerous obstacles, Poole and Loola manage to deepen their awareness of each other as human beings and not merely as animals, and at the end of the novel seem well on the way to escaping to a small community of normal people somewhere in northern California.

This rebirth of love in a world of hate, this vision of a tiny new phoenix rising out of the ashes, represents of course no guarantee that the whole process will not begin all over again: that the mad historical gyrations between ape and essence will not lead once again to apocalypse. But it does represent at least a chance to start anew, a hope that perhaps this time ape and essence will coalesce into true humanity. Significantly, the final expression of this hope occurs at the grave of William Tallis, deceased author of the script.

Tallis, as the introductory vignette of the same name tells us, was a recluse in the desert, a man who had removed himself from his fellows in the style of the ancient prophets in order to discern man's fate all the more clearly. From the desert, shortly before his death, he mails his epistle of doom to a Hollywood studio, which — as Huxley no doubt had good reason to know from his own experience — treats it in typical fashion by having it sent to the incinerator.* Only by the purest chance does it fall into the rescuing hands of the unnamed narrator and his acquaintance, Bob.

These two men are understandably intrigued at finding so extraordinary a work in a place where only sentimental drivel might be expected. Therefore, a short time later, they make a point of driving out to pay a visit to the author. Arriving at his house, they are met by the impoverished owners who inform them of Tallis's death. While the narrator listens patiently to the old couple's story, Bob, a shallow Hollywood type who suffers from sexual impotence at crucial moments, retires to the kitchen with their sixteen-year-old daughter, who possesses the face, the body and the prospects of a Lady Hamilton. Looking at her, as she returns from her conversation with Bob, flushed with the excitement of a promised screen test, and listening to the sound of diapers being rinsed in the toilet bowl by another, less Hamiltonian daughter, the narrator shrugs his shoulders and allows Tallis's script to begin.

This curious beginning makes one wonder what Huxley was about. Why did he feel it necessary to have this kind of manuscript-found-in-the-bottle introduction, and why did he bother to develop the history of Bob's dismal desires and affairs? And why such pains to describe the wretched existence of the owners of Tallis's desert retreat?

Perhaps one reason is to be found in the fact — announced in the very first sentence of the novel — that the action takes place the day of Gandhi's assassination (January 30, 1948). It is the day of the violent demise of the nonviolent, an ominous occasion which marks yet another rung in man-ape's progress to perdition.

*Huxley's original scenario survives in the Special Collections of the UCLA Library. It strikes me as considerably inferior to the published version. Not only is the prologue missing, but so are some of the best lines, like "More brassieres than Buffalo." Also the entire scene showing Loola and Poole and various others having sexual intercourse is cut. In another concession to Hollywood, the scenario ending has the mild-mannered Poole uncharacteristically beating the Arch-Vicar and locking him in a closet because he has overheard his and Loola's plan to escape northward.

Does this event serve to awaken anyone to danger? Bob Briggs, Lady Hamilton, and entourage stand ready to reply. The answer, uttered in various baboon accents, is very definitely no. Man-ape is much more concerned with pursuing the personal satisfactions of his actual or illusory sexuality, of expanding the authority of his selfish ego, than he is with reaching a greater awareness of the human condition. And when man-ape does turn his attention to the final end of man-ape, so the narrator sadly reflects, he turns it to such vast projections of his own bestiality as Marxism and fascism. Or else, if he happens to belong to the category of essence rather than ape, he limits himself to equally harmful speculations about a purely abstract truth. Only a very few possess the vision to transcend both ape and essence, and those few are all too often killed or forgotten in the desert.

Standing in the doorway, Bob Briggs and his Hamiltonian Rosie are as much archetypes for man and woman as Alfred Poole and Loola, winding their solitary way past Tallis's grave. Paradise, even the very imperfect sort known in California, so this prologue in Hollywood seems to tell us, is all too easily lost, and all too arduously regained. Without a clear understanding of man's place in the whole order of things, without an awareness of his *telos* (a word evoked by Tallis),* there can be no humanity to bridge the gulf between the monsters of monkey and machine.

*There is probably also a further allusion to Thomas Tallis (1505–1585), who after Byrd, was the most noted composer of English sacred music of the sixteenth century. The two Tallises not only share a desire to achieve harmony, but also envision that harmony as arising ultimately from a true perception of the nature of God.

CHAPTER VI

The Music of Eternity
The Later Novels

IT HAS been remarked by at least one critic of Huxley that the sexual mores of the inhabitants of the brave new world are strikingly similar to those recommended by Rampion in *Point Counter Point,* and that therefore Huxley, by satirizing these mores in *Brave New World*, is distancing himself from the Rampion/Lawrence ideal advocated in the earlier novel.[1] This, it seems to me, is clearly not the case. Sex, in Rampion's view and even more unmistakably in Lawrence's, was always understood as a sacrament. It was something that arose out of the indefinable, but nevertheless very real "deep passional soul" which, whatever else it may have been, was certainly not the seat of any impulse toward promiscuity. That is why, as Huxley notes in his introduction to *The Letters of D. H. Lawrence,* Lawrence was "profoundly shocked" when he read Casanova's memoirs.[2] To think of Lawrence as condoning free love in the manner of the Complete Man or of Lucy Tantamount is to mistake him "completely," which naturally does not prevent him from being frequently mistaken in this way. For "Lawrence's doctrine," as Huxley further observes, "is constantly invoked by people, of whom Lawrence would passionately have disapproved, in defence of behavior which he would have found deplorable or even revolting."[3]

It is therefore evident that when Huxley satirizes the casual and almost undifferentiated sexual couplings of the citizens of his anti-Utopia, he is not breaking with any ideal advocated by Rampion in *Point Counter Point* or by Lawrence anywhere else.

Nevertheless, it is important to realize that Huxley does not actually advocate Lawrence's ideas in *Brave New World*. The absence of a Rampion-like counterpoint is, in fact, what makes this novel a destructive satire and not a constructive one like *Point Counter Point*. Furthermore, in at least one respect, that is, the condemnation of the primitive Indian society as "insane" in the teeth of Lawrence's well-known admiration for such societies (for example, in *The Plumed Serpent*), Huxley has come to a definite parting of the ways with Rampion/Lawrence.

What seems to be happening in *Brave New World* is that Huxley is slowly returning to a pre-Lawrentian position regarding the nature and function of the body, although he does not come back full circle to the rather puritanical conclusion of *Those Barren Leaves*. Lawrence had made much too powerful an impression on Huxley to allow him ever to assume quite so simple a view again.* In *The World of Light*, a play first produced in 1931, a year before the publication of *Brave New World*, Huxley is still very much concerned with the problems of a Quarlesian intellectual who is completely cut off from life because he does not attend sufficiently to the needs of his body. Even in *Brave New World*, the Savage's endeavor to establish a deep emotional relationship with Lenina and his refusal to accept anything less are actions with which Lawrence would have been deeply sympathetic.

But there is evidence other than his disapproval of primitive societies to show that Huxley was beginning in the early and middle thirties to undergo a profound change. Klaus Mann, for instance, recounts in his autobiography how he visited Huxley at Sanery-sur-mer either in 1935 or 1936 and found the "once so

*Though he comes close in *After Many a Summer* (1939).

frivolous and skeptical intellectual *jongleur* and seasoned artist"
already in the first stages of his conversion to mysticism.[4] More
significantly, in his philosophical diary of a journey, *Beyond the
Mexique Bay* (1934), Huxley himself indicates at several points
that he does not find Lawrence's attitude toward the body and
its "dark forces" entirely satisfying. Lawrence, he notes with some
asperity, was wrong and even knew it himself. "The facts of his
life," he says, "are there to prove it" (page 312). For although
Lawrence is able to write passionately, eloquently, and "sometimes over-emphatically" of Oaxaca and Lake Chapala and "the
merits of that rank weed-life of the natural man," he is incapable
of tolerating it for extended periods of time (pages 249–250).
Only his fictional characters discover their blood consciousnesses
in remote corners of the world. Lawrence himself returns to Europe.

Even in the years when Huxley had been most strongly in-
fluenced by Lawrence, he had never been a mere puppet. When
he once remarked that in Rampion he had left out most of Lawrence, the statement cut two ways.[5] He certainly, as we have seen,
omitted most of what was truly vital in Lawrence, but, by the
same token, he also omitted much that was petty and weak. Rampion is an idealized portrait in the best and worst sense of the
phrase. There is none of the real Lawrence's refusal to get sensi-
ble treatment for the disease that was slowly killing him. "He
doesn't *want* to know how ill he is," Huxley wrote about Lawrence to his brother on July 13, 1929; "that, I believe, is the fundamental reason why he won't go to Doctors and homes" (L313).
Nor is there in Rampion any of Lawrence's double-dealing, a
trait which emerges clearly and repeatedly in H. T. Moore's edition of *The Collected Letters of D. H. Lawrence*.[6] Take, for example, his attempt to act as a middleman for S. S. Koteliansky,
who was trying to get a series of "intimate" confessions of modern writers together. Lawrence had agreed to write something as
well as to tackle Norman Douglas and Huxley. When both rather
understandably refused, he wrote Koteliansky on October 31,
1927, that he was "sorry about Douglas and Huxley — but rather

expected it. People are very small and mingy nowadays." His next communication to Koteliansky included the statement that "Huxley's 'Proper Studies' is a bore!" although he had written to Huxley a week earlier outlining some reservations, but concluding that the seventy pages he had read were "very sane and sound and good."* Then, in the early spring of the following year, in connection with an idea for an Author's Publishing Society, he tells Huxley that he does not like Koteliansky's letters: "sort of bullying tone he takes, with an offended Jewish superiority." Of course, Lawrence is probably the last man to be judged on his foibles, though this kind of gossip was characteristic of the man (and characteristic too was his dislike of gossipers). More serious were his famous flashes of irrational rage. Talking about these some twenty years after Lawrence's death, Huxley contends that the "rather savage outbursts which [Witter] Bynner talks about [in his *Journey with Genius*] were reactions in a sense to the enemy within, which was the disease. And that he projected it — I mean, for example — this particularly savage remark about Katherine Mansfield and her T.B., which seems very brutal. But I think it's perfectly comprehensible when you realize that what he was saying about T.B. was about his own."[7]

Huxley knew that Lawrence was a sick man, just as he knew that he was at times a vain one.† And though he liked and admired him profoundly, to the extent even of calling him "the most extraordinary and impressive human being I have ever known" (L332), he was reluctant to join Lawrence in every scheme that crossed his fertile and erratic imagination — from Rananim to Koteliansky's "intimate" confessions. What really made Lawrence sympathetic to him intellectually was that Law-

---

*The same is true of his reaction to *Point Counter Point*. Writing to Huxley in October 1928, he begins with the sentence: "I have read *Point Counter Point* with a heart sinking through my boot-soles and a rising admiration." Then in December he writes to Dorothy Brett: "Did you read Aldous' book? A bit cheap sensational I thought."

†About the relationship between Lawrence and Murry, he writes on March 1, 1962, that "Lawrence, like most other people, was fascinated by Murry at first, was convinced by his show of passionate enthusiasm — and also flattered, I'm afraid, by the ascription to himself of messianic qualities" (L930).

rence had arrived at a philosophical position in many ways astonishingly similar to his own. Like Huxley, "he was continually occupied, I think, with the relation of the individual with the given, not with the home-made superstructure which men make . . . He was interested in what the universe gives one on every level, but not with what our imagination and our intellect has fabricated on the basis of experience . . . His criticism, implied criticism is basically the same as that of [Alfred] Korzybski, insisting that words are not things, and that most of us live about seventy percent of our lives in a universe constructed wholly out of words."[8] This view is so close to the one Huxley was elaborating in his poems, essays, short stories, and novels well before he knew Lawrence intimately that he might almost be talking about himself rather than Lawrence.

Brave New World and Beyond the Mexique Bay both question the Rampion/Lawrence ideal — the former hesitantly and obliquely, the latter sharply and directly. But neither, despite this questioning, offers to replace it with anything specific. Both are profoundly skeptical works, the last of their kind which Huxley ever wrote. They reveal a Huxley who was looking, as he writes in a letter of November 5, 1932, for "an acceptable philosophical system which will permit ordinary human beings to give due value both to Lawrence's aspect of reality and to that other aspect, which he refused to admit the validity of — the scientific, rational aspect" (L365). These works mark an end, a definitive end this time, to the period of destructive satire. Only a few years later Huxley had found his answer. Already, as one can see from Klaus Mann's remarks, by 1935 or 1936 Huxley had picked up the shattered pieces of his ideal and had fused them into a mystical unity.

Ironically, as late as 1934, Huxley had written that mysticism as an attitude toward life was no doubt desirable, but, alas, also very likely illusory (Beyond the Mexique Bay, page 221). Human nature and the human condition were generally deplorable and an illusion might be satisfying; but if one were to be truthful, one had to put up with the best of a bad job by allowing oneself only the attitude of an amused detachment. However, at least by 1937, with the publication of *Ends and Means*, Huxley felt quite differently about these subjects. (The exact date may be 1935 when Huxley joined Canon Sheppard's Peace Pledge Union.)[9] Faced with the question of whether "the world as a whole possess[es] the value and meaning that we constantly attribute to certain parts of it," Huxley now answers with a resounding yes. To be sure, he admits that even "a few years ago" he would never even have posed such a question, "for, like so many of my contemporaries, I took it for granted that there was no meaning" (pages 269–270). Now all is changed, changed utterly. Now through mysticism, the world is charged with meaning; and the old "philosophy of meaninglessness" becomes a skeleton to be locked away in some closet. Satire, once the powerful instrument for exposing the "meaninglessness" of the human condition and the isolation of man, now changes explicitly into a weapon, along with "argument and persuasion," to prevent evil ideas — those of a mistaken religious zeal, for example — from causing harm (page 231).

The solution Huxley now proposes is that of a mystical "non-attachment." It is an ideal, so he notes with his usual display of erudition, endorsed by such authorities as Buddha, Lao-tzu, Jesus, John Tauler, and Spinoza; and which, despite the great variety of chronology, civilization, and geography of its adherents, is in all cases fundamentally the same. The agreement, he suggests, derives from the success of these men in freeing themselves "from the prejudices of their time and place," and in achieving liberation "by the practice of disinterested virtues and through direct insight into the real nature of ultimate reality" (pages 2–3). Huxley's ideal man is now the man who lives in the light of the mystical teaching: "The ideal man is the non-attached man. Non-attached to his bodily sensations and lusts. Non-attached to the objects of these various desires. Non-attached to his anger and hatred; non-attached to his exclusive loves. Non-attached to wealth, fame, social position. Non-attached even to science, art speculation, philanthropy. Yes, non-attached even to these" (pages 3–4). This nonattached ideal man is in some respects reminiscent of the nonattached Calamy at the end of *Those Barren Leaves*. Like Calamy, he is primarily interested in an "ultimate reality greater and more significant than the self" (page 4). But unlike him, he does not uncompromisingly reject the claims of the body or the beneficial interference of some "little ravishment." Sex *may* be evil when it takes the form of physical addiction or when it manifests itself as a way of satisfying the lust for power or for social distinction. But at the same time it is also and "at least as frequently the method whereby unpossessive and unselfish individuals achieve union with one another and indirectly with the world about them" (page 310). Sex, Huxley maintains, can be good or evil, depending upon the nature of the end for which it serves as the means.

Good and evil. It is a distinction which becomes the crux of Huxley's new attitude toward life, a distinction which Huxley, in *Ends and Means*, specifically defines for the first time. The single commandment of his new religion proclaims that "Good is that which makes for unity; Evil is that which makes for separateness" (page 303); or elaborated into more typically Huxleyan terms: "Goodness is the method by which we divert our attention from this singularly wearisome topic of our animality and our individual separateness" (page 298). Goodness is mystical nonattachment and the consequent overcoming of isolation, but not through subhuman or bestial means: not through a contemptible unity in the style of the Solidarity Services of *Brave New World*. Man must be a human being and an individual, and therefore separate, before he can attain genuine union. For one of the fundamental conditions of nonattachment is awareness. "Unawareness," Huxley says, "is one of the main sources of attachment or evil" (page 221). Man must be made to know that what he ordinarily conceives of as reality "is a private universe quarried out of a total reality which the physicists infer to be far greater than it" (page 296). He must be made aware that even this greater reality of the scientists is "a partial one — the product of their special competence in mathematics and their special incompetence to deal systematically with aesthetic and moral values, religious experiences and intuitions of significance" (page 269). Man, in short, must realize that, ordinarily, he is imprisoned in a preconception of reality, and that the only means of escape is through a proper understanding of the whole truth or the "ultimate reality." But to gain this final understanding is not easy. As a fundamental prerequisite, man must be relieved from fundamental biological pressures, both external and internal: "If he is to transcend the limitations of man's private universe he must be a member of a community which gives him protection against the inclemencies of the environment and makes it easy for him to supply his physical wants. But this is not enough. He must also train himself in the art of being dispassionate and disinterested, must cultivate intellectual curiosity for its own sake and not for what he, as an animal, can get out of it" (page 297). Only when he and his society have fulfilled these conditions can men and women "overcome the illusion of being completely independent existents and . . . realize the fact of their oneness with ultimate reality" (page 298).

Despite its dispassionately analytical tone, *Ends and Means* is not merely a disinterested, scholarly treatise on mysticism. Its avowed purpose is to be a tract against war. It purports to state an alternative to the reigning mythologies of the day, belligerent communism and belligerent nationalism; an alternative which would rescue man from the supposed bestiality and stupidity of these mythologies, and which would, if heeded, transform the world into a genuinely human society. *Ends and Means* was not Huxley's first literary attempt toward achieving this end. In *Eyeless in Gaza*, published a year earlier, Huxley had tried to do something of the same sort in the guise of a novel.

Eyeless in Gaza is not primarily a satirical novel — Huxley's first not to be so. It does contain characters and scenes (the protagonist's father or the social gatherings at Mary Amberley's, for example) which are satirical, but on the whole it is a serious, a desperately serious novel.

Of all Huxley's books, including even *Point Counter Point*, it is probably the one into which he wrote most of himself and, for this reason among others, it is pitched at the highest level of emotional intensity.* For the first time, one feels that Huxley is not merely laying aside, however brilliantly, the corrupt fleshy folds of a gangrenous society, but attempting to save the patient without at the same time destroying him. He has abandoned the drastic measures of surgery in favor of the milder restoratives of internal medicine. As written out in this lengthiest of his novels, his prescription occasionally makes for some rather puzzling reading, but in the end it can perhaps be deciphered as calling for massive doses of compassion and awareness, and for abstaining from the use of any sort of force.

This may make *Eyeless in Gaza* seem like a cliché, but then any attempt to distill the "message" of a serious work of art inevitably does. And in an important sense this novel is like a cliché: that is, in the sense that Huxley, or his main fictional persona, Anthony Beavis, no longer fears taking seriously a number of ideas which had seemed at best outdated to the earlier intellectual jongleur and his satirical masks.

The most important, though least overtly developed, of these concepts is God. The very title of the novel tells us that this is, as Huxley's detractors like to remind us, a "conversion novel." The blinded and embittered idealist who, as a defeated youth at the mill with slaves, had railed at an unjust fate imposed by the great topiarist on himself and his fellows, now becomes in middle

---

*So clearly was it based on recognizable family history that Huxley received what, judging from his own response (L409–410), must have been a very irate letter from his stepmother. In his reply he denied that Beavis senior was based on his own father, claiming that "the primary nucleus of the character came from an autobiographical poem by Coventry Patmore called 'Tired Memory,'" and most of the rest from the philologist Ernest Weekley, Frieda Lawrence's first husband. He did, however, admit to making "use of mannerisms and phrases some of which were recognizably father's." Brian Foxe, he also confessed, was "definitely" based on his brother Trevenen, who had committed suicide in 1914 and who, like Brian, had had both a stammer and an "ascetic obsession" (L409).

A clue to the intensity of the family feelings aroused by the novel is perhaps provided by the absence of any further correspondence with any survivors of his father's second family.

Huxley's cousin Gervas Huxley maintains that the pupils at Bulstrode are an amalgam of the boys at their old preparatory school, Hillside. See *Both Hands: An Autobiography* (London, 1970), pp. 38–41.

age the prophet of a resurrected hope. Unlike Samson, this new hero of our time does not aim at a violent and final destruction of his enemies, but at persuading them peacefully of the errors of their ways, even to the point of turning the other cheek. To achieve this end, however, he first must free himself from the impediment of an ego diseased with the memories and habits of the past.

Eyeless in Gaza is a demonstration of how the metaphorically blind are made to see. Simple enough in outline, the novel becomes complex in detail, even more so because of the fragmented and antichronistic way it is told. This disjointed narrative procedure has been the cause of disturbance for a good many readers and a few, notably David Daiches, have fulminated against it in print. Symptomatically, even a relatively well-disposed reader of Huxley, such as Harold Watts, unabashedly observes that *Eyeless in Gaza* could be rearranged into exact sequence without losing in the process any "essential meaning."[10]

The repeated failure of critics to understand that the peculiar time scheme of *Eyeless in Gaza* is an integral part of its "essential meaning" is probably due to their not seeing how much Huxley, from *Those Barren Leaves* onward, was becoming obsessed with the problem of time. Even the titles of some of his later books reflect this obsession: *After Many a Summer* with its allusion to the myth of the ever aging Tithonus; *Time Must Have a Stop* explicitly calling attention to time; *The Perennial Philosophy* revealing not merely the concern with but also an escape from time. The fragment of his last novel shows him still writing under this impulse, still trying to get at the reality of time and at the whole truth that reality would reveal. The presumptive hero of this novel, a historian in his seventies, is looking back to his eleventh birthday in 1900 and reflecting on "how easy it would be to construct a linear narrative, a straightforward tale that would read like the simple truth! But the truth is never simple. If the straightforward tale carries conviction it is precisely because it is not the truth, but an elegantly streamlined novelette. At the risk of seeming confused and digressive, I shall stick as closely as I can to the complex realities of the autobiographical process." And then, continuing, a few sentences later, in a vein very much reminiscent of *Point Counter Point*: "The bad Waverleys [Huxley's example of simple chronology and simplified truth] are straightforwardly plausible, the good ones are not. Inevitably so; for to be good, an autobiographical Waverley must necessarily be complicated, digressive and full of inconsistencies. Every life is a set of relationships between incompatibles. To get to know oneself, one must get to know all the disparate fields of which, at any moment, one is the center."[11]

Getting to know all these disparate fields is what the odd construction of *Eyeless in Gaza* is all about. And getting to know them as they really exist involves depicting not merely an Anthony Beavis as he is at any single point in time, or as he develops in a continuum, but also as he exists simultaneously at all points and throughout a whole duration of time. This is why the novel begins with the hero looking at a collection of snapshots out of his past. Intellectually, Anthony can place each photograph in exact time, but the memories which they evoke coexist simultaneously with the present. The Anthony of 1902 or 1914 continues to live quite as vitally as he ever did in the Anthony of 1933 or 1935, and vice versa. Time, as he realizes while making love to Helen Amberley on the roof of his Mediterranean villa, is a human fabrication without real existence. "Somewhere in the mind a lunatic shuffled a pack of snapshots and dealt them out at random, shuffled once more and dealt them out in a different order, again and again indefinitely. There is no Chronology" (pages 22–23).

This perception, uncertain though it is at this point in Anthony's pilgrimage, provides the clue to the seemingly confused labyrinth of his experience. It reveals his growing awareness that the apparently arbitrary process of his memory may not be arbitrary at all. Not that it is the result of a merely Freudian association, since the psychologists of this school are only the "victims of the pathetic fallacy, incorrigible rationalizers always in search of sufficient reasons, of comprehensible motives" (page 23). It derives, rather, in some obscure way from a conscious intention larger than his own, which has determined that this particular picture galley should be stored away in the recesses of the mind "for the sole and express purpose of being brought up into consciousness at this particular moment" (page 24). It begins to dawn on Anthony, when he realizes that the memory of dead Brian sheds a sudden illumination on his empty relationship to Helen, that the supposed lunatic dealing out these mental photographs may not be such a lunatic after all, and that, further, beyond the pointless universe of random thoughts, desires, and feelings, there may exist a more than Lucretian order.

Certainly, behind the façade of literary chaos, Huxley is stacking his cards very carefully, and dealing them out one by one to achieve calculated effects. There is nothing chancy about the way the novel begins. Anthony, at forty-two, is only a little past the *mezzo camino* of his life and, though he does not yet know it, he is also at its turning point. Looking back, like the Proust whom he reviles so bitterly and, as Helen perceptively points out, so personally, he has as yet only an inkling that his past life has a meaning. Weaving backward and forward in what seems to be a random fashion, superimposing one image on another, Huxley unfolds this past for us in a series of brilliant illuminations until he has achieved a fully developed and almost four-dimensional portrait. This jagged movement, though consciously deviating from standard chronology, is not without a sense of development and accompanying moments of climax. The obviously crucial but puzzling incident of the dog falling from the sky is placed near the beginning of the novel, but is clarified only much later. The almost equally crucial encounter with Miller, the account of Brian's suicide, the abduction of Ekki Giesebrecht, the semireconciliation with Helen, and Anthony's discovery of meaning in life, all crowd the final pages of the novel. And the very last scene, with Anthony about to set out alone to address a potentially hostile political meeting, is also chronologically the last event in the book.

Huxley, one is tempted to say, is cheating his readers here,

or at least having some of his nontemporal cake and eating it
too. Still, to attack him too harshly for doing so would be to be-
grudge him, and incidentally ourselves, this pleasure on too narrow critical grounds. The antichronistic composition of *Eyeless
in Gaza* is, in the event, unquestionably justifiable; it is the external correlative to Anthony's theoretical and (eventually) practical realization that human time is meaningless. But any too
rigid correlation on Huxley's part would probably have made the
novel much less satisfying. Only a fool, as Nigel Dennis once said,
rides a theoretical hobbyhorse, particularly a very good one, to
perdition.

What the discrete images of various Anthonies are meant to
reveal is the real existence of a variety of separate and distinct
personalities inadequately defined by the single name Anthony
Beavis. The being who seems to be a unity in the present is actually a diversity in the past and in the future. The jumble of
portraits of the sociologist as a young and middle-aged man show
how absurd it is to limit a person within a single identity; he is
all the identities he ever was, or at least all the identities he re-
members or will remember being. Which is why Anthony so passionately wishes to rid himself of all "superfluous memories," and
why he heaps such contumely on those who reveal, like Proust,
the multifaceted personalities refracted from the prism of past
memory (again through an antichronistic novel). What Anthony,
on the brink of a new realization, desperately desires is to confine
himself to a single identity, to play the "part he had long since
assigned himself — the part of the detached philosopher" (page
4), to be merely the impersonal sociologist who collects and
mounts people as if they were so many insects.

The intensity of his desire derives from his knowledge that
man has no single personality. He is fully conscious that most
men conceal a mass of often conflicting personalities behind the
superficially stable mask of a conventional identity. Writing
down a series of reflections on this subject as the basis for a future *Elements of Sociology,* the Anthony of December 1926 arrives at conclusions which in places echo those of his contem-

porary Philip Quarles. With Polonius's parable of the musical instruments as one of his points of departure, Anthony observes that "Polonius and the others assumed as axiomatic that man was a penny whistle with only half a dozen stops. Hamlet knew that, potentially at least, he was a whole symphony orchestra" (page 144). Passing on from Shakespeare to Blake (and further to Proust and Lawrence), he traces the growth of the doctrine he calls psychological atomism. For these later writers, he notes, "good and evil can be predicated only of states, not of individuals, who in fact don't exist, except as the places where the states occur. It is the end of personality in the old sense of the word" (pages 144–145). And with the end of the old confining psychology and its premise of a fixed personality, Anthony perceives the possibility of getting at a new kind of man: "the total man, unbowdlerized, unselected, uncanalized," the man who, like Hamlet, knows too much to have a personality, who is aware of his "total experience, atom by atom and instant by instant," and who accepts "no guiding principle which would make him choose one set of patterned atoms to represent his personality rather than another" (pages 147–148).

Although Anthony is aware of the pitfalls of a defined personality, his awareness is purely theoretical. Seeing the better, he nevertheless perversely insists on following the worse. It takes an explosion of blood to shock him out of his comfortable inactivity, and the further traumatic experiences of near death at the hands of a drunken gunman in the hinterlands of Mexico and the bloody removal of his friend Mark Staithes's leg, to bring him to the point of acting on his abstract knowledge. The dog who falls so dramatically from the sky, though perhaps not identical with Thompson's hound of heaven, is, as Helen later half-jokingly remarks, like a sign from God.* Naked a moment before and, in Helen's words, as if in the garden of Eden, they are suddenly

---

*The word dog is perhaps also to be read as an anagram for God. That it is a *fox* terrier is probably a pointed hint, particularly since the scene ends with memories of "Brian in the chalk pit, evoked by that salty smell of sun-warmed flesh, and again dead at the cliff's foot, among the flies — like that dog . . ." (p. 168).

covered, literally drenched with blood. Helen realizes immediately, though only subconsciously, the significance of what has happened, and departs. Anthony only gradually comes to a similar
and more conscious realization that the old life cannot go on as
before, that the detached and amused observer must give way to
a committed participant in the processes of life. For demonstrably, regardless of the sociologist's wishes to the contrary, life in-
trudes even into the remotest retreat.

Spurred on by this perception and by Mark Staithes's offer
to show him what life is like in a provincial Mexican revolution,
Anthony leaves his armchair existence and timidly embarks on a
life of action. This life of physical violence, as it turns out, is no
better than his previous intellectual detachment, but it takes
another sign from heaven, this time in human guise, to make him
realize it. His encounter with Miller, while on a seemingly hopeless mission to find a doctor for the injured Staithes, is as sudden
and miraculous as the earlier incident of the dog. In fact, "miracle" is the word used to introduce it. When Anthony shortly there-
after observes that had he been praying their meeting would have
made him "believe in special providence and miraculous inter-
ventions," Miller replies that nothing "ever happens by chance,
of course. One takes the card the conjuror forces on one — the
card which one has oneself made it inevitable that he should
force on one" (page 550).

It is no accident that Miller should use the same metaphor
that had occurred to Anthony at the opening of the novel. Things
are coming full circle, and Anthony's disjointed life is about to
be ordered by meaning. One aspect of this meaning is the knowledge that there is no chance: character is fate and the attempt to
fix personality and life in one direction provokes only a corresponding destructive counterblow from another direction. Or, as
Miller analyzes the situation from a specifically Buddhist point of
view, Anthony must cease to think and live according to a dual-
istic separation of body and spirit, and start thinking and living
as a physical and mental unit. For the wrong kind of thinking
will call forth an unfavorable physical reaction just as inevitably

as the wrong kind of eating will have an adverse spiritual effect.
Anthony must believe with the Buddhists that there are no special providences for individuals, but that there exists a "moral
order, where every event has its cause and produces its effect"
and where, returning again to the same metaphor, "the card's
forced upon you by the conjuror, but only because your previous
actions have forced the conjuror to force it upon you" (pages
554–555).

The final chapters of the novel alternate scenes detailing the
progress — or rather the deterioration — of Anthony's friendship
with Brian, and scenes from his journey into the heart of darkness with Mark Staithes. Both culminate in dramatic moments in
his life, moments as crucial for his development as the incident of
the dog falling from the sky: Brian's suicide and Anthony's consequent spiritual death; Staithes's accident, the encounter with
Miller, and Anthony's spiritual rebirth. The juxtaposition is
carefully and artistically handled. It makes us realize, almost as
if Anthony's memory were our own, that the two seemingly dia-
metrically opposed poles of existence which Mark and Brian represent are both false because both are arbitrarily manufactured.
Brian Foxe, like his namesake John Foxe, looks everywhere for
sainthood and martyrdom;* hence his vision excludes the claims
of the body, particularly when they are sexual. And Mark
Staithes, though in a more perverse way, does the same thing.
His asceticism is, if anything, even more rigorous than Brian's;
whenever possible, he subjects his body to physical torture. Anthony's suspicion that he wears a hair shirt is amusing but by no
means absurd. Brian the saint and Mark the diabolist, so different outwardly, join inwardly in this detestation of all things cor-
poreal. And significantly, both are punished for it, appropriately
enough, physically. Anthony escapes such punishment, but only
because Miller saves him by pointing out the way to overcome
the traditional dualism inherent in the Western tradition. Mill-

*John Foxe (1516–1587), English Puritan and author of the so-called
Book of the Martyrs, which deals chiefly with Roman Catholic oppression
of Protestants. Perhaps it is not accidental that Brian commits suicide in
Scotland, the seat of British Puritanism.

er's solution may appear to be eccentric and at times almost ridiculous: for example his diagnosis of Anthony's constipation, or
his Tolstoyan censure of the eaters of roast beef. Still, the eccen-
tricity — like Miller's mysticism — demonstrably produces good
results in a way the more accepted attitudes of Brian and Mark
do not. Miller's "practical" mysticism works. And that, Anthony
decides, is what is most important: even more important than the
risk of playing the fool or of getting pummeled by the self-ap-
pointed guardians of British manhood.

There is no escape from the past, whether mental or physical. It is impossible to fit one's former selves into a narrow conception of one's present self; any such effort is doomed to failure.
That is the lesson Anthony learns from Miller and the lesson
Mark Staithes refuses to grasp. Like Spandrell in *Point Counter
Point,* Staithes approaches life with a rigidly fixed attitude; rather than conform to life, he wishes to make life fit his own perverse bed of Procrustes. His inability to do so echoes Spandrell's
earlier unsuccessful attempt, but this time without any overtones
of ambiguity. Here the fact of extreme physical pain is perceived
not as the arbitrary *acte gratuit* of a topiarist god, but as the inescapable consequence of incorrect modes of mental and physical
behavior. It is Staithes's refusal to recognize that he cannot impose his will on external reality that precipitates the injury which
eventually leads to the amputation of his leg. It is his similar
refusal to recognize the humanity of his fellows that is the cause
of his own lack of humanity.*

Actually, the basic situation of *Point Counter Point,* not just
of Spandrell, is recapitulated in the Beavis-Staithes-Miller tri-
angle of the concluding chapters of *Eyeless in Gaza,* even to the
point, as we have seen, of picking up once again the same metaphor: man as penny whistle or man as a whole symphony orchestra. But this time it is resolved successfully. The reason for the
success is that in this instance Huxley uses Miller to move beyond

*That Staithes, like Spandrell and Richard Greenow before him, repre-
sents another "state" of Huxley/Beavis is indicated by the antipathy both
feel toward humanity in the mass. Even the terms of Staithes's revulsion —
for example, the graphic description of the smell of the civet used as a base

Rampion/Lawrence to a position much closer to Spandrell's, but without Spandrell's melodramatic Baudelairean gestures. It is almost as if he had fused Rampion and Spandrell to achieve Miller, and had thereby attained a reconciliation of God and man. Not that either Rampion/Lawrence or Spandrell/St. Augustine is rejected; they are merely transcended. Miller believes in an impersonal God and in the divinity of man, and he communicates his belief to the Quarlesian intellectual Beavis. At the end of the novel both are therefore able to confront Staithes/ Spandrell with a resoundingly major positive point beside which his negative one seems decidedly minor.

Which is not to say that *Eyeless in Gaza* closes with an assertion that all's right with the world. On the contrary, very little is. The inevitabilities of pain, of division, of being born to one condition while bound to another continue to be inevitable, as Anthony clearly sees in the extended meditation on this subject that composes the final chapter of the novel. But what he sees now and what he never saw before — at any rate, before Miller* — is

for Mary Amberley's perfume — recall an early poem (1912) Huxley had written about soap:

> Sitting round the Cauldron, we
> Manufacture soap.
> Eglantine and Rosemary
> Thyme and Heliotrope
> You'd suppose would go to make
> One delicious, scented cake.
> No, No! oxens' bones and hide,
> Hoofs and horns and hair,
> Boil, until they're jellified,
> In the cauldron there.
> Almost anything you've got
> We can take to feed the pot.
> In the cauldron on the trivet,
> Stirred into the jelly,
> Exquisitely smelly.
> This is how our soapcake gets
> Scent of thyme and violets.

In the notebook (now in the Stanford Manuscript Collection) in which this poem is written, there is an accompanying illustration of three figures seated around a fire at night and a large cauldron suspended over the blazing flames.

*Whose name may be an allusion to the being who had created the mill for slaves.

the unity of all men and of all life, the fundamental unity beneath the superficial diversity. Though his own self is broken up into fragments of many selves, and though these selves are separate from the selves of other men, and these separate from all other manifestations of life, nevertheless they are united by being formed in "identical patterns, and identical patternings of patterns" (page 692). It is this unity that may be called God, synonymous also in Anthony's mind with goodness, despite His also being "an ultimate Dark God, much darker, stranger and more violent than any that Lawrence imagined" (page 489). For here lies the paradox which earlier Anthonies had failed to understand or understood only as pointless or as a practical joke: the paradox that a God of Unity and goodness has created a world of separation and evil. But "now at last it was clear, now by some kind of immediate experience he knew that the point was in the paradox, in the fact that unity was the beginning and unity the end, and that in the meantime the condition of life and all existence was separation, which was equivalent to evil. Yes, the point, he insisted, is that one demands of oneself the achievement of the impossible. The point is that, even with the best will in the world, the separate, evil universe of a person or physical pattern can never unite itself completely with other lives and beings, or the totality of life and being. Even for the highest goodness the struggle is without end; for never in the nature of present things can the shut become wholly open; goodness can never free itself completely from evil" (pages 616–617).

It is this perception which has dropped the scales from Anthony's eyes and has allowed him a glimpse into the workings of eternity. And it is the same insight which now moves him, armed with love and awareness, to try to bring down the temples of hate. His success, as we can infer from the example of his preceptor Miller, will not be dramatic. No great masses of stone will come crashing down on the heads of the Philistines, but that is not what matters most. Complete success, complete unity, and destruction of hate are impossible. What Anthony must do, like Faust, is strive eternally, knowing full well the ultimate futility of doing so. For that is the point to which there is no counterpoint.

In *After Many a Summer*, Huxley returns once again to satire, and returns to it with force. But it is a force which is now explicitly directed at a specific end, the need for living life from the perspective of eternity. Just as Rampion was the static judge of characters and events in *Point Counter Point*, Propter in this novel unvaryingly and unflaggingly declaims and persuades in the name of the mystical ideal. To be sure, Propter is a little less obtrusive in his pedagogy. Huxley keeps him in the background by using another more kinetic character, Pete Boone, as the funnel for his ideas. And in any case Rampionesque haranguing would be unsuitable for a professing mystic. Still, Propter does turn out to be something of a gasbag; his very name, identical with the Latin preposition "because of," points to his function as wise explicator of all things.* Compared with his immediate, eccentric, and much more sympathetic predecessor, Miller, he is a passive, inactive preacher. Quarles or Beavis one could imagine turning into Propter (they all share sedentary intellectual pasts), but never Miller. Miller is altogether a different type.

Even in its outward shape, *After Many a Summer* harks back to the novels of the twenties. There is the house party with its usual quota of oddities, bores, and intrigues to keep the conversation flowing and the plot moving. With the possible exception

*In his interview with *The Paris Review*, Huxley, besides pointing to the Latin meaning of the name, quoted from memory Edward Lear's poem "Incidents in the Life of My Uncle Arly," in which the name occurs in the context of "Propter's Nicodemus Pills." (It is when one stumbles on something like this that one realizes that Huxley, even at his most pious, never lost his sense of humor.) In a letter to his brother, dated April 12, 1938, Huxley writes of seeing "Ralph Borsodi, whose work you probably know and who has set up what he calls a 'School of Living' for giving practical effect to his ideas about decentralization and small-scale production" (L434). Annotating this passage, Grover Smith observes that in *After Many a Summer* "Borsodi's theories were shown in practical application." On the most usual critical identification of Propter with Gerald Heard, Huxley once commented: "Propter does resemble Gerald in some ways, but rather remotely." (From the original typescript of the interview made by George Wickes and Ray Frazer on November 18, 1959, p. 13. In the Special Collections of the UCLA Library.)

of the millionaire Stoyte, all of the characters are old Huxley standbys. Jeremy Pordage, for example, is Denis Stone grown older but no wiser, still preferring the reality of books to that of life. He is intelligent enough to realize that there may be something in what Propter keeps drilling into him, just as Denis senses the possible validity of some of Scogan's criticisms; but like him and, for that matter, almost all intelligent people in Huxley's early novels, Jeremy enjoys the comfort of his intellectual rut. He prefers not to make the effort of laboriously finding his way to a greater and more truthful reality.

The same is true, though in quite a different way, of Dr. Sigmund Obispo, personal physician to Stoyte and researcher into the biological processes of aging. Obispo is a kind of Scogan grown young, a cynical hedonist whose inflexible "scientific" attitude refuses to take into account any sort of idealistic justification, particularly for love. He refuses, for instance, to seduce Virginia Maunciple on anything but his own rigid terms: "No Romeo-and-Juliet acts, no nonsense about Love with a capital L, none of that popular-song claptrap with its skies of blue, dreams come true, heaven with you. Just sensuality for its own sake" (page 139). For Obispo, tragedies are mainly pharmaceutical and lyrical sentiments are the result of tuberculosis, alcohol, or drugs. He makes a particular point of insisting that all of man's striving for higher goals is caused by various kinds of physical malformation. Like Spandrell (or Chelifer or Coleman or Mark Staithes) before him, his cynicism is really inverted idealism. Which is why he enjoys torturing Virginia's already much tortured conscience: torture, like sensuality, for its own sake. Even his name symbolizes the self-division (to return to Fulke Greville's phrase) at the hard core of his personality: on the one hand, the Sigmund of Freudian materialistic explanations of spiritual life; on the other, the Spanish bishop's (*obispo*) repressed religious and idealistic nature.*

---

*Huxley's statement to his interviewers that the name merely refers to the town of San Luis Obispo must be a red herring. His knowledge of Spanish, as ample quotes in this novel and elsewhere illustrate, was excellent.

Jo Stoyte, based on William Randolph Hearst and representing the epitome of American vulgarity despite occasional Anglicisms like "chaps" in his conversation, is a materialist on a much simpler level.* Beneath the pose of the hard-nosed, hardhearted money-maker, Stoyte has remained the same spiritually obese and lonely adolescent who used to be called "Fatty." Living in the splendid isolation of his mock medieval castle, a kind of super-Wemmick surrounded by moats and precipices, Stoyte has managed to make himself almost wholly proof to the dangers of the outside world and, except for an occasional visit by his old friend Propter, to any of its spiritual benefits. Almost, but not completely. For despite his continual protestations that "God is Love," the Calvinistic fear of death and eternal damnation keeps creeping into his mind. Tactless office managers who remind him of his designated burial place may be dismissed, but he himself cannot forget that one day he must die. His only hope is that through Obispo's discoveries he will be able to buy off death just as he has managed to buy off everyone else.

Virginia Maunciple, Stoyte's child mistress and, as her name implies, official caterer of affection, has no such ugly awareness to hide from or struggle against. In her natural state she is a more

*That this "chaps" is only an infrequent lapse is probably owing to Anita Loos's having checked the manuscript of the novel for just such anglicisms (L446).

Another, and much less incisive, illustration of Huxley's oft-repeated adage that "nothing fails like success" is contained in the unpublished scenario "Success" which Huxley wrote in 1937. There the focus is on the almost unlimited power of advertising to condition the masses and make practically anyone into a public figure of major importance. That Huxley should have imagined Hollywood would even touch a manuscript with this kind of a subject (when it was clear that only fascists indulged in propaganda) reveals how little he knew about the industry when he first began working for it. The scenario is now in the Manuscript Collection of the Stanford University Library.

Though Jo Stoyte and Virginia Maunciple are clearly based on Hearst and Marion Davies, Huxley had already dissected an almost identical relationship in "Chawdron," a short story first published in *Brief Candles* (1930). The reason for Huxley's sudden attention to these men of purely material success is perhaps to be found in an entry in Quarles's journal in *Point Counter Point*: "No predominantly acquisitive character has appeared in any of my stories. It is a defect; for acquisitives are obviously very common in real life" (p. 411).

elementary Anne Wimbush who simply avoids the unpleasant
things either by not bothering to think about them or else by
making some show of repentance to the Virgin Mary. Until Obispo puts an end to her old existence, she is "happy in limitation,
not sufficiently conscious of her personal self to realize its ugliness and inadequacy, or the fundamental wretchedness of the human state" (pages 197–198). Her seduction by Obispo jolts her out
of this happy stupidity into a stupid unhappiness. But Obispo
cannot, because he will not, save her by jolting her further into
a state beyond the merely human.*

Only Propter, in this novel, can do so. Only Propter is neither animal nor confined to a necessarily human state of separation. Only he is nonattached and therefore understands the whole
truth about the human condition. He knows that goodness is possible on only two levels, a lower and a higher. "On the lower
level, good exists as the proper functioning of the organism in
accordance with the laws of its own being. On the higher level,
it exists in the form of a knowledge of the world without desire
or aversion; it exists as the experience of eternity, as the tran-
scendence of personality, the extension of consciousness beyond
the limits imposed by the ego" (page 120). In other words, the
only possible alternatives to evil are a regression into animality
or a progression into superhumanity. For to be merely human
means being individual, and being individaul means being isolated, and being isolated means being evil. The chain of logic is
unbreakable. Therefore, as Propter tirelessly and tiresomely re-
peats, it is folly to seek to be human.

But this position, logical though it may be for Propter, lands
Huxley in considerable difficulty. For it produces a situation in
which the ideas of the novel pull in one direction and the events
in another. According to the strict wording of Propter's principles, the fifth earl of Gonister ought to be commended for having transformed himself, however inadvertently, into a fetal ape.

---

*There is an echo here too of the Lenina-Savage relationship in *Brave
New World*. Like Lenina, Veronica is made to discover, at the cost of her
own infantile happiness, a new and terrible "adult" world.

After all, he has only followed Propter's directive to seek goodness on one of two possible levels. That he has found the lesser good on the animal level makes him only less rather than more praiseworthy.

This fundamental contradiction between theory and practice leads to further confusions. Logically, it should prevent Huxley from condemning (or at least satirizing) Virginia's prelapsarian animalistic unawareness; but satirize her he does. Moreover, Propter himself is not always sure of his footing in this gradually deepening ethical quagmire. Only an hour or so after his enunciation of the principle of two goods, he suffers from a gross lapse of memory. Without warning he makes one good grow where two grew before. Animality is inexplicably devalued to "no-track idiocy" characteristic of the *homme moyen sensuel* or the cultural idiot like Stoyte. Now the route via superhumanity remains the only acceptable escape from the human condition: "There are a million wrong tracks and only one right — a million ideals, a million projections of personality, and only one God and one beatific vision. From no-track idiocy most of them pass on to some one-track lunacy, generally criminal. It makes them feel better, of course; but pragmatically, the last state is always worse than the first. If you don't want the only thing worth having, my advice is: Stick to idiocy" (page 154). By leaving the reader unsure of his bearings, Huxley exposes himself to being hoist with his own petard — or at least with that of his mouthpiece, Propter. For like the literature which Propter finds so sorely lacking in systematic justification, this novel in the final analysis offers no convincingly worked out theory of life, but only the attempt at such a theory, only an ethical collage.

Even so, the intention of the novel is plainly to suggest mysticism as the only correct mode of understanding man's fate. But, as both *Beyond the Mexique Bay* and *Eyeless in Gaza* pointed out, mystical comprehension involves seeing life *sub specie aeternitatis*. Or as Propter puts it: "Potential evil is *in* time; potential good isn't. The longer you live, the more evil you automatically come into contact with. Nobody comes automatically into con-

tact with good. Men don't find more good by merely existing
longer" (page 108). This statement and this conception of time
have an obvious bearing on the events of the novel. They serve,
for example, to place in proper perspective for the reader both
Stoyte's attempts to remain alive for as long as possible and the
fifth earl of Gonister's success in doing so. They explain, furthermore, as Huxley's outmoded science no longer will, why the
earl must be metamorphosed into an ape.* And, finally, they
clarify some of the implications of the title.

The source of that title, as the hero of Christopher Isherwood's *A Single Man* informs his ill-read pupils, is Tennyson's
poem "Tithonus." In that rather melodramatic monologue, an
old Tithonus laments his fate to his ever youthful bride, Aurora,
asking for a return of his humanity and, with it, the power to die.
In having learned to wish for death and for an escape from time
(defined as a continuous process of change and hence still appli-
cable to Tithonus, though immortal), Tithonus, Huxley implies,
has learned a lesson which Stoyte, the earl of Gonister, and the
mass of humanity never learn. Stoyte, for example, with the results of the earl's experiments confronting his eyes and nose, is
still determined to repeat that success.

What Huxley, however, does not seem to realize is that his
Tennysonian title cuts two ways. For in the poem it is precisely
the folly of humanity's desire for superhumanity which is condemned. Tithonus is made to see how far more preferable it
would have been to refuse the gifts of the gods, how much better
it is to be merely a man than a man-who-would-be-god. This perception runs directly counter to every ethical premise in Huxley's
novel.

So does Tithonus's wistful memory of the bliss of sexual
love. For in this novel, at least insofar as Propter is a trustworthy
guide to it, all sex is necessarily evil because in human beings sex

*Though there is no obvious reason to think of "influence," a good deal
of this fantasy suggests similar symbolic fantasies by Kafka. When Klaus
Mann visited Huxley in August 1940, not long after the publication of *After
Many a Summer*, he found him much occupied with that author. See *Wendepunkt*, p. 365.

is never the simple impulse it is in animals.* Even when men think they are being most animalistic in their sexual behavior, so Propter advises us, they are still behaving as humans, which means "they were still self-conscious, still dominated by words — and where there were words, there, of necessity, were memories and wishes, judgements and imaginations" (page 229). In short, sexuality is always and inevitably mentalized, which is Lawrence's position taken to semantic extreme.

Huxley's attack on time involves an attack on everything that is in time, even, or especially, the very means of perceiving time and expressing it. To this end, Propter adopts and elaborates the opposed concepts of a limiting personality and a liberating union with an impersonal God, much as Anthony Beavis had developed them in the closing pages of *Eyeless in Gaza*. For Propter, as for Beavis, personality as such is evil; it is by definition a state of separation and imprisonment, or to use Propter's own favorite metaphor, a "spatiotemporal cage" of the memory and slowly changing body (page 271). Liberation from this cage is not possible through identification with or devotion to causes larger than the "swarming self," even those as supposedly "selfless" as art and science. Such devotion merely translates the smaller swarm into a larger. True liberation can be achieved only by allowing "eternity to experience itself within the temporal and spatial cage," that is by voluntarily quieting down the swarm of self sufficiently "to render possible the emergence of profounder silence" (page 272).†

In practical terms, this means on the one hand an almost complete rejection of any kind of mediated or verbal knowledge. For true understanding, as we discover in Propter's extended

---

*But Huxley's antipathy to sex seems to extend even to animals. "How human!" Virginia exclaims, while watching the indiscriminate mating of baboons.

†Huxley thought highly enough of this section of his novel (roughly pp. 270–273 in the *Collected Works Edition*) to allow it to be printed separately under the title "Beyond the Swarm." A note at the end informs us that "300 copies of this excerpt have been printed by permission of the author for the friends of Josephine, Judith, and Jake Zeitlin by the Ward Ritchie Press, Los Angeles, December, 1939."

meditation on the nature of God, must be immediate and non-linguistic. Words, after all, are human and temporal, and therefore represent obstacles to knowing the absolute.* Hence there is the formidable attack against the arts mounted in this novel, and the selection of verbal, verbose Jeremy Pordage as one of the prime satirical butts: this is what devotion to the arts leads to. Hence also the provisional exception that is made in favor of satire. For good satire is not only "much more deeply truthful" and "much more profitable than good tragedy," it is also the only art form really prepared to attack human values. But unfortunately, "so few satirists were prepared to carry their criticism of human values far enough" (page 227). Even Candide could do no more than advocate the ideal of harmlessness. No, the best art, so we are led to conclude, is that which best destroys man qua human being. The best art, by a strange Platonic paradox, is that which commits suicide.

By these criteria, *After Many a Summer* makes a rather good showing, but fortunately not only by these. For with Huxley, as with Propter, theory and practice do not always go hand in hand. Though both recognize the futility if not wickedness of language, Propter continues talking and Huxley writing; though both know that time is evil, neither seems inclined to take his own life; though both realize theoretically the stupidity of devoting themselves to merely human causes, Propter keeps on working for the good of man in his carpentry shop and Huxley in his study. In the end, though both very clearly see the better, both follow the more humane.

Time Must Have a Stop† is first mentioned in Huxley's cor-

*While he was still working on the novel, Huxley wrote to his brother on July 30, 1939, of his growing interest in words and their meanings. "There is obviously no hope of thinking or acting rationally about any of the major issues of life until we learn to understand the instrument we use to think about them" (L443). Almost a year later he reverts to the same question and comes to the same conclusion. "I don't know whether there is any solution to human problems; it seems doubtful. But if there is, it lies, I am convinced, in applied semantics and applied religion" (L453).

†As Huxley points out in the novel itself (p. 290), the title is taken from Hotspur's final speech in *Henry IV*, Part I. Huxley had also thought

respondence as a "kind of novel" (L483). At that time — November 1942 — it was still very much in the planning stage, but even after it had been published it remained only a "kind of novel." Not that it differed in this respect from most of Huxley's other longer works of fiction. With the exception of *Point Counter Point, Eyeless in Gaza,* and *The Genius and the Goddess,* all of Huxley's novels are in a very real sense "kind of novels." And even these exceptions are at times what the others are as a rule: blends of the utterly fantastic and the completely ordinary. Fantasy and naturalism are the two poles between which Huxley's imagination moved. And it is of course this continual fluctuation which made him, like Swift, so powerful a satirist.

In this novel, the fluctuation is made explicit, at least in its later sections. Here Huxley dares what perhaps no serious novelist since the Romantic period had dared to do, namely pursue one of his main characters into the afterlife. It is probably such daring that led his critics to conclude that Huxley had gone off the deep end, that he had become so serious as a religious thinker that he should cease to be taken seriously as a novelist.

And yet Huxley no doubt was right when he maintained that he had "deliberately kept light" (L498) the characters and events of this curious story. Nowhere in the novel, not even in the sections describing Eustace Barnack's posthumous experiences, is there so heavy and indigestible a pill to swallow as that which Propter offers us in *After Many a Summer.* Even these sections are "kept light" by their brevity and by being occasionally filtered through the spiritualistic medium of an imbecile's brain. Also the figure of the mystical Bruno Rontini is muted, and probably quite consciously so if we consider that Huxley excluded from the final version a chapter in which Rontini assumes a more didactic role.* The focus throughout the book as Huxley

of calling the novel "Time's Fool" or "Glassy Essence" (from *Measure for Measure*) or even "The Barnacks" (L499).

*This chapter shows Sebastian and his father traveling by train from Genoa to Florence. Sebastian is distracted from watching the landscape (which is beautifully described in a manner reminiscent of *Those Barren Leaves*) by the drawings and conversation of a man who later turns out to be Bruno Rontini. Rontini and Sebastian then talk at length about semi-

finally published it is on the flawed characters of Eustace and his nephew, Sebastian Barnack.

This is not to say that we are ever in doubt about how to read the moral of this story. The counterpoint of divine with human comedy (L501) clearly exists in order to allow us to judge the events of the novel *sub specie aeternitatis*. The conscious parallel with Dante's *Divine Comedy* (quite as important as the parallel with *The Tibetan Book of the Dead*)* must make us realize that Huxley, like Dante, is showing us hell and purgatory — here combined — only in order to reveal the bliss of heaven all the more effectively.

The story is treated rather subtly. It was perhaps for artistic as much as moral reasons that Huxley later confessed that of all his novels he liked this one best.[12] The basic format is again the house party with the usual collection of oddities. Of the two main characters, Sebastian is, with his poetical ambitions and fantasies about women, clearly a younger and less awkward version of Denis Stone, and his uncle, Eustace, is a Scogan or Cardan mellowed by an almost limitless bank account.†

The house party scheme is, however, not adhered to strictly. The novel is, in fact, as much a *Familienroman* as it is a Peacockian satire. Part of the action takes place in London — the time is 1929 — in the bourgeois home of Sebastian's aunt, part in Eustace's Florentine villa, and the remainder in heaven. There is a good deal of the old satire of homemade universes, but in almost every case the butts are chosen rather carefully to show that alternatives to the mystical solution are impractical. For example, Sebastian's father, John Barnack, is exposed again and again as a small-minded and vengeful puritan who has subconsciously adopted socialism as a way of gaining power legitimately over others. On a more intellectual level, he is the equivalent of Fred

mystical subjects. (The manuscript of this chapter is in the Special Collections of the UCLA Library.)

*For a good discussion of the use to which Huxley put *The Tibetan Book of the Dead* in this novel, see Peter Bowering's *Aldous Huxley*.

†What with his love of wine, sex, and off-color limericks, Eustace seems pretty clearly modeled on Norman Douglas.

Poulshot, businessman in the City and intolerable tyrant at home, a ghoul who considers any expression of high spirits sacrilegious.

But these are satirical small-fry compared to Eustace. For Eustace is to John as John is to Fred Poulshot. He moves on another level altogether. He recognizes how others are trapped in their own narrow doctrinal universes; he sees through John's egocentric puritanical socialism and Fred's egocentric puritanical capitalism. He sees through everyone except, of course, himself (and Bruno Rontini). Or rather, he does see through himself; he sees his own limitations, his own indolence and tolerant hedonism, but likes what he sees. The worse, even though he knows it to be morally worse, invariably proves more attractive to him; unlike Calamy or Anthony Beavis, he is not bothered by the *meliora video, deteriora sequor* dilemma. His whole value system is hedonistic. The total reality he aims at is the total reality of pleasure, intellectual, emotional, spiritual. He has developed an impeccable taste for good painting, good poetry, good music, good conversation, good cigars, and less than good women. Though his indulgence in these pleasures has made him dangerously obese, Eustace is incapable of restraining himself from indulging further. Now, on top of his distastes for serious thoughts about what, after Haeckel, he likes to call the Gaseous Vertebrate, comes a Stoyte-like fear of them. When Bruno tells him that God can even forgive him "for being a human being . . . can forgive your separateness so completely that you can be made one with him" (page 104), Eustace simply smiles and declines the invitation of a merger between solid and gaseous vertebrates. Eustace prefers his "sepulchre of privation" (page 106), his pleasurable death in life. But for a moment "an enormous and blissful brightness streamed into him" (page 107). He reacts to it with an outburst of anger and fear, accusing Bruno of trying to hypnotize him. Bruno remains silent: "He had made his final desperate effort to raise the lid; but from within the sarcophagus it had been pulled down again" (page 107). Bruno gives Eustace up as a lost cause.

Quite rightly, as it turns out. For when later that same evening Eustace dies and ascends to eternity, he still refuses to raise the lid and accept a nonpersonal resurrection. Once again, but on a cosmic scale, he makes the same withdrawal into separateness and away from the unifying light. To be sure there is a struggle, but the outcome is never really in doubt. "For an immense duration the two awarenesses hung as though balanced — the knowledge that knew itself separate, knew its own right to separateness, and the knowledge that knew the shamefulness of absence and the necessity for its agonizing annihilation in the light" (page 140). Eventually the awareness of being separate wins out, and the intolerably bright light begins to dim. In the renewed darkness, memories briefly and irregularly pulse through his consciousness and the entity known as Eustace Barnack is slowly reconstituted. That entity is doomed to the continual remembrance of things past, doomed because salvation lies not in the regaining of time or memory, but in their total annihilation, in the denial of a separate personality. Only the prospect of beginning the whole laborious cycle all over again in a new reincarnation faces him, and, in the meantime, like Satan, he is condemned to fighting the incursions of the light which hereafter was "always his enemy" (page 228).

The remaining characters of the novel (always with the exception of Bruno Rontini) share Eustace's fate, at least on earth. This is particularly true of Veronica Thwale, the attractive companion of Eustace's "Queen Mother"-in-law. She is a well-bred would-be Eustace without Eustace's money and hence without his easygoing charm. Veronica has a very thorough understanding of the elementary libidinal and ego-satisfying drives in man, and with single-minded determination applies that understanding to her chosen victims. Not that she is without humor. But it is a humor of a very wry and black sort, and it is never directed at herself. Her policy is to commit some signal outrage, some *acte gratuit,* making certain all the while that she will never become personally or emotionally involved in the consequences of her action. Her seduction of Sebastian is motivated by this perverse impulse. What for her is merely "an interesting scientific experiment" (page 214) is for the inexperienced youth an almost surrealistic experience of "cannibals in bedlam" (page 223). Unlike Sebastian she never bothers to calculate what the repercussions of her "experiments" might be in terms of emotional and physical suffering. Like the Einsteins of *Ape and Essence* she is simply interested in her version of science for its own sake. But, of course, running a laboratory of scientific pleasures of this sort requires a good deal of financing, and so Veronica does her best to lure the wealthy American Paul de Vries into marriage.

Paul, as Sebastian recognizes, is intelligent. He knows a little about everything, and is willing to talk about that little a great deal. He knows, for example, that the human condition is basically evil, and that the only real escape from it is through a mortification of the flesh and a destruction of the ego. He is a kind of Jack of all sciences and arts, intelligent, but "also a fool" (page 227). A fool because his ideas remain always ideas, mere conversation pieces, because the "bridges" which this self-avowed *pontifex minimus* builds are invariably destined to remain illusory; a fool, lastly, because he does not realize why Veronica really married him, because he does not know that Sebastian (*e pluribus unus*) is his wife's lover.

Among this small crowd of satirical butts, the only character who seems to have any chance of transcending himself and reaching the absolute is Sebastian, despite his having started out with several distinct disadvantages. For, as Bruno remarks, Sebastian is, like his saintly namesake, fate's predestined target. He is young, good looking, intelligent, talented. He must therefore be tempted at every turn by the pleasures both of the mind and of the body. His escape from the sarcophagus of separation will consequently be extremely difficult. As it is, the chances are slim enough even for ordinary men; by Bruno's calculations, only one out of every ten thousand will ever make it. Sebastian's intelligence and good looks render the odds even greater and more unfavorable. Nevertheless, at the end of the novel there is some indication that Sebastian will succeed.

He will owe his success to Bruno. It is through Bruno that he first becomes aware of the complicated moral echo set up by any evil action, or by any attempt to further the self in whatever disguise. He becomes aware of it not primarily through what Bruno says, but by what happens to Bruno. When he sees Bruno led away by fascist police, he realizes that his carelessness and his selfishness are in good part responsible. His realization, however, does not bring about more than a temporary resolve to change his ways. It is only when he meets Bruno again many years later in Paris and sees what imprisonment and torture have done to him that there is a possibility of permanent amelioration. In the fifteen weeks preceding Bruno's death, Sebastian concentrates the illuminations of a lifetime. It is then that he learns that "there's only one effectively redemptive sacrifice . . . the sacrifice of self-will to make room for the knowledge of God" (page 282). It is then that the slow and laborious process to gain a mystical understanding of life begins. Observing it take place is a moving experience; moving because Bruno, unlike those earlier protagonists of virtue, Rampion and Propter, is not merely a phonograph record in the shape of a man, but a living, changing, and suffering human being — and in the end a dead one. This "being" of Bruno's, this essential nobility and calm in the face of suffering, is what finally convinces Sebastian, not Bruno's talk. It is because, as he tells his father years after the event, "Bruno could somehow convince you that it all made sense. Not by talking, of course; by just being" (page 305).

Time Must Have a Stop is filled with the echoes of Dante, of *The Tibetan Book of the Dead,* even of a kind of Miltonic war in heaven. There is a calm and detached ascetic quality about it which recalls the mood of *Grey Eminence,* and which, like that brilliant historical biography, is probably in part due to Huxley's depression about the war. Of all of Huxley's novels, including even *Island,* it is the most otherworldly, the one which breathes most deeply the conviction that there is no hope for the things and creatures of this world.

In this respect, *The Genius and the Goddess* is quite different.* It reverberates with the laughter of the Homeric gods, though for the narrator, John Rivers, the sounds are muffled by the passage of more than thirty years. Of all Huxley's longer works of fiction, it is the only one to exude this sense of the richness of merely physical experience. Not that it is content to remain always at that level, but the older John Rivers's memories evoke again and again the warmth of human emotions and the heightened awareness of the beauty of flowers, stones, houses, people, conferred by purely human love. Perhaps it is this fact of filtering the whole story through the nostalgic sensibility of an older and wiser man that makes its bittersweetness almost tangible in the way that the coloring of a remembered Combray seems to the older Marcel much more intense than the real thing. And, of course, the greater human immediacy of this novel is also due to the way most of the characters are presented, particularly Katy and Rivers himself. Like Anthony Beavis in *Eyeless in Gaza,* they are seen from within, a mode of characterization which, as John Rivers knows quite well, cannot produce the harsher response of satire or farce. "In real life," he remarks to his narrator friend, "farce only exists for the spectators, never for the actors" (page 100). Lypiatt, the artist manqué in *Antic Hay,* had earlier arrived at much the same perception.

The laughter, then, provoked by *The Genius and the Goddess* is chiefly laughter for its own sake, and not directed at any particular person or idea. Oddly enough, this least embittered and satirical of all of Huxley's books was composed at a time of greatest personal suffering. The "easiness," as he wrote to his English editor, Ian Parsons, on November 30, 1954, "was horribly difficult to get" (L715). This alludes, one almost cannot help inferring, not just to "writing and rewriting the thing for months," but obliquely as well to seeing his wife grow progressively weaker in her struggle against cancer. In a moving passage near the beginning of the novel which refers quite clearly to

*Page references are to the first edition (London: Chatto and Windus, 1955).

Huxley's own situation, Rivers recalls that his wife Helen "knew how to die because she knew how to live — to live now and here and for the greater glory of God. And that necessarily entails dying too there and then and tomorrow and one's own miserable little self. In the process of living as one ought to live, Helen had been dying by daily instalments. When the final reckoning came, there was practically nothing to pay" (pages 10–11). Rivers then goes on to tell of how he himself had been "pretty close to the final reckoning," when he had contracted pneumonia, an illness of which Huxley nearly died himself in the spring of 1938.*

In fact the personal element may be far more deeply interfused. The Maartens menagerie is somewhat reminiscent of Cherwell, the home of the distinguished Oxford physiologist John Scott Haldane, whom Huxley had already portrayed as the scientist Lord Tantamount in *Point Counter Point*. Huxley, as we can see from Naomi Mitchinson's recollections of him in the *Aldous Huxley Memorial Volume,* as well as from his own *Letters,* frequently visited and stayed at Cherwell during the First World War and in the years immediately preceding. There, besides being able to observe a scientist's household at first hand, he became friendly with Haldane's daughter Naomi — who had a habit of showing him her poems — and her brother Jack. To judge from Ronald Clark's biography of him, Jack Haldane, with his eccentricities and repeated marriages, fits the bill for Maartens much better than his father. It is perhaps this circumstance of looking back in tranquillity at his own youth, however greatly the resemblance has been transformed and made to appear "purely coincidental" (page 11), that enabled Huxley to capture so beautifully the flavor of a happier past.†

*In view of this, Laura Archera Huxley's assertion that Huxley did not know his first wife was dying seems almost certainly mistaken. See *This Timeless Moment* (New York, 1968), p. 11.

†Part of the intensity of the portrait of Katy may be attributable to her descent from Frieda Lawrence. In a letter to the actress who played Katy in the ill-starred production of the stage version, Huxley says so in so many words: "I used to know very well a specimen of the breed. This was Frieda Lawrence, the wife of D. H. Lawrence. I think I told you the other day about the miraculous way in which she raised Lawrence almost from

In any case, it was this harking back that seems to have primarily interested Huxley in this novel.* In a statement to his *Paris Review* interviewers which was not published or edited and therefore reads rather awkwardly, Huxley noted that "the point of the story — what gave it a certain value — was . . . that you had this extra dimension given by the fact that it was told by the man in old age looking back at his past. So you got a certain enrichment, I think, of the character of the young man . . . by the story being told by the same man when he is old. That for me was the interesting part of the story."[13] That Huxley's interest was not merely an abstract Henry Jamesian one in shifting points of view or limited narrative perspectives emerges clearly from the novel itself. "The point of the story" — at least the point of telling it in this way — is to try to get at as large a segment of the truth as possible. Or as John Rivers says, " 'Maybe one could take a hint from the geometers. Describe the event in relation to three co-ordinates.' In the air before him Rivers traced with the stem of his pipe two lines at right angles to one another, then from their point of intersection, added a vertical that took his hand above the level of his head. 'Let one of these lines represent Katy, another the John Rivers of thirty years ago, and the third John Rivers as I am today. Now, within this frame of reference, what can we say about the night of April twenty-third, 1922 [the night when John and Katy became lovers]? Not the whole truth, of course. But a good deal more of the truth than can be conveyed in terms of any single fiction' " (pages 89–90). What Huxley was after in this story was the same "whole truth" he had been chasing all his novelistic life. In this respect, *The Genius and the Goddess* is very firmly established in the Huxley canon. The contrast of the old and the young Rivers exists, as it were, to show

death when he was ill with influenza (superimposed upon chronic and deepening TB) in my house. Katy's miracle with Henry is merely a transcription of what I myself saw, thirty years ago . . . Frieda (and Katy is a non-German and less Rabelaisian version of Frieda) was a woman of enormous strength and vitality, completely untouched by the neuroses of the Age of Anxiety" (L831).

*This would probably have been more apparent if Huxley had been permitted to retain his own title, "The Past Is Prelude" (L715n).

that you cannot step in the same Rivers twice. It is not to be read as revealing a sudden taste for the purely literary techniques of fiction.

There are other ways in which *The Genius and the Goddess* conforms to the general outlines of Huxley's writing, even though, as we have seen, the critics were not altogether wrong in viewing the novel as something rather new for Huxley. For example, in reply to a remark of this sort by his *Paris Review* interviewers (again from the unpublished tape), Huxley observed that its "method was something which I had used before, in some of these long short stories or novelettes which I had written in the past, like 'Two or Three Graces.' " The comparison is accurately drawn: the same device of a narrator looking back on events in which he had participated himself, the same focus on human relationships, though here they are mostly observed from the outside.* But interesting as these similarities may be, they are not specifically or characteristically Huxleyan. More to the point is the fact, not immediately noticeable because of the complex mode of narration, that this novel follows fairly closely the traditional Peacockian house party format. Almost all of the action, after all, takes place in the Maartens's home in St. Louis. Even the device of the "visitor" to open the story recurs. Rivers's arrival, like that of Denis, Calamy, Pordage, and to some extent Sebastian, sets the plot in motion. The assemblage of various striking and extraordinary characters, though here on a considerably diminished scale, is also reminiscent of the earlier novels.

This may be the reason why Huxley was convinced that this story could be successfully adapted to the stage. This, plus the fact that it had, for a Huxley novel, an unusually strong plot. In theory Huxley was probably right. In practice, as it turned out, he was wrong. The play, mangled by various people who thought

*Of his novelettes in general and "Two or Three Graces" in particular, Huxley observed to his *Paris Review* interviewers (unpublished tape): "When is a novel not a novel? Actually, I mean, one always feels so delighted to get away with it. Publishers ask for 80,000 words and you get away with thirty. That's really a great coup, I feel." Part of the plot, as well as one of the more important characters of "Two or Three Graces" seems to be derived from Paul Verlaine's story "L'Obsesseur."

they knew more about the practical requirements of the stage than the supposedly abstruse Huxley, failed dismally. The farcical history of Huxley's compromises and legal entanglements, as recounted in the *Letters* (particularly L834ff), would probably make a rather good play in itself. One imagines for it a title something like *Die Idioten proben das Genie*. Huxley's luck with the theater seems always to have been bad, from the very beginning when he tried his hand at writing a "melodrama about Bolshevism" (L183), to the relative failure of both the adaptation of *Point Counter Point* and his original play *The World of Light*. The only theatrical success he ever had, and even that qualified, came with the film and stage versions of his short story "The Giaconda Smile." Why Huxley persisted in writing for the stage is a mystery, unless his early conviction, expressed in a letter to his brother on July 21, 1918, carried over to old age — namely that "plays are obviously the things one must pay attention to. Imprimis, they are the only literary essays out of which a lot of money can be made; and I am determined to make writing pay" (L157). If this indeed was his reason, then he certainly could have occupied himself more profitably had he never tried to write plays at all.

Perhaps a minor but contributing factor in the failure of *The Genius and the Goddess* as a play was that the material was simply too British to prove attractive to an American audience. The idea of contrasting an older and totally cosmopolitan sophisticate with a young man of twenty-eight who has been conditioned to believe that the "most wonderful wedding present a man could bring his bride was his virginity" (page 14) must have been simply too much for most audiences to swallow. Not that such male virgins are intrinsically improbable in an American context, but the traditions which might conceivably produce such people in a caste society like the English — with its male public schools and almost exclusively male universities turning out men who from a heterosexual point of view at least are virgins — are not in the mainstream of America, or, at any rate, were not in the mid-fifties (or twenties, the period when Rivers first meets Katy Maartens). Brian Foxe, for example, another Huxley character who suffers from similar problems, seems impossible to transplant from his English background.

What satire there is in this novel — and it is very little compared to most of Huxley's novels — is directed not at Rivers's puritanism or at Katy's paganism, as it might very well have been had these characters appeared in, say, a novel like *After Many a Summer*. They are allowed to pass more or less unscathed, though it is made very clear that theirs are very limited and distorted views of the total reality. Nor is there much more than a mild attack on Ruth, the young would-be Salome, whose jealousy and ignorant self-seeking, like Sebastian's egotism in *Time Must Have a Stop*, have enormous repercussions, leading ultimately to her own death and that of her mother. No, the satire is focused on quite another victim, on Henry Maartens, Nobel Prize winning physicist and the genius to whom the title refers. Like the novel which preceded this one, *Ape and Essence*, or like Huxley's last completed book, *Literature and Science* (1963), science and its dehumanizing effects become a major theme.

But perhaps it is not so much science as scientism — that is, science confused, like paganism or puritanism, with the whole of reality. Scientism is far more dangerous than either of these alternatives, not only because it happens to be the reigning mythology of our day, but because it is peculiarly fitted to allow its priests to become, like Henry, "psychological equivalent[s] of a foetus" (page 41). The reason Henry can be satirized in this novel, whereas the other two main characters cannot, is that Henry remains much the same whether seen from inside or outside. In other words, both Katy and Rivers are able to empathize with another person either emotionally or intellectually: Katy with the apparently dying Maartens, Rivers with the Katy who, in a double sense, has lost her virtue. Maartens is totally incapable of this sort of thing. Intellectually he is a giant, emotionally a dwarf. He simply cannot accept the separate existence of anyone outside himself. And, of course, scientism, which contains or accepts no human value system, does nothing to discourage such infantile egotism. Maartens is, in the framework of the novel, the archetype of modern man. Katy is primitive woman, amoral, almost purely emotional, almost a primeval mother goddess. Rivers — at least the younger Rivers — is humanistic, moral, romantic. Together they represent stages in the development of humanity. Maartens is the end product, in much the same sense, if in quite a different direction, that the fifth earl of Gonister at the conclusion of *After Many a Summer* is another end product. Maartens adds to his stupendous intellectual equipment the worst traits of the other two. He is primitive and amoral, but self-centered; Romantic, but not humane. Which is why it is impossible for him to grow as the others have done, to die dramatically like Katy, or to mellow and become wise like Rivers. For him, another fate is reserved, namely to become his own cenotaph. On and on he drones, brilliantly but as if he were not there, a voice but not a man, *vox et praeterea nihil*.

Island occupies a very special place in the long list of Huxley's novels, if for no other reason than that it is his last.* But there are other reasons. To begin with, it is the one novel, or even book plain and simple, wherein Huxley outlines at length and in detail (as his fictional Raja puts it) what's what and what to do about it — especially what to do about it. This may seem rather tiresome in the abstract, and compared to some of Huxley's earlier novels, in practice it sometimes turns out to be. Inevitably, perhaps, for Utopias are by definition "good places" and descriptions of the good, as Huxley would have been the first to admit, too often tend to be goody-goody. The *Letters* testifies repeatedly to Huxley's efforts to combat this tendency. Writing to his son Matthew in the late summer of 1959, Huxley commented that "it may be that the job is one which cannot be accomplished with complete success" (L875), and then went on to

*Page references are to the first edition (London: Chatto and Windus, 1962).

observe that complete success in the genre had never been achieved. Still, he hoped to "lighten up the exposition by putting it into dialogue form, which I make as lively as possible" (L875). A few months later he told his British editor that, pressed by self-doubts about the strength of the plot to carry so much exposition, he had consulted Christopher Isherwood, and on his advice had added another character to the story* (L886).

Perhaps those doubts were justified, at least in part. Many of the reviewers certainly thought so. And yet they had been wrong before. More important, even if they should have been right, they were probably right, so far as Huxley was concerned, for the wrong reasons. For most of them were searching, like Pavlovian dogs who had grown older but no wiser, for the Huxley they were conditioned to expect in the twenties and thirties. Now they were barking angrily up another Huxley, without really bothering to investigate whom he had changed into.

Not that Huxley had become totally different. *Island* is, after all, as he admitted himself, a "kind of reverse *Brave New World.*"[14] This is not just another way of stating that the later novel is Utopian and the earlier one anti-Utopian. That hardly needs saying. What does need saying is that in a considerable number of important aspects the two novels are mirror images. This becomes easier to grasp the moment we see Will Farnaby, the intruder into Pala, as the equivalent to John the Savage in *Brave New World.* For Will too is a savage. In comparison with the Palanese, all his ideas about reality and his persistence in not

*Huxley does not say which character this was. The most likely candidate, I suspect, is Susila MacPhail.

When I asked Christopher Isherwood if he had any recollection of which character it might have been, he wrote to me (February 28, 1971) that he did not, but went on to say: "I do remember that Huxley gave me part of *Island* to read in ms and that we later discussed it, but since I didn't get to see the whole early draft of the book (if indeed the draft *was* completed at the time) I don't know how much he changed it. All I *do* remember is that I protested to Aldous because he had made the heavies (Col Dipa in his relations with Murugan) homosexual. I pointed out that this was becoming a cliché — homosexual Nazis and other fascists abounded in the literature of the period. Weren't 'good' homosexuals welcome on his island? He saw the justice of this, of course, and the question is touched on (page 83). But I haven't answered your question! Sorry!"

taking yes for an answer are just so much insane barbarism. This does not mean that they regard him as some odd and rather ridiculous sort of zoological specimen in the way the inhabitants of the New World thought of John. For one thing, even if they were disposed to do so, which they are not, they could not afford to. For Pala is isolated in more ways than one; it is an island literally and an island spiritually. It is surrounded on all sides by insane and powerful and threatening barbarians. Moreover, the Palanese themselves are fully aware how difficult it is to be sane and human and civilized. They know that it is a full-time job which engages all the faculties and requires continual attention and compassion. That is why the innumerable mynah birds on the island keep calling out the word "attention" in English and Sanskrit — making, as it were, a kind of mystical Muzak.

In *Brave New World* a good deal of Huxley's satire was directed at possible — or probable — abuses of science. Here again the situation is reversed. Or, more accurately, here once again we have a mirror image, for a simple reversal would have involved a rejection of science in the manner of *Erewhon*. Huxley is much too realistic and much too much of a Huxley to do that. Take, for example, one of the most memorable features of the Fordian civilization, its baby hatcheries. In Pala one might expect to find such institutions repudiated. And, of course, they are, but not by means of a simple negative. The Palanese, after all, have their own version of the hatcheries: eugenics and artificial insemination. They practice genetic control almost as rigorously as the lunatics of A.F. 632, but with the enormous difference of doing it voluntarily and in order to improve themselves intellectually, physically, artistically, spiritually — in every conceivable way — and not to perpetuate a rigid caste system. So too with the state conditioning of children, another essential feature of the New World. In Pala, there is also conditioning. Will, for example, watches and eventually participates in a behaviorist treatment of a child which, as he says, is "pure Pavlov" (page 190). The purpose of this training is to have the child make physical contact with a thing, an animal, or a human being, and, while being caressed by the mother, have the word "good" uttered repeatedly in his ear. Furthermore, there is a systematic examination of all children to ferret out those who are hypersuggestible. These children, who supposedly constitute about twenty percent of any random sampling, are considered potentially dangerous because they could be indoctrinated to do practically anything. In Pala "they can be hypnotized and systematically trained *not* to be hypnotizable by the enemies of liberty" (page 204). And even more dramatically, they can be taught to "distort time" (page 204), that is, be conditioned to go into a deep trance in which they can accomplish mental work in a subjective time which is only a fraction of the duration required to do the same work in real time.

Besides officially sanctioned conditioning of children, both states also share an intense suspicion of the traditional familial basis of society. When Will asks Susila MacPhail about her mother, she tells him that she hardly sees her anymore, and then goes on to explain that "in our part of the world 'Mother' is strictly the name of a function. When the function has been duly fulfilled, the title lapses; the ex-child and the woman who used to be called 'mother' establish a new kind of relationship" (page 89). This, to be sure, is still different from the total rejection of blood ties in the New World, where "mother" is the dirtiest of words, but the direction, if not the impulse, is the same. This becomes even more apparent when we discover that children in Pala are free to choose among about twenty sets of parents in a so-called Mutual Adoption Club. If for any reason whatever a child becomes unhappy with his natural parents (who, because of artificial insemination, may not even be his natural parents), he can seek redress elsewhere. The result, of course, is that the family, as most Western cultures conceive of it, ceases to exist.

Of the other parallels between the two worlds, the most striking is probably the use of drugs or druglike medicaments.*

*Not much of value has been written about Huxley's involvement, theoretical and practical, with drugs. For a brief survey, however, see Günter

In the Fordian state, the masses were kept quiet and happy by periodic dosings of *soma,* a drug which immediately translated them into realms of idiotic bliss. The corresponding druglike substance in Pala, *moksha,* is at times applied for vaguely similar reasons. That is, when a criminal case proves particularly difficult, the ordinary methods of treatment — group therapy, other medication — may be supplemented with the *moksha* medicine. By and large, however, the functions of this psychedelic are quite different from those of *soma.* The point of *moksha,* as Will discovers when taking it with Susila, is to increase awareness rather than diminish it. The point is to get to know more not only about what is positively good and beautiful in life, but also about what is bad and ugly, and the whole multitude of intervening shadings. This is why the medicine occupies a central position in the Mahayanistic initiation rite which all Palanese children undergo at roughly the age of puberty. After first being taken high into the mountains and made to climb precipices in order to experience the essential precariousness of life, they are given *moksha* as a group in an old Buddhist temple. How different from the orgy-porgian Solidarity Services of the Fordian world! And yet how much the same. For the aim here is to bring home as vividly as possible the essential solidarity of men, the community of experience in the mystical light. But it is a community and a light seen in the context of all the other aspects of the human condition, particularly man's morality and inherent solitude. That perhaps is the greatest difference between *moksha* and *soma,* or between the Buddhist and the Fordian worlds, namely that in the former the purpose is everywhere to realize one's individuality as completely as possible, and then transcend it; whereas in the latter individuality is a crime. Hence the Fordian solidarity is merely bestial, whereas the Palanese is spiritual and consciously willed. The Palanese use *moksha* to catch a glimpse of a higher reality; the Fordians take *soma* to escape themselves. And the Palanese never forget that the higher reality

Witschel, *Rausch und Rauschgift bei Baudelaire, Huxley, Benn und Burroughs* (Bonn, 1968).

is based on a lower one, and that a life lived with attention posits a death died in the same way.

For death is not, as in the world outside Pala, a dirty word. The dying are not separated from the rest of mankind, shot full of drugs, and rendered as incapable as possible of feeling what is happening to them. That of course is the fate of the Savage's mother and what outrages him profoundly. But the opposite happens to Will's aunt and that outrages Will just as deeply. Here again the Palanese do the reverse. They try as best they can to make the pain bearable by psychological means, largely hypnotic; but they try also to keep the dying person conscious — fully conscious — even to the moment of death itself. So much is death an accepted part of the whole of life that Will, almost a total stranger, is invited to the deathbed of Robert MacPhail's wife, Lakshmi.

As Will leaves, very much moved but unwilling to admit it, he sarcastically remarks that the attractive nurse is now probably trotting off for a little *maithuna* with her boyfriend. Susila's response is that she finds nothing incompatible between death and love — and in the final section of the novel she proceeds to demonstrate this to Will.* Though it never comes to actual physical lovemaking, it is clear that what gradually grows between them during that night is love. The whole episode takes place in a relatively short time, but perhaps not quite so short as the birth of Lenina's desire for the Savage. And it is perhaps with Lenina and John in the back of our minds that Huxley wanted us to look at Will and Susila. Both women are products of a sexually liberated society, both men of sexually inhibited ones. But how different they are! For Lenina sex — or at any rate the pursuit of physical pleasure — is "woman's whole existence," for Susila it is merely "a thing apart," stimulating and worthwhile no doubt, but never to be confused with the totality of human relations. It is as if here, and everywhere else in this book, Huxley were repeating again and again that the worst thing you can do is take the part for the

---

*This too seems a conscious echo of the "death-conditioning" practiced in the new world.

whole, the mistake all known civilizations have committed and the one for which he so mercilessly lashed the Fordian world.

Not that he neglects to distribute a few well-directed lashes here as well, but essentially *Island* is not a satirical novel — certainly it is not what one reviewer called it, a "lethal satire."[15] In fact, from some points of view, it may not even be a novel. At any rate, those who insist that a novel should first and foremost tell a good story will not get much satisfaction here. And perhaps they should not. For, despite Huxley's attempts to get a "fable" strong enough to bear the weight of the ideas, it would have been a mistake to have constructed too effective a plot.* A plot that is too good, after all, distracts from the ideas, and it is in the ideas that Huxley is ultimately interested. The age-old device (one recalls Plato's Athenian Stranger) of using an outsider to lead into the descriptive sections of the novel is skillfully handled, though now and again a seam does show. For example, it is highly unlikely that Will Farnaby, an international journalist with several years' experience and a special commission to do some skulduggery for a large oil company, should be surprised to learn that all Palanese speak English. And surely the unusual phenomenon of a society like Pala would already have been fully documented, with at least one team of American sociologists on the spot. But these are minor matters. It is more important that Huxley does succeed in putting the various elements of his new society before us in as natural a way as possible. The idea of using a journalist to do this was an excellent one. That of involving him at the same time in the nefarious dealings of an oil tycoon was a stroke of genius. For the developing intrigue between international oil interests and the local Rani and her underage Raja son, in conjunction with

---

*Like *Brave New World*, part of the plot and some of the figures of the novel are derived from Shakespeare's *Tempest*. Will Farnaby's shipwreck echoes Ferdinand's and his love of Susila that of Ferdinand for Miranda. Prospero is here split into the two founders of Pala, Dr. Andrew MacPhail and the Raja, whereas Syrcorax, Caliban, and the malignant Antonio appear in the guises of the Rana, Murugan, and Colonel Dipa, respectively. In fact, *Island* follows the pattern of *The Tempest* much more closely than does *Brave New World*, where at first reading Shakespeare seems so much more important.

the imperialistic machinations of a neighboring Sukarno-like dictator to take over Pala and make it over in his ugly image, provides the necessary moving background before which Huxley can unfold his fundamentally static ideas. In the end, when Huxley has finished sculpting his intellectual statuary, foreground and background join, and disaster ensues.

It is this ever present sense that Pala is on the brink of annihilation that prevents *Island* from seeming smug and condescending in the way so many other Utopias do. And besides, "if one is to be realistic," as Huxley observed, that is how Pala must end — another and better Atlantis brought down by an explosion of human ignorance and greed.[16]

"If one is to be realistic" — and Huxley did try to be realistic. From the Aristotelian epigraph, "In framing an ideal we may assume what we wish, but should avoid impossibilities," to the sounds of gunfire and loudspeakers blaring at the end of the novel, we are aware of Huxley's intention to make his fiction fit, as the mynah birds have it, into the here and now. This intense concentration on the present is probably what makes *Island* so radically different from the brave new world — or from the contemporary American consumer society on which that world was based. "Here and now" permit no escape into an illusionary technological paradise. Everywhere he has "avoided impossibilities": the Palanese have no special gadgets, no secret knowledge, no mysterious recipes for success. Traced to their original sources, their institutions can be recognized as either already existing somewhere in the world or else having been experimentally proved to be feasible. All Huxley has done is gather up the various individual pieces, execute the very difficult task of fitting them together, and then exhibit the completed puzzle. For example, the cooperative economics of Pala exist full-blown in Israel and, somewhat less completely, in some of the Scandinavian countries. The systematic improvement of agriculture is modeled, as is stated several times in the novel, on the work of the Rothamstead agricultural station in England. The psychologically discriminated and differentiated education of children is based on

William H. Sheldon's published researches on psychology as related to physical types. A good deal of the loose social organization can be traced to experiments like the Oneida community and to anarchistic theories like that of Kropotkin. The *moksha* medicine is clearly mescalin or LSD, which early experiments indicated were not merely vision-inducing but helpful in treating psychotics.* Even the system of banking is based on that devised by Wilhelm Raffeisen in Germany in the nineteenth century.

Island is realistic all right — and is becoming, as we are discovering now to our distress, more and more realistic every day. The great problems of population and ecology which Huxley tried to resolve in 1962 are only now beginning to dawn on us in all their enormous and horrible proportions. "Nature never did betray the heart that loved her." But how terribly she betrays the hearts, minds, stomachs, and souls of those who do not. In Huxley's simultaneously ideal and real state every sexually mature citizen, besides practicing *coitus reservatus,* receives a thirty-day supply of contraceptives in the mail at the beginning of each month. Homosexuality is just as accepted as heterosexuality. On the ecological level, children are educated to know and respect nature from the moment they enter school. The result is that everybody has enough to eat because there are no excess mouths to feed. In Pala, man has achieved the most difficult task of all, a balance between himself and nature.

All this is of course only possible in a society in which all individuals are responsible and aware. The story of Will Farnaby's discovery of how the society of Pala functions is also the story of his discovery of how he himself functions. What began,

*At that time — the early sixties — there was not much real evidence about harmful side effects. Huxley's partial responsibility for the spread of knowledge about psychedelics is undeniable; but that he was the "Daddy of LSD" is not true. Witness part of a letter he wrote to Humphrey Osmond on July 22, 1956, in which he turns down an offer to appear on television to discuss psychedelics: "As you say in your letter, we still know very little about the psychedelics, and, until we know a good deal more, I think the matter should be discussed, and the investigations described, in the relative privacy of learned journals, the decent obscurity of moderately high-brow books and articles. Whatever one says on the air is bound to be misunderstood . . ." (L803).

perhaps, as a mere device for introducing the ideas ends by being an integral part of the novel. For just as ecology is the knowledge of how all the activities of nature and man relate to each other — both for good and for evil — so too there is an ecology of the spirit. The Palanese learn this over a period of years in school. Will must learn it in a few days under Susila's direction. With her help and that of the *moksha* medicine, he comes to understand that man is not alone, not separated from the rest of creation by the unbroachable wall of his own inevitable individuality. Brought down by Susila from the heaven revealed by the psychedelic to a hell of insects copulating, devouring each other and being devoured in their turn at his feet, and then raised again at last to a midpoint where he finds and touches Susila's face — humanity — Will suddenly senses that he is alone no longer. Senses it, perceives it, but does not and cannot explain it: "One touches and, in the act of touching, one's touched. Complete communication, but nothing communicated" (page 278). Earlier Will had witnessed — but obviously not understood in quite the same way — the identical lesson being taught more abstractly to some children in a school. The teacher had told them the story of the Buddha and the flower. It is a parable of how the Buddha, surrounded by a group of followers anxious to be wise, instead of giving them the expected sermon, simply picked up a flower and showed it to them. Only his disciple Mahakasyapa smiled. Only he understood — in what really matters words have no meaning.

A good many people, reading *Island* for the first time, must have been reminded now and again of Book IV of *Gulliver's Travels*.* Of course, the wise Palanese are human and not equine,

*As I have suggested before, Huxley's satire is in many respects closer to Swift than to either Peacock or Douglas, the two models whom critics usually cite. Late in life Huxley confessed that as a young man he had been "very fond of Swift." And, indeed, almost all of his early poetry, short stories, and even his first novel, *Crome Yellow*, betray that fondness: they could fairly be described as solid English eighteenth-century structures with French symbolist façades. With advancing age, to be sure, Swift's impact diminishes — just as Huxley's satirical impulse diminishes — but it never disappears. The attack on Swift in *Do What You Will* (1929) was written in

but their remote island habitat, the superb regulation of all aspects of their lives — if nothing else, the fact of Will's shipwreck — evoke that most enigmatic and powerful of Swift's satires. The evocation, as Huxley's *Letters* shows, is not wholly accidental. Writing to Humphrey Osmond, the man who introduced him to mescalin, in March 1956, Huxley outlined his plans for a novel which, though substantially the same as *Island*, differed markedly in a number of important respects. To begin with, the whole business with Dr. Andrew MacPhail and the Raja of the Reform is missing. In their stead, there is an enterprising and somewhat unethical Englishman who, after helping himself to the spoils of India, comes to Pala, undergoes "a kind of psychological conversion" (L791), and remains. He is still alive when another Englishman, with quite a different background, comes to the island. This second stranger has recently been released from an asylum for the insane. His mental problems have their roots in an Evangelical upbringing, here resembling somewhat MacPhail's Calvinistic childhood. On the island he becomes for the first time "a really sane and fully developed human being" (L791), a circumstance which causes him, once he returns to England, to be locked up again.

Though it is difficult to make a judgment on the basis of a mere outline which has not even begun to be fleshed out, this plot — qua plot — seems a good deal stronger than the one Huxley finally adopted. It also resembles the plot of the fourth voyage rather more closely, particularly the sections after Lemuel Gulliver has returned home. It is in England, after all, that Gulliver,

the fullness of his enthusiasm for Lawrence's ideas, and hence provides an unbalanced view of his overall response. Aside from very possibly modeling the character, some of the opinions, and the style of the fifth earl of Gonister in *After Many a Summer* on Swift, Huxley in 1941 was thinking of writing a Utopian novel which would employ as the "narrator a grandson of Lemuel Gulliver" (L466). Unfortunately nothing seems to have come of the project. Of course Huxley was in his later years completely opposed to Swift's intense misanthropy, though he certainly understood it well enough to come close occasionally to matching Swift's invective — for example in the figure of Mark Staithes in *Eyeless in Gaza*. Also the whole discursive, ironic, Utopian bent of Huxley's genius is evocative of Swift's. And both, if not congenital novelists, were certainly born satirists.

transformed by his lengthy sojourn among the Houyhnhnm *animalia rationales*, is regarded as insane by his merely *animalia rationis capaces* human fellows. The distinction between the rational Houyhnhnms and the irrational Yahoos, so central to Swift's satire, is also very much at the heart of Huxley's original conception of the book — and a good many traces of this remain in the final version.

Why then did Huxley change his mind? There is no fixed answer to this question. But we can speculate that the greater focus on the sane-insane dichotomy would have distracted readers from what Huxley really wanted them to concentrate on, namely Pala. Perhaps he also wanted to avoid too close a parallel with Swift's fantasy, since that would have allowed the critics to chase this hare ad infinitum, thereby avoiding again the essential issues. Perhaps — and this is the most contingent perhaps of all — he knew this would be his last novel and he wished to leave behind him a testament of hope rather than despair.

In an odd way, the four voyages of Gulliver evoke other associations with Huxley. They correspond — very roughly of course — with what one might for a moment be excused for calling the four stages of development in Huxley's novelistic career. The first voyage — that to Lilliput and Crome — is concerned with the great and the small, and with the relation of man to his social environment: Swift and politics, Huxley and postwar England; Gulliver and the Lilliputians, dwarfish Sir Hercules Lapith and his normally monstrous son. The second — to Brobdingnag and Rananim — treats the problem of man's relation to what is greater than himself, how he must come to an understanding with powers that are larger than life, particularly those within his own mind: Gulliver and the monkey, Walter Bidlake and Lucy Tantamount; Glumdalclitch in a world of greed and lust, Rampion surrounded by stupidity and egotism. The third voyage — to Laputa and the New World — deals with lunacy, with man's presumption in thinking he knows better than God or nature, in believing that just because he can perform a few technological tricks, he can effectively control his own destiny: the flying island named after a whore, the hatcheries where men are bred like chickens. And finally the last voyage, to the Houyhnhnms and to Pala, to wisdom(?) and to wisdom, to an impossibility and to a possibility which, in some shape or other, had better become a reality if we are to survive. But striking as these parallels may be, they are in one respect at least profoundly wrong. Wrong, in that they suggest a limitation to Huxley's work and life. Huxley had a mind that was always voyaging. That, if anything at all, was its essential characteristic. Unlike Gulliver, he never came home. In the end, the real parallel is not with Gulliver but with Faust.

NOTES

Notes

Introduction

1. Frank Swinnerton, *The Georgian Scene: A Literary Panorama* (New York, 1934), p. 441.

2. George Wickes and Ray Frazer, "Aldous Huxley," in *Writers at Work: The Paris Review Interviews,* 2nd ser. (New York, 1963), p. 208.

3. Aldous Huxley, *Essays New and Old* (New York, 1927), p. 118.

Chapter I. The Defeat of Youth and the Victory of Age

1. Ronald Clark, *The Huxleys* (New York, 1968).

2. André Maurois, *Prophets and Poets* (New York, 1935), p. 288.

3. Laura Archera Huxley, *This Timeless Moment: A Personal View of Aldous Huxley* (New York, 1968).

4. Robert R. Kirsch, in Lawrence C. Powell et al., *Aldous Huxley, 1894–1963: Addresses at a Memorial Meeting Held in the School of Library Service, February 27, 1964* (Los Angeles, 1964), p. 4.

5. Kirsch, in Powell, *Huxley,* p. 3.

6. Gervas Huxley's recollections in *Aldous Huxley, 1894–1963: A Memorial Volume,* ed. Julian Huxley (London, 1965), p. 160.

7. L. A. G. Strong, *Green Memory* (London, 1961), p. 180.

8. A. E. Coppard, *It's Me, O Lord!* (London, 1957), p. 165.

9. Clark, *The Huxleys,* p. 152.

10. Frank Swinnerton, *Swinnerton: An Autobiography* (Garden City, N.Y., 1936), p. 310.

11. Stanley J. Kunitz and Howard Haycroft, eds., *Twentieth Century Authors: A Biographical Dictionary of Modern Literature* (New York, 1942), p. 698.

12. Michael Holroyd, *Lytton Strachey: A Critical Biography,* vol. 2 (New York, 1968), p. 182.

13. Harold Acton, *Memoirs of an Aesthete* (London, 1948), p. 76.

14. Osbert Sitwell, *Noble Essences or Courteous Revelations* (London, 1950), p. 39.

15. Christopher Hassall, *Edward Marsh* (London, 1959), p. 411. Actually other poets, like Ezra Pound, had declined the honor earlier.

16. [Virginia Woolf], "Review of *Defeat of Youth*," *TLS*, October 10, 1918, p. 477.

17. Acton, *Memoirs*, p. 75.

18. F. A. Lea, *The Life of John Middleton Murry* (London, 1959), p. 66.

19. Derek Patmore, *Private History* (London, 1960), p. 157.

20. Dilly Tante, ed. [*sic*], *Living Authors: A Book of Biographies* (New York, 1931), p. 191.

21. J. W. N. Sullivan, *Contemporary Mind: Some Modern Answers* (London, 1934), p. 141.

22. Edwin Muir, "Aldous Huxley: The Ultra-Modern Satirist," in Raymond Weaver et al., *Aldous Huxley: A Collection of Critical and Biographical Studies* (Garden City, N.Y., 1930), p. 22. Originally published in *Nation*, February 10, 1926.

23. Kunitz and Haycroft, *Twentieth Century Authors*, p. 698.

24. Sullivan, *Contemporary Mind*, p. 145.

Chapter II. Double War and Triune Peace

1. Harold Monro, *Some Contemporary Poets (1920)* (London, 1920), p. 124; Herbert S. Gorman, "Review of *Leda*," *NYTBR*, September 19, 1920, p. 24; John Middleton Murry, "Review of *Leda*," *Athenaeum*, May 28, 1920, pp. 699–700; and Desmond MacCarthy, "New Poets I — Mr. Aldous Huxley," *New Statesman*, 15 (September 4, 1920), 595.

2. From a taped interview conducted by George Wickes and Ray Frazer on October 9, 1959, now in the Special Collections of the UCLA Library. This portion was omitted from the version published later in the *Paris Review*, and then republished in *Writers at Work: The Paris Review Interviews*. The published version is actually a composite of two separate interviews, the first made on the date given above, the second on November 18, 1959.

3. The manuscript of this talk is in the UCLA Library.

4. [Aldous Huxley], "Marginalia," *Athenaeum*, December 3, 1920, p. 762.

5. This story was first published in the *Palatine Review*, 4 (1916), 5–13, and later republished in *Limbo* (1920).

6. Aldous Huxley, "What, Exactly, Is Modern?" *Vanity Fair*, 24 (May 1925), 94.

7. First published in *Limbo* (1920).

8. [Aldous Huxley], "Marginalia," *Athenaeum*, August 27, 1920, p. 274.

9. Aldous Huxley, "The Modern Spirit and a Family Party," *Vanity Fair*, 18 (August 1922), 55.

10. "Review of *Limbo*," *Spectator*, 124 (April 10, 1920), 494. [Virginia Woolf], "Review of *Limbo*," *TLS*, February 5, 1920, p. 501. Bj., "Review of *Limbo*," *Freeman*, 1 (August 4, 1920), 501.

11. Swinnerton, *Swinnerton*, pp. 311–312.

Chapter III. The Music of Pan: The Early Novels

1. Weaver, et al., *Aldous Huxley*, p. 14.

2. Aldous Huxley, "One Sunday Morning," *Art and Letters* (London), 3 (Spring 1920), 25–32, 35.

3. Aldous Huxley, "A Country Walk," *Coterie* (Autumn 1920), 69–73. Further references to this story are incorporated in the text.

4. Aldous Huxley, *The Defeat of Youth and Other Poems* (Oxford, 1918), p. 36.

5. José Bataller Ferrandiz, "Aldous Huxley y la Novela," *Revista de literatura*, 16 (July–December 1959), 59.

6. According to Charles M. Holmes, *Aldous Huxley and the Way to Reality* (Bloomington, 1970), this copy is now in the Houghton Library, Harvard.

7. Peter Quennell, "Ottoline Morrell," *Bonniers Litterära Magasin*, 7 (September 1938), 548. See also his essay "Camp-Follower," in *The Sign of the Fish* (London, 1960).

8. Grant Overton, *Cargoes for Crusoes* (New York, 1924), p. 110. See also Huxley's remarks on literary characterization in Wickes and Frazer, "Aldous Huxley," pp. 210–211.

9. Donald Joseph Dooley, "The Impact of Satire on Fiction," Ph.D. dissertation (State University of Iowa, 1955), p. 154.

10. Weaver et al., *Aldous Huxley*, p. 63; and Raymond Mortimer, "Bombination; Review of *Crome Yellow*," *Dial*, 72 (June 1922), 631–633.

11. Frank Swinnerton, *The Georgian Scene: A Literary Panorama* (New York, 1934), p. 441.

12. Evelyn Waugh et al., "A Critical Symposium on Aldous Huxley," *London Magazine*, 2 (August 1955), 52.

13. Edwin Muir, *Transition: Essays on Contemporary Literature* (New York, 1926), p. 110.

14. William Wordsworth, *The Poetical Works*, ed. Thomas Hutchinson, ed. and rev. Ernest de Selincourt (London, 1960), p. 377.

15. G. U. Ellis, *Twilight on Parnassus: A Survey of Post-War Fiction and Pre-War Criticism* (London, 1939), p. 271.

Chapter IV. The Music of Humanity: *Point Counter Point*

1. See John Atkins, *Aldous Huxley: A Literary Study* (London, 1956), p. 103; Ludwig Borniski, *Meister des modernen englischen Romans* (Heidelberg, 1963), pp. 236–237; David Daiches, *The Novel and the Modern World* (Chicago, 1939), p. 209; André Gide, *Journal 1889–1939* (Paris, 1948), p. 1037; Wyndham Lewis, *Men without Art* (London, 1934), p. 302; D. S. Savage, *The Withered Branch: Six Studies in the Modern Novel* (London, 1950), p. 141; and Virginia Woolf, *A Writer's Diary*, ed. Leonard Woolf (London, 1954), p. 238.

2. Daiches, *The Novel*, p. 209.

3. For example, Frank Baldanza, "*Point Counter Point*: Aldous Huxley on 'The Human Fugue,'" *South Atlantic Quarterly*, 58 (Spring 1959), 248–257. To date the most complete analyses of the musical structure of *Point Counter Point* are Maren Selck, "Der Kontrapunkt als Strukturprinzip bei Aldous Huxley," Ph.D. dissertation (University of Cologne, 1954); and chap.

3 of Alden Dale Kumler's "Aldous Huxley's Novel of Ideas," Ph.D. dissertation (University of Michigan, 1957).

4. Reprinted as "Crébillon the Younger," in *The Olive Tree* (1936).

5. Baldanza, *"Point Counter Point,"* p. 254.

6. *New York Times*, May 6, 1933, p. 14.

7. *The Collected Letters of D. H. Lawrence*, ed. Harry T. Moore, vol. 2 (New York, 1962), p. 1096.

8. G. U. Ellis, *Twilight on Parnassus*, p. 278.

9. André Gide, *Journal des Faux-Monnayeurs* (n.p., NRF, 1927), p. 112.

Chapter V. The American Dream: *Brave New World* and *Ape and Essence*

1. The 1946 preface to the novel reprinted in the *Collected Works Edition*, p. x.

2. Aldous Huxley, "Brave New World," *Life*, 25 (September 20, 1948), 63–64, 66–68, 70.

3. Aldous Huxley, "The Outlook for American Culture, Some Reflections in a Machine Age," *Harper's Magazine*, 155 (August 1927), 265–270.

Chapter VI. The Music of Eternity: The Later Novels

1. Herman Clay Bowersox, "Aldous Huxley: The Defeat of Youth," Ph.D. dissertation (University of Chicago, 1943), p. 131.

2. D. H. Lawrence, *The Letters*, ed. and intro. by Aldous Huxley (London, 1932), pp. xii–xiii.

3. *Ibid.*, p. xiii.

4. Klaus Mann, *Der Wendepunkt: Ein Lebensbericht* (Frankfurt, 1963), pp. 286–287. My translation.

5. "D. H. Lawrence Round-Table Conference," Los Angeles, March 7, 1952. The unpublished tape of this discussion, featuring Huxley and Frieda Lawrence, is in the Special Collections of the UCLA Library.

6. H. T. Moore, ed., *The Collected Letters of D. H. Lawrence* (New York, 1962). All subsequent citations are to this edition. To avoid still more footnotes, I have taken the liberty of giving only the date of the letters, not the pagination.

7. "D. H. L. Roundtable."

8. *Ibid.*

9. *An Encyclopaedia of Pacifism*, ed. Aldous Huxley (London, 1937), pp. 90–91.

10. Harold Watts, *Aldous Huxley* (New York, 1969), p. 90.

11. As quoted in Laura Archera Huxley, *This Timeless Moment: A Personal View of Aldous Huxley* (New York, 1968), p. 213.

12. Wickes and Frazer, "Aldous Huxley," p. 206.

13. From the taped Wickes and Frazer interview with Huxley at the UCLA Library.

14. Wickes and Frazer, "Aldous Huxley," p. 198.

15. Eric Keown, "Review of *Island*," *Punch*, April 11, 1962, p. 585.

16. Wickes and Frazer, "Aldous Huxley," p. 199.

INDEX

Index

Acton, Harold, 14, 17, 18
"After the Fireworks," 94
After Many a Summer, 5, 24n, 25, 26, 147, 157, 165, 176, 177, 187n: characters in, 158–160; analysis of, 161–164; source of title, 162
Aldous Huxley, Satire and Structure, 4
Aldous Huxley Memorial Volume, 27, 172
Alice in Wonderland, 26
Antic Hay, 18, 22, 38, 52, 54, 88, 96, 105, 120: analysis of, 64–69, 73, 78, 80; characters in, 70–73, 77–79; and theme of imbalance, 74–76; compared to *A Handful of Dust*, 76–77
Ape and Essence, 26, 121, 133, 169, 176: compared to *Brave New World*, 134–135; analysis of, 135–137
Arabia Infelix, 28
Aristophanes, 46
Arnold, Julia (Mrs. Leonard Huxley), 12
Arnold, Matthew, 12
Art of Seeing, The, 24
Athenaeum, The, 19, 21, 112
Auerbach, Erich, 8

Baldanza, Frank, 99
Balliol College, Oxford, 12

Balzac, Honoré de, 42
Bedford, Sybille, 11
Bell, Clive, 16, 19, 44
Bennett, Arnold, 15
Beyond the Mexique Bay, 23, 140, 142, 161
Bloomsbury group, 5, 16, 21: criticizes Huxley, 62–64
Borsodi, Ralph, 157n
Brave New World, 37, 42, 55, 115, 117, 144, 160n: as anti-Utopian satire, 119–121; and *Crome Yellow*, 122–123; and theme of uniformity, 123–124; analysis of, 125–126, 129–133; and Dostoevsky's Grand Inquisitor, 126–128; compared to *Ape and Essence*, 134–135; sexual mores portrayed in, 138–139; destructive satire of, 139, 142; compared with *Island*, 178–182
Brave New World Revisited, 121n
Brooke, Rupert, 13
Brothers Karamazov, 126
Browning, Robert, 31
Buddha, 143
Burning Wheel, The, 15
Bynner, Witter, 141
Byron, Lord George, 22

Campbell, Roy, 13, 15
Carrington, Dorothy, 59n